Mothering, Time, and Antimaternalism

This book aims to broaden understanding of the diverse positions and meanings of motherhood by investigating understudied and marginalized mothers (rural itinerant, African American, and Irish Catholic American) between 1920 and 1960.

Fueled by anxieties around feminism, a perception of men's loss of status and masculinity, racial tensions, and fears about immigration, "antimaternalism" discourse blamed mothers for a wide range of social ills in the first half of the twentieth century. *Mothering, Time, and Antimaternalism* considers the ideas, practices, and depictions of antimaternalism, and the ways that mothers responded. Religion, class, race, ethnicity, gender, and immigration status are all analyzed as factors shaping maternal experience. The book develops the historical context of American motherhood between 1920 and 1960, examining how changing ideas—scientific motherhood, time efficiency, devaluation of domesticity, racial and religious bias—influenced the construction and experiences of motherhood.

This is a fascinating and important book suitable for students and scholars in history, gender studies, cultural studies, and sociology.

Mary K. Trigg is Associate Professor, Department of Women's, Gender, and Sexuality Studies, Rutgers University.

Interdisciplinary Research in Motherhood

The Maternal in Creative Work
Intergenerational Discussions on Motherhood and Art
Edited by Elena Marchevska and Valerie Walkerdine

Intersections of Mothering
Feminist Accounts
Edited by Carole Zufferey and Fiona Buchanan

Refiguring Motherhood Beyond Biology
Edited by Valerie Renegar and Kirsti Cole

Mothering, Time, and Antimaternalism
Motherhood Under Duress in the United States, 1920-1960
Mary K. Trigg

https://www.routledge.com/Interdisciplinary-Research-in-Motherhood/book-series/IRM

Mothering, Time, and Antimaternalism
Motherhood Under Duress in the United States, 1920-1960

Mary K. Trigg

LONDON AND NEW YORK

First published 2023
by Routledge
4 Park Square, Milton Park, Abingdon, Oxon OX14 4RN

and by Routledge
605 Third Avenue, New York, NY 10158

Routledge is an imprint of the Taylor & Francis Group, an informa business

© 2023 Mary K. Trigg

The right of Mary K. Trigg to be identified as author of this work has been asserted in accordance with sections 77 and 78 of the Copyright, Designs and Patents Act 1988.

All rights reserved. No part of this book may be reprinted or reproduced or utilised in any form or by any electronic, mechanical, or other means, now known or hereafter invented, including photocopying and recording, or in any information storage or retrieval system, without permission in writing from the publishers.

Trademark notice: Product or corporate names may be trademarks or registered trademarks, and are used only for identification and explanation without intent to infringe.

British Library Cataloguing-in-Publication Data
A catalogue record for this book is available from the British Library

ISBN: 978-1-032-36966-2 (hbk)
ISBN: 978-1-032-36969-3 (pbk)
ISBN: 978-1-003-33471-2 (ebk)

DOI: 10.4324/9781003334712

Typeset in Sabon
by Deanta Global Publishing Services, Chennai, India

Because this book is about the future as well as the past,
I dedicate it to my grandsons Aiden Davis, Julian Wilson,
Henry Davis, and Raphael Wilson.

Contents

List of figures		viii
Acknowledgments		ix
	Introduction	1
1	Alarm Clocks in the Soul: Scientific Motherhood, Temporal Regulation, and Antimaternalism	16
2	A Promaternal Narrative and Archive: Dorothea Lange's Photographs of Rural Mothers	56
3	Reclaiming Maternity: African American Mothers and Maternal Grief as a Counter-Narrative	103
4	Herself: Irish American Catholic Mothers, Maternal Power, and Antimaternalism	151
5	Antimaternalism and the Work of Care: How Is This Showing Up Today?	191
	Index	221

Figures

2.1	Dorothea Lange, *Migrant Mother*, March 1936	59
2.2	Dorothea Lange, *Mexican Mother in California*, June 1935	64
2.3	Dorothea Lange, *Two Tobacco Tenant Mothers*, July 1939	65
2.4	Dorothea Lange, *While the Mothers are Working in the Fields*, November 1936	69
2.5	Dorothea Lange, *Young Migrant Mother with Six Weeks Old Baby*, April 1939	70
2.6	Dorothea Lange, *Tulare County, Mother and Child*, May 1939	71
2.7	Dorothea Lange, *Mother and Two Children on the Road*, September 1939	78

Acknowledgments

I have many to acknowledge for their contributions to *Mothering, Time, and Antimaternalism*. Rutgers undergraduates have been involved in this book from its inception in the fall of 2012. I thank Dawn Angelicca Barcelona, Deyana Ibrahim, Judy Wu, and Meghan Valdes for their early, invaluable research assistance. I especially thank Kim LeMoon for her meticulous research skills and influential insights. I thank the Rutgers University Aresty Research Program for giving me the opportunity to work with these fine students. In addition I must acknowledge the inspiration I have received from my students in the seminar on the history of motherhood, which I first taught in 2014 and have continued to teach each spring. They have stimulated my thought and reinforced my belief in the importance of motherhood studies in the discipline of women's, gender, and sexuality studies. That seminar and its students have played an important role in this decade-long project.

I thank my family for supporting my writing and helping me to carve out the time to write, revise, and complete this book. First, as always, I thank my husband Ron Rapp for his friendship, love, investment in my work, and unquestioning commitment to our family. He helped me to become a mother, one of the most meaningful experiences of my life. I thank my daughters Laurel Rapp and Sarah Rapp, who both became mothers in the course of my writing this book. Not only did they each come to my class to generously share their experiences of childbirth, they have kept me connected to, and cognizant of, young motherhood. I thank them for sharing their maternal insights, which I utilized in the final chapter of this book. My oldest grandson Aiden came with his mother Laurel to my class at the tender age of four months. I thank my sons-in-law Adam Wilson and Matt Davis for being such great dads, and for writing about fatherhood, an important area of work that needs more attention. They too provide caring labor and experience the time squeeze that is one of the subjects of this book. I thank my niece Kelly Kaems for her warm friendship and consistent interest in this book. I thank my late mother for her boundless love that has carried me through life. Virginia Woolf wrote, "We think back through our mothers if

x *Acknowledgments*

we are women." I have thought back through my mother in this book, and her loving and enduring influence has been with me as I wrote it.

I thank both Rutgers University and Routledge for their belief in, and support of, *Mothering, Time, and Antimaternalism*. The Rutgers School of Arts and Science has sustained my research through funding and leaves, which allowed me to write and complete the manuscript. I thank then-Dean Michelle Stephens for her support while I was department chair and her belief in the value of my research. For their friendship and encouragement I thank Lisa Hetfield, Sasha Taner, Rebecca Mark, and Emily Haran, my teammates and fellow adventurers at the Institute for Women's Leadership. I thank my colleagues in the Department of Women's, Gender, and Sexuality Studies, especially Harriet Davidson, Judy Gerson, Charlotte Bunch, Radhika Balakrishnan, Ethel Brooks, Ed Cohen, Marisa Fuentes, Maya Mikdashi, and Zakia Salime. I thank Routledge Press, especially editor Alexandra McGregor for her sustained interest in the manuscript over many years, and Eleanor Catchpole Simmons for her assistance throughout the publication process. I am indebted to the two readers of my manuscript for their perceptive comments and generous appraisals. Finally, I thank Heather Aimee O'Neill for her brilliant insights into this manuscript and her patient work with me as I thought about time and fiddled, rewrote, and reconceptualized motherhood under duress, 1920 to 1960.

For permission to replicate their material I acknowledge and thank:

Toi Derricotte: Excerpt from "Natural Birth" by Toi Derricotte, copyright 1983, 2000 by Toi Derricotte. Reprinted by permission of Toi Derricotte.

Library of Congress, Prints & Photographs Division, FSA/ OWI Collection, for the replication of Dorothea Lange's photographs.

HarperCollins: Excerpt from "Place" by Jorie Graham.

Introduction

Mothers are not given the resources they need to mother. This is as true in the twenty-first century United States as it was in the early to mid twentieth century, the period I explore in this book. The critical lens on motherhood, the unrealistic expectations placed upon mothers, and the lack of cultural and institutional support offered to mothers can be traced to ideas that took root in the post-1920 years. In *Mothering, Time, and Antimaternalism* I consider the ideas, practices, and depictions of what historians have called antimaternalism in the years between 1920 and 1960, and the ways that mothers responded. I pay particular attention to how time was used as a tool of maternal control and oppression. I also consider the effects that antimaternalism continues to have, and the fear of maternal power that motivates it.

Antimaternalism blames mothers for everything from emasculated sons and disorganized families to larger-blown social issues like masculinity-in-crisis and welfare dependence. During World War II, antimaternalists compared mothers to Nazis "with swastikas for hearts," and blamed them for American battle fatigue, male sexual dysfunction, and psychoneuroses.[1] Julie Stephens has described antimaternalism as "a resentment-fuelled, hate-filled discourse about mothers," which in the twenty-first century is applied to "Mothers in general, but feminist mothers in particular, liberal mothers, 'helicopter mums,' teenage mothers, professional educated mothers and so-called 'welfare moms.'"[2] Antimaternalism goes beyond discourse to influence policies that affect the lives of, and resources available to, both mothers and their children. Because it is linked to a devaluation of motherhood, domesticity, and care, antimaternalism—which at times has included feminist voices—belittles women's traditional labors, which include the creation and maintenance of homes and the bearing and rearing of children. Antimaternalists in the 1920 to 1960 years deployed a variety of tools to control the mother—whom they associated with disorder and unruliness—including scientific motherhood and time discipline. How this came to be, and how it affected in particular the lives of marginalized mothers, is the focus of this book.

DOI: 10.4324/9781003334712-1

2 *Introduction*

In "New Directions in Motherhood Studies," Samira Kawash noted that what is needed in scholarly work on motherhood is a broadening of our awareness and understanding of the diverse positions and meanings of motherhood.[3] This book attempts to respond to that need by investigating the experiences and representations of understudied and marginalized mothers during four decades of dramatic change in the United States.[4] I echo Sarah Knott's conclusion that carrying and caring for children are time and place dependent (they are also race and class dependent), and that "grasping what mothering has been means getting plural and specific, exploring its immense variety."[5] In *Mothering, Time, and Antimaternalism* I investigate three kinds of American mothers during these decades: rural itinerant mothers, African American mothers, and Irish American Catholic mothers. All were outliers to the maternal ideal. Poor mothers, migratory mothers, black mothers, and immigrant mothers have always been stigmatized and otherized in the United States. I wanted to examine the reasons why, the role antimaternalism played in this othering, and the ways that these mothers responded.

I also had personal motivations for choosing this topic, and these particular groups of mothers, to investigate. My respect and love for my own mother, who bore and raised five daughters and ran a household in the 1940s, 1950s, and 1960s drew me to this time period and topic, as did my earlier research on the history of feminism in the early twentieth-century United States. Both projects have helped me understand more fully the ways that some strands of feminism have ignored, belittled, or devalued the contributions of mothers, while others have fought for their rights. I chose the three groups of mothers investigated here out of personal and intellectual interest. I wanted to include immigrant mothers, and chose my own ethnic and religious heritage of Irish Catholicism to focus one chapter upon. My grandmother emigrated from Ireland to the United States in the early twentieth century and gave birth to five children here, only two of whom (one my mother) survived to adulthood. She died at age 34 in the influenza epidemic of 1918, just months after giving birth to my mother. As immigrants who entered a Protestant culture, Irish American Catholic mothers like her faced religious and ethnic discrimination, and I wanted to understand that history more fully.

African American mothers faced greater discrimination yet, and throughout American history have fought for their right to be mothers. In light of the contemporary Black Lives Matter movement and the significant roles that African American mothers have played in social justice movements, it was important to me to include them in this book. In addition, I have admired the ways that African American culture has valued children and mothering, and the grace and resilience African American mothers have displayed in the face of hardship. Interested in motherhood under duress, I also chose to investigate often-overlooked rural mothers, specifically the itinerant farm working mothers of the 1930s that Dorothea Lange captured in her iconic photographs. As a graduate student in the 1980s I read the classic texts *Let Us Now Praise Famous Men* (James Agee and Walker Evans) and *Mothers of the South* (Margaret Jarman Hagood), and was moved by the perseverance of tenant farm women and men during the depression years.[6] As a mother, and now a grandmother, I am interested in norms of ideal mothering and their history, and the ways that mothers across class, race, and time have responded to that messaging. I have also contemplated and experienced how time speeds up, slows down, and disappears in mothering, and the time poverty mothers face. This understanding also motivated me to write this book.

A revolution in ideas about mothering occurred during the four decades between 1920 and 1960. The idea of maternalism, espoused by social reformers (and some feminists) who helped craft the early welfare state in the late nineteenth and early twentieth centuries, had largely shaped the ways Americans interpreted motherhood before 1920. Historians Seth Koven and Sonya Michel first defined the term:

> maternalism exalted women's capacity to mother and extended to society as a whole the values they attached to that role: care, nurturance and morality … it extolled the private virtues of domesticity while simultaneously legitimizing women's public relationships to politics and the state, to community, workplace and marketplace.[7]

Maternalist narratives existed in relation to other discourses—about citizenship, class, gender, and national identity, among others.[8] Maternalist thinking ultimately reinforced gender roles as it emphasized women's responsibilities within the family. Its prescriptions modernized gender inequality by politicizing and codifying social roles and relations. Maternalist ideas impaired women's ability to operate in the labor market as equal workers with men. In connecting women's citizenship to the maternal ideal, such prescriptions ultimately denigrated the role of women's paid labor, and legitimated a gender-segregated work force.[9] Yet, maternalism was a powerful vision that included a caring state in which women played roles as voters, policy makers, administrators, and workers, both within and outside the home and it was their roles or potential roles *as mothers* that prepared them for these functions.

Historian Rebecca Jo Plant has highlighted a transformation in the middle-class cultural construction of motherhood that occurred during the interwar years and World War II, when cultural critics and psychological experts rejected these core doctrines of the pre-1920 ideas of maternalism. These earlier ideas included the beliefs that the mother role was full-time and lifelong, incompatible with wage-earning; that motherhood was not just a private, familial role, but was the foundation of female citizenship; that mothers should bind their children to the home with love in order to guarantee their moral development; and that motherhood involved physical suffering and self-sacrifice.[10] In the years after 1920 scientific motherhood replaced the nineteenth-century maternal ideal: medical and scientific advice aimed to displace mothers' traditional reliance on instinct, common sense, and the guidance of extended family and friend networks. Scientific motherhood, according to historian Rima Apple, "advanced the belief that women need assistance in raising their families healthfully and they expected that this assistance would be in the form of medical and scientific expertise."[11]

The "assault on moral motherhood" led to the rise of antimaternalism, a negative interpretation of mothers that came to predominate in the post-1920 United States. Antimaternalism reflected the belief that motherhood was too laden with political meaning and burdened with sentiment. Motherhood should instead be understood as a biologically based familial role, interpreted in a more narrow and sensible manner. Three kinds of people expressed antimaternalist arguments in the 1920–1960 period: critics who rejected sentimentality, hypocrisy, and sexual repression; social scientists and psychologists who wanted to apply their professional expertise; and women (especially young women) who wanted to tear down the Victorian construction of motherhood, with its overtones of self-sacrifice and suffering.[12] In this book I pay particular attention to the second group: social scientists, psychologists, and other experts, and the messages they offered mothers on time management and time efficiency. The demise of moral motherhood and the rise of a new maternal ideal both reflected and facilitated white, middle-class women's gradual inclusion in the political and economic order as individuals rather than as wives and mothers.[13] Yet, as early as the 1920s, the rise of male experts and social scientists' psychologically oriented critiques of motherhood for the first time included middle-class mothers with poor mothers as targets of mother blaming, and replaced the positive image of American mothers with increasingly negative ones. I argue that the marginalized groups of women I explore here never accepted the post-1920 ideas about motherhood, but held to the earlier ideals. While those earlier constructs may seem outdated and overly sentimental, they did at their root value mothers and their essential contributions to families and societies.

The reasons for twentieth-century mother blaming, and the anxieties that triggered it, were many. One was the success of the feminist movement. American women won the suffrage in 1920, and women—including mothers—could not only vote, they also continued to enter the labor force in growing numbers, which some found threatening. A fear of men's loss of status and masculinity, triggered by male unemployment during the economic crisis of the Depression along with the impact of two world wars on men's mental health, contributed to antimaternalism. So did a changing racial climate in the United States, as African Americans won landmark victories in access to housing, education, and voting rights that threatened the (male) white power and privilege structure. Emotions about the exploding consumerism of the 1920s and 1950s; the consolidation of a bureaucratic, post-industrial society; immigration; and concerns about democracy in light of the rise of European fascism and Nazism can all be seen in ideas about, and depictions of, antimaternalism. Freud's influence on American ideas about sexuality and the bonds between mothers and their children also played a role, as did twentieth-century feminist writers like Simone de Beauvoir and Betty Friedan.

Ruth Feldstein has argued that several key cultural changes in the 1930s altered the meaning of motherhood. The psychology profession became more established and influenced political discourse, promoting the idea that "bad" mothers and dysfunctional families were responsible for broken citizens and impaired men. Second, by now "good" and "bad" women were not as easily tied to notions of the public and private spheres. Before the 1930s, "bad" women were those who wielded power in the public sphere. By the 1930s, society criticized women for their behavior in the private sphere of the home. Feldstein asserts that the most outspoken critics of motherhood were neither conservatives nor traditionalists but liberals who espoused progressive ideas on race and social welfare. "Women became suspect," she wrote, "because they wielded too much power in the private sphere *as mothers*." Dangerous women and (bad) mothers became interchangeable: "the categories of 'woman' and 'mother' blurred. Thus ideas about motherhood impacted all women, regardless of race or maternal status."[14] These misogynist interpretations would culminate in the "Momism" of the 1940s and 1950s, but the idea moved forward later in the century and into the twenty-first, as well.

Concerned that mothers would dominate their children, early twentieth century experts began to raise the daunting specter of maternal influence. Some parent educators spoke out about the dangers of over-attentive mothers. One of them was child psychologist Helen Wooley, who stated at a 1926 parent education conference about the stay-at-home mother: "Either she dominates, makes the child too dependent on her; or she is oversolicitous and fearful and communicates her fear to the child." Some mothers reflected on their own culpability in loving their children too much. A settlement-house mother confessed:

> I have one fault—I give him too much affection. I yearn over him. That is because I have no baby. But I am learning to suppress my emotions. I am gradually withdrawing because I want him to be independent.

A woman enrolled in a Minnesota Home Bureau mother's group admitted a similar shortcoming: "I now realize under the guise of too personal interest that I have made my children over-dependent on me. I should read more about 'mental weaning.'"[15]

6   Introduction

Sigmund Freud delivered his pivotal lecture on "Femininity," which transformed ideas about child rearing and maternal power, in 1933. In it he described infants' intense attachment to their mothers—for sons and daughters, the primary object of love is the mother: "The first object-cathexes occur in attachment to the satisfaction of the major and simple vital needs," Freud stated. Part of the work of healthy psychological development, Freud argued, was for boys/men to sublimate the Oedipus complex (their unconscious desire to murder their fathers and marry their mothers), and for the girl/woman "to change her erotogenic zone and her object."[16] Freud believed that the mother–infant relationship was the archetype for all love relationships, and "contains elements of romance and eroticism along with such functions as nurture, protection, and education."[17]

Jacqueline Rose has argued that mothers are hated in modern-day Western culture, and are held accountable for the ills of the world.[18] Why? One reason she points to is maternal power, the critical fact that, as Adrienne Rich noted in her seminal book *Of Woman Born: Motherhood as Experience and Institution*, "all human life on the planet is born of woman." "There is much to suggest," Rich wrote in 1976,

> that the male mind has always been haunted by the force of the idea of *dependence on a woman for life itself*, the son's constant effort to assimilate, compensate for, or deny the fact that he is "of woman born."[19]

Rose asks of our contemporary moment:

> do the conservative anti-mother crusaders (against single mothers, immigrant mothers) draw on "their own vaguely remembered years of utter dependency ... that they are trying to repudiate?" [do they] ... have the echo of the baby in the nursery hovering somewhere in the back of his or her—mostly his—head?[20]

We should ask the same of the antimaternalists of the 1940s and 1950s. The history of motherhood in the 1920–1960 decades includes very real struggles over maternal power. As Momism illustrates, maternal power was, and continues to be, deeply threatening.

One central area of attention that antimaternalists focused upon was mothers' use of time. In the maternalist vision, the "tender mother" was required to "secure *time*" for her children: in *Letters to Mothers* (1838) poet Lydia Sigourney tried to persuade mothers, whose duty was to make "lasting impressions" on young children, to prioritize childrearing above all else. Yet, there is a danger here—as the nineteenth century moved into the twentieth, surplus maternal tenderness became increasingly suspect: it produced children who lacked drive toward the future—children who could not separate and take their place in the capitalist social order. The mother's pleasure in the presence of the child could not set itself against the laws of time by seeking to defer the child's inevitable growth.[21] As scholar Dana Luciano notes, the sentimental home's primary affective bond existed "in a doubled temporality, at once timeless and of necessity transient, insofar as children were both to be cherished and to be raised, and hence to grow away from the mother who remained behind at home."[22]

In considering time as a tool of control that is linked to antimaternalism, it is important to recognize the gendered double standard in access to time, which has especially affected the lives and opportunities of mothers. Individuals' use of time involves negotiation with others, including employers, partners and spouses, children, and authorities. Thus, time is relational: it must be understood in relation to others' time.[23] Men and women have differing access to time, which is replicated in other social hierarchies. According to Karen Davies, "women's specific subordinate position in society influences how their time may be used and what power they may exert in these negotiations. Thus time is genderized on different levels."[24] Julia Kristeva has described time as patriarchal in nature, and argues that the very concept of time undergirds the patriarchal structure.[25]

Women throughout history have had less freedom to claim time as their own. Women's relation to time is often characterized by task-orientation, and in the home, those tasks are largely tied to domesticity, childcare, and housework. The amount of control that individuals have over time is an indication of power: "[t]he feeling of possessing time," Kerry Daly concludes, "is a function of autonomy, control, and status."[26] While time might be conceived of as an equally distributed resource, the fact that family members often assume women are responsible for housework and caring work means they believe they have the right to lay claim to women's time. The time that women take for themselves and their own interests is often given little, or no, priority.[27] Researchers have documented a gender gap in access to free time, or time when one is not working or occupied. Women spend significantly less time on leisure than men.[28] This is intensified for women who are mothers, and even more pronounced for single mothers.[29] Mothers pay an emotional and intellectual price for this gendered double standard in access to time. Writer Rachel Zucker noted,

> Sometimes I work on this essay in the cracks of time and then have to rush out or give a reading or go to the dentist or pick up the kids and it feels like walking around in the middle of open-heart surgery.[30]

One of the important achievements of feminists in the twentieth century was to make women's time visible, to insist that care work was indeed work, and to note that caring labor was unpaid. As early as the 1920s, United States feminists led a "Wages for Housework" campaign, and in 1926, Doris Stevens named the "double shift" which forced wage-earning women to shoulder a second round of unpaid household labor when they returned home.[31] Nineteenth and twentieth-century feminists like Charlotte

Perkins Gilman and Simone de Beauvoir pointed to women's lack of control over their own time.[32] But even in the twenty-first century, feminists have not been able to achieve gender parity in access to time, especially in the home. The COVID-19 pandemic has only made this gender disparity, especially for mothers, more apparent.[33] Women, and mothers in particular, are still time-poor. A twenty-first century woman in the United States described voluntary childlessness as a conduit to what she called "the male-kind of time." "I think [being childless has meant] a certain freedom—financial, time, ability to identify with career, ability to be good in what you're doing because you have the male-kind of time," she told an interviewer. The author concluded, "This woman suggested that the only way to obtain the freedom of 'male-kind of time' was by rejecting motherhood."[34] The kinds of expectations and demands that expert proponents of scientific motherhood placed on early twentieth century mothers added to their burdens and increased their time poverty, and this has trickled down to our own time.

In part because of maternity and the demands of care, women have traditionally been associated with the circular, or cyclical, model of time. Philosopher Fanny Soderback describes how the linear "male" model of time is associated with forward movement:

> Women, so often relegated to the natural realm and to embodiment, have become the bearers of cyclical time, while men, who have taken upon themselves the task of subordinating nature and the body in the name of culture and reason, have come to lay claim to linear time and the progress associated with it.[35]

In these temporal models, woman is an embodied creature and man a cerebral, rational subject unfettered by the body. In *The Second Sex*, Simone de Beauvoir connected these two models of time and their genderedness with the sexual division of labor. She argued that as upholders of reproduction and bearers of children, women have had to carry the responsibility and physical labor of the daily sustenance and caregiving that is needed to allow men to live life as cerebral, un-embodied beings.[36]

Society's expectations about ideal maternal care can lead to mothers' feelings of guilt and a perception of their lack of control over time. Poet and young mother Rachel Zucker describes a telling dream in which she leaves both her own toddler and a friend's child alone in a market, as she goes off for a drive with her father. Realizing with horror what she has done, she leaps out of the car and starts running, jumping through doorways and windows, trying to fly in order to quickly get back to the children. "I am terrified to tell [her husband] what happened—that I am now a person who has left two toddlers unattended in a busy market." Although the children are both safe upon her return, when the mother of the other child discovers what this mother has done, she slaps her, screaming, "What kind of person are you? Never, never, never speak to us again!" And then, the guilty mother (who had tried to become a super hero in order to return to the children) realizes in the dream that she had simply glided out of time.

> She describes my crime—how I left the babies—but in talking about it I realize that I'm missing (in memory) a large section of time. That I had slipped out of time completely, that I wasn't "there" at all. I try to explain this, not as an excuse, but just to explain, to clarify. She slaps me again. I wish it were harder.[37]

The mother who is not-in-time cannot be held responsible for neglecting her children, or those in her care, but she still feels deserving of punishment. Antimaternalists might view this as a mother's ultimate act of carelessness with time, leaving it altogether.

Like other historians of motherhood, I have searched for sources where I could find them. There are many more sources demonstrating what American culture *told* mothers they should do and be, then on how mothers responded. This is in part because of the time poverty that mothers have historically experienced.[38] As Sarah Knott beautifully stated:

> Even in the best-lit corners of past and present, caring for an infant interrupts thinking, punctures reflection, or leaves a book half read. The richest records, such as letters and diaries, often stop exactly as they are getting interesting. A piece of correspondence is left off, mid-sentence; the letter writer called away by a cry, or a diary suspends, because both hands are needed to hold the baby.[39]

Not surprisingly, there are many more existing sources written by middle-class mothers than by working-class mothers. To address this paucity I have woven through this text quotations and ideas gleaned from letters, memoirs, and oral histories (when I could find them), along with magazines of the period like *The Crisis*. I have also utilized artistic representations of, by, and about mothers—photographs, short stories, lynching plays, films, novels, and poetry. Chapter 4, which focuses on Irish American Catholic mothers, was the most difficult to write because the sources were so elusive. Janet Nolan, who has published one of only two monographs on Irish American women, noted, "Irish women's voices are rarely heard in the historical records. Women ... have been largely lost to Irish history as a result."[40] This seems to be as true for Irish American women as it is for Irish women, and doubly true for mothers across race and ethnicity. Irigary has described "the deadly silence" of maternal history. It is that silence that I seek to address in this volume.[41]

Mothering, Time, and Antimaternalism is organized into an Introduction and five chapters. Chapter 1 considers the ways that the cultural imperative of time discipline affected mothers. This chapter develops the historical context of American motherhood between 1920 and 1960, as it considers how changing ideas about time influenced the construction and experiences of motherhood. Mothers were to raise their children in ordered, efficient homes where daily routines structured time toward maximum productivity. Scientific motherhood, which celebrated time discipline and the "experts," sought to force a rigid interpretation of linear time onto a set of tasks (mothering) that require flexibility and more complicated temporalities. As an ideal, it was largely out of reach for the primarily working-class mothers I examine in this book. Scientific motherhood eventually succumbed to broader forces of political and global change. As the 1930s Depression moved into the World War II years and the uber-domestic 1950s, scientific strategies gave way to more child-centered parenting practices. A growing movement for breastfeeding and natural childbirth challenged ideas of time discipline and temporal regulation and suggested a different vision of the relationship between mothering and time. Simultaneously, a rising antimaternalism swept across the United States.

In the second chapter I focus on four years of the Great Depression, as I turn to Dorothea Lange's photographs of migratory mothers and their children that she took for the Farm Security Administration (FSA) between 1935 and 1939. Through them I aim to interpret the representation and experiences of rural, itinerant mothers struggling to support their children and sustain their families during the crisis depression years. Rural mothers were burdened with so many different tasks that the ideals of time discipline and order that experts advocated were impossible to meet. Many of Lange's ennobling photographs of mothers and their children served as a counter-narrative to the antimaternalism of the time. A few depict the lengths to which some poor, itinerant mothers went to strive for domestic economy and the ordering of time that scientific motherhood proponents advocated. Lange's loving, dignified images fly in the face of antimaternal dictates of experts warning of the dangers of mother's love and announcing the demise of maternal sacrifice. Lange's personal struggles as a mother and an artist illuminate the emotional ambivalence that also runs through the history of motherhood. I have embedded two mini-biographies in the book, of Lange and Mamie Till Bradley, as another way to try and grasp the experiences and emotions of mothers during these years.

While Julia Kristeva posits that motherhood—in that it involves the eventual, inevitable separation between mother and child—always involves loss, African American mothers have borne a disproportionate share of maternal grief, which I consider in Chapter 3.[42] They have also shown resilience, resolve, and joy in their mothering. Burdened with racism, less access to resources, a greater need to combine care work with waged labor, and concerns for the safety of their children, African American mothers carried heavy loads in these years.[43] In addition, white Americans have stereotyped blacks in their relationship to time, associating them with disorganized families, a lack of temporal discipline, and a disregard for efficiency and productivity.[44] In this chapter I draw on visual and material culture—photographs, sculptures, cartoons, lynching plays, short stories—to investigate the ways that African American artists and writers of the era depicted mothers' grief. These representations reject white, Eurocentric notions of motherhood, including cultural messaging cautioning mothers not to love their children too much. These images of maternal grief serve as another counter-narrative to the antimaternalism of the time. The chapter also considers the past and memory as a kind of maternal reclaiming. I approach this through analysis of three genres or events: 1920s' memorial funerary portraits of children; the pilgrimages of African American Gold Star mothers between 1930 and 1935; and the example of Mamie Till Bradley, whose teenaged son Emmett Till was lynched in 1955.

The fourth chapter considers the ways that xenophobia and ethnic and religious bias constructed the Irish-American Catholic mother as "other" to the motherhood ideal, as well as Irish American dissemination of antimaternalism. The chapter traces this by first considering white Protestant bias toward the Irish in general, including their racialization, then using memoirs, oral histories, and historical studies to examine the lives, challenges, and experiences of Irish American Catholic mothers in these years. White Anglo Saxon Protestants feminized Irish men, whom they labeled as poor and emotional. In response the Catholic Church and Irish American culture expected women—especially mothers—to mask their own considerable strengths while they buttressed the male. The last section analyzes how Catholicism constructed the "good mother" and concludes by describing early to mid-century antimaternalist writings by Irish American Catholic male writers James Farrell (a novelist) and Andrew Greeley (a sociologist and Catholic priest), who penned scathing portraits of the Irish American Catholic mother, which I examine. Yet working-class Irish American Catholic mothers persisted, playing a critical role in the survival of the Irish Catholic family and its upward mobility in the United States in the twentieth century.

The final chapter serves as the conclusion to the book, focusing on antimaternalism and the work of care, and considering how the antimaternalism I trace manifested in the years after 1960, and how it is showing up today. It also considers contemporary mothers in the United States, and the relevance of this research on motherhood and antimaternalism to the lives and challenges of diverse mothers in the twenty-first century and during the COVID-19 pandemic. It closes by considering the potentially radical idea of mothering, and what women need to mother. For the most part, I have kept my focus in the first four chapters on the 1920–1960 years, straying at times to provide a broader historical context I thought was essential to the story at hand.

In *Of Woman Born*, Adrienne Rich made the critically important distinction between two meanings of motherhood, one superimposed on the other: "the *potential relationship* of any woman to her powers of reproduction and to children; and the *institution*, which aims at ensuring that that potential—and all women—shall remain under male control." The institution of motherhood "has a history ... an ideology" and stands in contrast to the daily practice of mothering, which can, as we will see, be a source of joy, deep reward, and challenge.[45] Were the mothers I investigate able to claim and retain their powers of reproduction—the capacity of their bodies to conceive, to carry a child, to give birth, to breastfeed—and their relationships with their children in light of the messaging and maneuvers coming from the institution, which sought to keep motherhood under male control? How did the working-class mothers I try to summon and materialize here respond to messaging about motherhood and time efficiency and discipline—which were a manifestation of antimaternalism and the institution of motherhood? How can we interpret the fragments and anecdotes mothers left behind, as they lived the hours, days, months, and years of their lives?[46] These questions lie at the heart of this book.

Notes

1. The "swastikas for hearts" quote is Edward Strecker's, from *Their Mothers' Sons: The Psychiatrist Examines an American Problem* (Philadelphia, PA: J.B. Lippincott, 1951), 133.
2. Julie Stephens, "Mother Hate: The Anti-Maternal Fantasies of the Alt-Right," *Arena Magazine*, No. 160 (June–July 2019): 36–39. See 36.
3. Samira Kawash, "New Directions in Motherhood Studies," *Signs*, Vol. 36, No. 4 (Summer 2011): 969–1003.
4. Rima D. Apple and Janet Golden, eds., *Mothers and Motherhood: Readings in American History* (Columbus, OH: Ohio State University Press, 1997), introduction.
5. Sarah Knott, *Mother is a Verb: An Unconventional History* (New York: Farrar, Straus and Giroux, 2019), 8.
6. James Agee and Walker Evans, *Let Us Now Praise Famous Men* (Boston, MA, and New York: Houghton Mifflin, 2001 ed. Originally pub. 1939); Margaret Jarman Hagood, *Mothers of the South: Portraiture of the White Tenant Farm Woman* (New York and London: W.W. Norton & Company, 1977; Originally pub. 1939).
7. Seth Koven and Sonya Michel, eds., *Mothers of a New World: Maternalist Politics and the Origins of the Welfare State* (New York: Routledge, 1993), 4, 6.
8. Seth Koven, "Borderlands: Women, Voluntary Action, and Child Welfare in Britain, 1840 to 1914," in Seth Koven and Sonya Michel, eds., *Mothers of a New World: Maternalist Politics and the Origins of the Welfare State* (New York: Routledge, 1993), 94–135.
9. Gwendolyn Mink, *Wages of Motherhood: Inequality in the Welfare State, 1917–1942* (Ithaca, NY: Cornell University Press, 1995), 8; Alice Kessler-Harris, *In Pursuit of Equity: Women, Men, and the Quest for Economic Citizenship in 20th-Century America* (New York: Oxford University Press, 2001), 33–34.

10 Rebecca Jo Plant, *Mom: The Transformation of Motherhood in Modern America* (Chicago, IL: The University of Chicago Press, 2010), 87.
11 Rima D. Apple, *Perfect Motherhood: Science and Childrearing in America* (New Brunswick, NJ, and London: Rutgers University Press, 2006), 22.
12 Plant, *Mom*, 7–8.
13 Plant, *Mom*, 2, 13.
14 Ruth Feldstein, *Motherhood in Black and White: Race and Sex in American Liberalism, 1930–1965* (Ithaca, NY: Cornell University Press, 2000), 7.
15 All quoted in Julia Grant, *Raising Baby by the Book: The Education of American Mothers* (New Haven, CT: Yale University Press, 1998), 142, 143.
16 Sigmund Freud, "Lecture XXXIII: Femininity (1933)," in Graciela Abelin-Sas Rose et al., eds., *On Freud's Femininity* (London and New York: Taylor & Francis Group, 2010), 25–49. See 32–33.
17 Suzanne Juhasz, "Mother-Writing and the Narrative of Maternal Subjectivity," *Studies in Gender and Sexuality*, Vol. 4, No. 4 (2003): 395–425. See 416.
18 Jacqueline Rose, *Mothers: An Essay on Love and Cruelty* (New York: Farrar, Straus and Giroux, 2018), 6.
19 Adrienne Rich, *Of Woman Born: Motherhood as Experience and Institution* (New York and London: W.W. Norton & Company, 1986), 11.
20 Rose, *Mothers*, 30.
21 Julia Kristeva, Alice Jardine, and Harry Blake, "Women's Time," *Signs*, Vol. 7, No. 1 (Autumn 1981): 13–35.
22 Dana Luciano, *Arranging Grief: Sacred Time and the Body in Nineteenth-Century America* (New York and London: New York University Press, 2007), 122.
23 Karen Davies, *Women, Time and the Weaving of the Strands of Everyday Life* (Aldershot, Hampshire, UK, and Brookfield, VT: Gower Publishing Co., 1990), 15.
24 Davies, *Women, Time and the Weaving*, 9.
25 Kristeva et al., "Women's Time."
26 Kerry J. Daly, *Families & Time: Keeping Pace in a Hurried Culture* (Thousand Oaks, CA and London: Sage Publications, 1996), 107.
27 Davies, *Women, Time and the Weaving*, 15.
28 Daly, *Families & Time*, 168–169.
29 Jillian M. Duquaine-Watson, *Mothering by Degrees: Single Mothers and the Pursuit of Postsecondary Education* (New Brunswick, NJ, and London: Rutgers University Press, 2017). See Chapter 3, "Clocks and Calendars."
30 Rachel Zucker, *Mothers* (Denver, CO: Counterpath, 2014), 107.
31 Davies, *Women, Time and the Weaving*, 38, 140; Mary K. Trigg, *Feminism as Life's Work: Four American Feminists through Two World Wars* (New Brunswick, NJ, and London: Rutgers University Press, 2014), 129–130.
32 Charlotte Perkins Gilman, *Women and Economics* (London: G.P. Putnam's Sons, 1906); Simone de Beauvoir, *The Second Sex* (New York: Knopf, 1952).
33 Andrea O'Reilly and Fiona Joy Green, eds., *Mothers, Mothering, and COVID-19: Dispatches from the Pandemic* (Ontario, Canada: Demeter Press, 2021).
34 Maura Kelly, "Women's Voluntary Childlessness: A Radical Rejection of Motherhood," *Women's Studies Quarterly*, Vol. 37, Nos. 3–9 (Fall/Winter 2009): 157–172. See 169.
35 Fanny Soderback, "Revolutionary Time: Revolt as Temporal Return," *Signs*, Vol. 37, No. 2 (Winter 2012): 301–324. See 301.
36 de Beauvoir, *The Second Sex*. See also Soderback, "Revolutionary Time," 302.
37 Zucker, *Mothers*, 201–204.
38 On the ways that motherhood has impacted women's time and ability to write, see Tillie Olsen, *Silences* (New York: Dell, 1978).

39 Knott, *Mother is a Verb*, 5.
40 Janet Nolan, "Silent Generations: New Voices of Irish America," *American Literary History*, Vol. 17, No. 3 (Autumn 2005): 595–603.
41 Luce Irigaray, "The Bodily Encounter with the Mother," in Margaret Whitford, ed., *The Irigaray Reader* (Oxford: Basil Blackwell), 34–46. See 44.
42 Julia Kristeva and Arthur Goldhammer, "Stabat Mater," *Poetics Today*, Vol. 6, No. ½ (1985): 133–152.
43 Deborah Gray White, *Too Heavy a Load: Black Women in Defense of Themselves, 1894–1994* (New York and London: W.W. Norton & Company, 1999).
44 Brittney Cooper, "The Racial Politics of Time," *TEDWomen*, 2016, https://www.ted.com/talks/brittney_cooper_the_racial_politics_of_time
45 Rich, *Of Woman Born*, 13, 33.
46 Knott, *Mother is a Verb*, 7.

Reference List

Agee, James Agee and Walker Evans. *Let Us Now Praise Famous Men*. Boston, MA and New York: Houghton Mifflin, 2001. Originally pub. 1939.

Apple, Rima D. *Perfect Motherhood: Science and Childrearing in America*. New Brunswick, NJ and London: Rutgers University Press, 2006.

Apple, Rima D. and Janet Golden, eds. *Mothers and Motherhood: Readings in American History*. Columbus, OH: Ohio State University Press, 1997.

Cooper, Brittney Cooper. "The Racial Politics of Time." *TEDWomen*, 2016, https://www.ted.com/talks/brittney_cooper_the_racial_politics_of_time

Daly, Kerry J. *Families & Time: Keeping Pace in a Hurried Culture*. Thousand Oaks, CA and London: Sage Publications, 1996.

Davies, Karen. *Women, Time and the Weaving of the Strands of Everyday Life*. Aldershot, Hampshire: Gower Publishing Co., 1990.

Feldstein, Ruth. *Motherhood in Black and White: Race and Sex in American Liberalism, 1930–1965*. Ithaca, NY: Cornell University Press, 2000.

Freud, Sigmund. "Lecture XXXIII: Femininity (1933)." In Graciela Abelin-Sas Rose et al., eds., *On Freud's Femininity*. London and New York: Taylor & Francis Group, 2010, 25–49.

Grant, Julia. *Raising Baby by the Book: The Education of American Mothers*. New Haven, CT: Yale University Press, 1998.

Hagood, Margaret Jarman. *Mothers of the South: Portraiture of the White Tenant Farm Woman*. New York and London: W. W. Norton & Company, 1977. Originally pub. 1939.

Irigaray, Luce. "The Bodily Encounter with the Mother." In Margaret Whitford, ed., *The Irigaray Reader*. Oxford: Basil Blackwell, 34–46.

Juhasz, Suzanne. "Mother-Writing and the Narrative of Maternal Subjectivity." *Studies in Gender and Sexuality*, Vol. 4, No. 4 (2003): 395–425.

Kawash, Samira. "New Directions in Motherhood Studies." *Signs*, Vol. 36, No. 4 (Summer 2011): 969–1003.

Kelly, Maura. "Women's Voluntary Childlessness: A Radical Rejection of Motherhood." *Women's Studies Quarterly*, Vol. 37, Nos. 3–9 (Fall/Winter 2009): 157–172.

Kessler-Harris, Alice. *In Pursuit of Equity: Women, Men, and the Quest for Economic Citizenship in 20th-Century America*. New York: Oxford University Press, 2001.

Knott, Sarah. *Mother Is a Verb: An Unconventional History*. New York: Farrar, Straus and Giroux, 2019.

Koven, Seth. "Borderlands: Women, Voluntary Action, and Child Welfare in Britain, 1840 to 1914." In Koven, Seth and Sonya Michel, eds., *Mothers of a New World: Maternalist Politics and the Origins of the Welfare State*. New York and London: Routledge, 1993, 94–135.

Koven, Seth and Sonya Michel, eds. *Mothers of a New World: Maternalist Politics and the Origins of the Welfare State*. New York and London: Routledge, 1993.

Kristeva, Julia, Alice Jardine, and Harry Blake. "Women's Time." *Signs*, Vol. 7, No. 1 (Autumn 1981): 13–35.

Kristeva, Julia and Arthur Goldhammer. "Stabat Mater." *Poetics Today*, Vol. 6, No. ½, The Female Body in Western Culture: Semiotic Perspectives (1985): 133–152.

Ladd-Taylor, Molly, ed. *Raising a Baby the Government Way: Mothers' Letters to the Children's Bureau, 1915–1932*. New Brunswick, NJ and London: Rutgers University Press, 1986.

Luciano, Dana. *Arranging Grief: Sacred Time and the Body in Nineteenth-Century America*. New York: New York University Press, 2007.

Mink, Gwendolyn. *Wages of Motherhood: Inequality in the Welfare State, 1917–1942*. Ithaca, NY: Cornell University Press, 1995.

Nolan, Janet. "Silent Generations: New Voices of Irish America." *American Literary History*, Vol. 17, No. 3, Symposium Issue: Race, Ethnicity, and Civic Identity in the Americas (Autumn 2005): 595–603.

O'Reilly, Andrea and Fiona Joy Green, eds. *Mothers, Mothering, and COVID-19: Dispatches from the Pandemic*. Bradford, ON: Demeter Press, 2021.

Plant, Rebecca Jo. *Mom: The Transformation of Motherhood in Modern America*. Chicago, IL: The University of Chicago Press, 2010.

Rich, Adrienne Rich. *Of Woman Born: Motherhood as Experience and Institution*. New York and London: W.W. Norton & Company, 1986.

Rose, Jacqueline. *Mothers: An Essay on Love and Cruelty*. New York: Farrar, Straus and Giroux, 2018.

Soderback, Fanny. "Revolutionary Time: Revolt as Temporal Return." *Signs*, Vol. 37, No. 2 (Winter 2012): 301–324.

Stephens, Julie. "Mother Hate: The Anti-Maternal Fantasies of the Alt-Right." *Arena Magazine*, No. 160 (June/July 2019): 36–39.

Strecker, Edward. *Their Mothers' Sons: The Psychiatrist Examines an American Problem*. Philadelphia, PA: J.B. Lippincott, 1951.

Trigg, Mary K. *Feminism as Life's Work: Four Modern American Women through Two World Wars*. New Brunswick, NJ and London: Rutgers University Press, 2014.

Tronto, Joan. "Time's Place." *Feminist Theory*, Vol. 4, No. 2 (August 2003): 119–138.

Vandenberg-Daves, Jodi. *Modern Motherhood: An American History*. New Brunswick, NJ and London: Rutgers University Press, 2014.

White, Deborah Gray. *Too Heavy a Load: Black Women in Defense of Themselves, 1894–1994*. New York and London: W.W. Norton & Company, 1999.

Zucker, Rachel. *Mothers*. Denver, CO: Counterpath, 2014.

1 Alarm Clocks in the Soul
Scientific Motherhood, Temporal Regulation, and Antimaternalism

Early twentieth-century proponents of temporal regulation, who connected time management to scientific motherhood, valorized time efficiency and applied it to motherhood and the home. Parent educators, journalists, social workers, psychologists, physicians, home economists, and efficiency experts joined forces in the 1920s and 1930s to argue that mothers needed training in time discipline and scientific child-rearing methods. Time management applied to mothering was one symptom of antimaternalism in the United States during the 1920s and 1930s, intended to control the mother, to rein in her power. Time discipline and closely watching and measuring time became the ideal for responsible, conscientious, "perfect" mothers.

These experts advised mothers to raise routinized and independent children. Behaviorists like John Watson, who dominated child-rearing advice at the time, connected time management to the dissolution of "unhealthy" ties between mothers and children. This not only ratcheted up the demands placed on mothers but it also made them question their own maternal instincts about care, and the pleasure they took in their children. Watson advocated strict "scientific" schedules and limited physical contact between mothers and their children. In his widely read *Psychological Care of Infant and Child* (1928), Watson condemned "The Dangers of Too Much Mother Love," warning mothers against the hazards of cuddling and kissing their children, and arguing that kissing baby was "at bottom a sex-seeking response."[1] Meanwhile, Watson was a noted anti-feminist, asking in *The Nation*'s 1927 series "These Modern Women" (in an essay titled "The Weakness of Women"): "Does their demand for this mystical thing called freedom imply a resentment against child bearing?"[2] Watson believed that conditioning could shape human and animal behavior, without appeal to thoughts and feelings. The behaviorist agenda focused on the "routinized" child, advocating clock-driven and unyielding schedules for bedtime and mealtimes. Doctors told mothers: "make a machine of the little one. Teach it to employ its various functions at fixed and convenient times."[3] Historian Jodi Vandenberg-Daves noted that early psychologists seized upon the factory system as a model for child rearing, as they envisioned children "as inputs into impersonal factory-production-like systems, with medical men

DOI: 10.4324/9781003334712-2

serving as the crucial mediators in the production of better products."[4] In this scenario, the clock—along with the advice of medical experts—would replace maternal instinct and mother love.

Proponents of scientific motherhood and time discipline played a large role in proclaiming and publicizing the dissolution of close ties between mother and child in the years after 1920. As Watson's dictates make clear, cultural commentators re-evaluated the ties between mothers and their children in the post-Freudian years. Historian Julia Grant has suggested that in the nineteenth century, sentimental literature popularized the idea that mothers across class and race had a special bond with their children and were prepared to sacrifice for them. In the twentieth century, the notion of "universal motherhood" came to focus on the problems of child rearing rather than on the affective links between mother and child. These links had once symbolized the ties that knit the nation together; in the years after 1920, the mother–child connection appeared to be unraveling. A bond that Americans had considered to be sacred and strong, by the 1920s Grant writes, "appeared to be fragile, uncertain, and of questionable desirability."[5]

A new emphasis on schedules, routines, and "science" aimed to distance mothers emotionally and physically from their children. One 1938 advertisement in *Parents* magazine captured this philosophical sea change: "Add science to love and be 'a perfect mother,'" it directed.[6] Watson's stress on the danger of overly close relationships between mothers and their children reflected changing advice from cultural critics and psychological experts. Their rejection of earlier tenets of motherhood—that mother love was pure and unrelated to sexual desire; that equated motherhood with self-sacrifice and children's debt to their mothers; and that believed that mothers should forge emotionally intense relationships with their children, especially their sons (to keep them on the path of virtue)—was complete by the late 1950s. This revolution in ideas about motherhood essentially pathologized mother love.[7] While Victorians idealized "Mother" because of her self-sacrifice and influence in molding character in her children, postwar psychological experts portrayed the benefits of mother love in narrower and more psychological terms. Plant argued that this critique intensified in the decade after World War II, when pundits and specialists "expressed a wariness of mothers and maternal influence that Victorian Americans could scarcely have fathomed."[8]

Advocates of efficiency and routines in child rearing linked time management to capitalism, and to the role of mothers in raising children to enter the capitalist system. Earlier generations of domestic advisors had suggested that efficiency could be domesticated, that what is effective in business can be equally effective in the home.[9] A century earlier in *The American Frugal Housewife* (1835), Lydia Maria Child advised her readers on the first page that "Time is Money," and suggested they "gather up all the fragments of *time* as well as materials."[10] Six years later in the popular *A Treatise on Domestic Economy* (1841), educator Catharine Beecher directed American women to perfect themselves as Christian wives and mothers by mastering the economic logic of modern time. Invoking time as God-given, Beecher instructed her readers: "Christianity teaches that for all the time offered us, we must give account to God; and that we have no right to waste a single hour."[11] Beecher was echoing Biblical ideas about the Christian mother, noted in Proverbs 31:27–28: "She looks well to the ways of her household/ and does not eat the bread of idleness. Her children rise up and call her blessed;/her husband also, and he praises her." Beecher theorized the importance of time and used it to create a template for a morally perfect, capitalist America. "A wise economy is nowhere more conspicuous," Beecher wrote, "than in the right apportionment of time to different pursuits."[12]

In Beecher's analysis, homemakers and mothers should run their homes like time efficient factories where children are conditioned to eventually take their places in the capitalist order. Wives and mothers should exemplify temporal thrift:

> A woman is under obligations to so arrange the hours and pursuits of her family, as to promote systematic and habitual industry; and if, by late breakfasts, irregular hours for meals, and other hinderances [sic] of this kind, she interferes with, or refrains from promoting regular industry in others, she is accountable to God for all the waste of time consequent on her negligence.[13]

Beecher argued that clock time should be the foundation of the social world of the household, and that the home shared the same logic as business and commerce. Significantly, she placed her strictures about time management in the context of Protestant theology.[14] In this approach, as scholar Thomas Allen has noted, the domestic sphere and the business sphere became parallel and adjacent cultural spaces organized by the same temporal logic.

> For Beecher, the definition of virtue in the domestic sphere lies in doing the same things at the same times every day, and at the same time as the other members of the family. Meals must be eaten at regular hours. Everyone must arise early and at the same time. And in order for this punctuality to really constitute character formation, it must be habitual; that is, it must be internalized so as to become natural and effortless. This model of the family moves the language of spending, saving, and wasting from the public economic discourse of market capitalism into the private sphere of the home and makes it the basis of middle-class personhood. The language of clock time makes it possible for these economic metaphors to cross the threshold of domesticity—in both directions, as these newly minted persons then move outward from the domestic sphere into every other arena of American life.[15]

Or as Elizabeth Freeman described Beecher's domestic vision: "middle-class femininity became a matter of synchronic attunement to factory rhythms, but with the machinery hidden."[16]

Ideas that linked maternal care to capitalist ideas of time efficiency grew out of industrialization and American ideas about time as a scarce resource. In mapping the history of time, historians most often have turned to the development and institutionalization of the machinery that tracked and quantified time: Americans especially elevated the importance of such measuring devices as clocks, railroad schedules, wristwatches, and calendars. As Dana Luciano notes, these devices offered an illusion of certainty and impartiality, as they "bespoke time as objectively given, concrete, measurable, orderly, and ultimately productive."[17] Scholar JaneMaree Maher has shown how these new tools of quantification affected temporal awareness: "starting and finishing bells, payment of hours worked and new measures of productivity—... inaugurat[ed] a new form of time consciousness in western subjects, where time was scarce and utilized in discrete blocks."[18] In the eyes of Western capitalists and industrialists, time's scarcity led to the idea of time as a resource. The more power and influence we have, the more we can decide how we and others spend that resource, and the greater capacity we have to resist social control and negotiate time.[19] A commodity that can be counted, measured, and ultimately controlled, time is related to power, as Rutz noted: "representations of time become ideologies that legitimize the exercise of power."[20]

The temporal order of industrialization thus became a form of social control that experts applied to motherhood. Elizabeth Freeman has written about the use of time to organize individual human bodies toward maximum productivity. She writes that people internalize the uniformity of managed time and feel "bound to one another, engrouped, made to feel coherently collective, through particular orchestrations of time," which they interpret as "seemingly ordinary bodily tempos and routine, which in turn organize the value and meaning of time."[21] Male experts applied this coercive temporal social control to mothers, who had less social power than they did.

Foucault addressed the topic of temporal discipline, and in his writings showed how social institutions like prisons, schools, hospitals, and factories became instruments of social control and domination that subjugate individuals. In *Discipline and Punish* he described a timetable established in monastic communities that those in power later applied to social institutions. This timetable established rhythms, imposed particular occupations, and regulated the cycles of repetition. Temporal modernization involved temporal programming: "Time penetrates the body and with it all the meticulous controls of power," he wrote. The "well-disciplined body" made use of every second with maximum speed and efficiency. Foucault argued that the rising twentieth-century professions of clinical medicine, psychiatry, and child psychology impacted the hospital, the school, the factory (and the home) and could be used as instruments of subjection.[22]

The Temporalities of Care

One form this social discipline took for American mothers in the 1920s and 1930s was through temporal regulation. Temporal regulation moved the authority on how to best utilize time in infant care and child rearing from mothers to experts, who believed they knew best. The rigid time discipline that experts imposed upon mothers in the 1920s and 1930s was a form of antimaternalism in which time was used as a tool of oppression. Scientific motherhood's emphasis on clock time hindered what mothers needed to do to care for their children. Scientific motherhood flew in the face of maternal instinct, made mothers second guess themselves, and made their jobs even more difficult. Temporal regulation conflicted with mothers' natural rhythms of care, and the kind of immediacy and flexibility that care requires. Care is based on a different relationship to time than strict adherence to clock time: "In reproductive work the clock is less important; rather it is the task at hand that is definitive." Maternal tasks respond to immediate needs, involve emotion, and are characterized by short cycles that are frequently repeated.[23] Care work of all kinds requires quick response to human needs, or a more flexible relation to time.

Not only does temporal regulation conflict with mothers' natural rhythms of care, it also conflicts with the natural rhythms of childhood. Young children experience a different temporality than adults—not tied to an awareness of productivity or profit, their use of time is exploratory, experiential, playful. To be with children and care for them requires a slowing-down and patience: sometimes for caregivers, time passes slowly, it drags. Caregivers are often asked to renounce their own needs. Yet, at the same time children require schedules: meals, naps, playtime, diaper changes, doctors' appointments, and school. It was this need that experts seized upon in the early twentieth century, as they constructed what they envisioned as the ideal temporal regulation of motherhood.

Political scientist Joan Tronto locates care outside conventional industrial time measures altogether, asserting that "time spent caring is not about mastering and control but maintenance and nurturance." Care, she suggests, including care for the ill and dying, demonstrates to humans our limits in forcing our wills upon the world.[24] Tronto argues that feminized notions of care, "which have traditionally taken whatever time they have needed to take and which traditionally have been women's domain, have shaped women's relation to time." Davies has argued that "process time," with its focus on the variability of needs and the multiple undertakings that care requires, is a more accurate way to conceptualize the temporalities of care than is linear, clock time.[25] While much of women's care work has concentrated on children, women have also traditionally cared for the sick, including the terminally ill, who summon a broader understanding of time, temporality, and the body. Thus the advice that the expert community gave mothers in the 1920s and 1930s was directly opposed to the ways that mothers organize, and utilize, time in their caregiving.

Some feminists have belittled the rhythm and outcome of maternal and domestic care and related both to women's subordination. In the 1940s Simone de Beauvoir equated housework, pregnancy, and child-rearing with repetition, which she placed in opposition to creativity, transcendence, and the future.[26] Men, even if they took on household and care work, still performed that work within a broader context of creative and productive pursuits. In contrast, domesticity and maternity bounded women's worlds in repetition, which—according to de Beauvoir—only reinforced the inferior nature of maternal and domestic labor:

> The woman who gave birth did not know the pride of creation; she felt herself the passive plaything of obscure forces ... in any case begetting and suckling are not *activities*, they are natural functions; no project is involved ... Man's case was radically different; he furnished support for the group, not in the manner of worker bees by a simple process ... but by means of acts that transcended his animal nature. *Homo faber* has from the beginning of time seen an inventor: the stick and the club ... became forthwith instruments for enlarging his grasp on the world ... he created, he burst out of the present, he opened the future.[27]

De Beauvoir argued in *The Second Sex* (1949) that because of women's devotion to habit and repetition, they remain mired in the present. "Few tasks are more like the torture of Sisyphus than housework," she wrote, "with its endless repetition: the clean becomes soiled, the soiled is made clean, over and over, day after day. The housewife wears herself out marking time, she makes nothing, simply perpetuates the present."[28] de Beauvoir critiqued not only the daily rituals—like feeding a child—that she believed circumscribed a woman's life, she also appraised the static form of women's work through the centuries. Not only are women's days unchanging, she argued, but the elision of their roles as historical actors was static as well. "The domestic labors that fell to [woman's] lot," de Beauvoir stated, "because they were reconcilable with the cares of maternity imprisoned her in repetition and immanence, they were repeated from day to day in identical form, which was perpetuated almost without change from century to century."[29] Thus, in what Kristeva considers a patriarchal interpretation, de Beauvoir—who was not a mother—connected women to the present, and men to the future. A writer reviewing *The Second Sex* in the African American magazine *The Crisis* in 1953 commented of de Beauvoir: "She seems to detest children and to be completely unaware of the compensations of motherhood, and sometimes the reader wonders if she doesn't detest all women—except the intellectual and artistic few."[30] Gender scholar Penelope Deutscher describes de Beauvoir's belief in the superiority of the future: "Transcendence, imagination and creation distinguish us from animality and have temporal implications: the human project is not to repeat oneself in time: it is to take control of the instant and mould the future."[31]

Other feminists writing about the temporalities of care have argued for a more complex understanding of what is involved in care, including the idea that repetitive care tasks involve a sense of progress. Davies posited that women's activities—and their use of time in care—should be understood as a spiral, one that involves forward movement despite the fact that the task is largely repetitive or circular.[32] Maher maintains that caring labor, especially the kind practiced by mothers, although involving repetitive acts like bathing, dressing, and putting a child to bed, are all focused on a future outcome. She advocates a more fruitful approach to thinking about the temporalities of care, one that "move[s] beyond the dichotomy of the industrial time of paid work and the fluid time of care since many caring activities are undertaken with a sense of temporal progress clearly in mind."[33] Thorne reasons that, because of the very nature of raising children, which involves repetitive tasks on a daily and weekly schedule that are set within a different temporality (the time of "growing up"), motherhood involves a multiplicity of temporal orders. These temporal orders include days, months, years, and decades and, in Thorne's words, "allude to a mix of daily, cyclical time (get up, get dressed, eat breakfast, pack lunches, head for school and work) and the sweep of cumulative time entailed in the passage from child to adult."[34] It is this multiplicity of temporal orders, and mothers' acute awareness of them, that leads to potential sorrow at the passage of time. As Eula Biss wrote, "The mother of an adult child sees her work completed and undone at the same time."[35]

In combining care work with other kinds of labor, mothers have demonstrated the multiple ways in which caring time intersects, and collides with, other temporalities. Historian E.P. Thompson described the exhausting contradiction in the forced conjunction of two simultaneous obligations—wage labor and home care—associated with different temporal measures. He quoted eighteenth-century British mother and Washer-Woman Mary Collier, who described the double duties that mothers carry:

> ...When we Home are come,
> Alas! We find our Work but just begun;
> So many Things for our Attendance call,
> Had we ten Hands, we could employ them all. ...
> Our Toil and Labour's daily so extreme,
> That we have hardly ever *Time to dream*.[36]

Many mothers, both in the decades examined here and in other historical periods, have combined wage labor with maternal care. Although sociologist Eviatar Zerubavel has asserted that time acts as a segmenting principle that can segregate the public and private through temporal boundaries, others have argued that these temporal boundaries are actually quite porous.[37] The public sphere of work and the private sphere of home may flow into one another, as may public and private time for the caregiver. Mothers thus are required to perform a kind of temporal code-switching: "[w]hat I am trying to make apparent here," Davies writes, "is that the make-up of women wage-earner's daily lives—as well as their lives seen in a longer perspective—consists of different temporal structures which weave complicated patterns and which demand a switching between different forms of temporality."[38]

As many scholars writing on work-life conflicts have demonstrated, caring time is often fragmented, episodic, and complex. Maher has argued that even without the interference of paid employment, mothers' obligations to their children are often experienced as fluid and unending temporal commitments, which must necessarily interconnect with the temporalities of other institutions like doctors' hours, school schedules, and the mother's own need for food or personal care.

> [F]luid caring temporality intersects with and is generated within and in relation to other measurable time units and industrial temporal orders. The time of care always already encompasses fragmentation and forward movement even as it has circularity, repetition and a sense of timelessness. The organizing principle of all these diverse temporalities of care is the desire to accumulate well-being; in the child, the family, the self. Each moment of care—fluid, discrete, contemporaneous with other activities, interrupted or partial—is focused on this accumulation.[39]

Maternal care overlaps with other obligations, and mothers' movements between different spheres and demands can be disorienting and fraught with anxiety. As a young mother speeding home on the New Jersey highway from my university job in order to be on time to meet my children at the bus stop after school, or to not be late for a school event or parent–teacher conference, I was stressed and had a visceral image of myself as a chameleon. I felt that I had to adopt a different persona to be accepted as a mother in my conservative, suburban community: not present myself as a feminist scholar, but as a person whose identity and use of time flowed singularly from motherhood. When I returned to the academic community, I had to shed my mother identity and assume a scholarly, professional, and work centric persona. In my movements between such different environments, I felt initially that I had left behind some essential piece of my identity, my self. My body was in those spaces, but there was a lag time before my full, integrated self and spirit could be fully present. My maternal identity, demands, and desires bled into my work setting, whether through my need to carry my sleeping child, home sick for the day, into faculty meetings; fielding calls in the office from day care, school, or babysitters; or simply missing my children. Similarly, my work identity and burdens inserted themselves into my time with my children. Temporal regulation—or the ways that those in power have used time to regulate bodies—is relevant to the history, identities, and experiences of motherhood.

Experts Spread the Gospel of Time Efficiency in Mothering

The emphasis on schedules, routines, and "science" in motherhood grew out of a cultural obsession with time efficiency in the late nineteenth and early twentieth century United States. The ideas of Frederick Winslow Taylor, a mechanical engineer and leader in the Efficiency Movement, were highly influential from the 1890s through the 1920s. Capitalizing on Americans' fascination with the concept of efficiency, Taylor used stopwatch time study to revolutionize industrial management practices.[40] One historian of the (Progressive) era stated, "efficient and good came closer to meaning the same thing in these years than in any other period in American history."[41] Taylor began his studies of time, motion, and productivity as a foreman in a machine shop at Midvale Steel Works. Focusing on the human component of production, Taylor believed that workers (and their managers) could maximize productivity by breaking each job down into component parts, timing each part, and rearranging them into the most efficient method of working. Excitement about what Taylor termed "scientific management," which he promoted in his 1911 book, *The Principles of Scientific Management*, spread throughout the business community.[42] Historian Laurel Graham has argued that scientific management fueled a growing efficiency craze that endorsed science and technology as the solutions for a myriad of physical, psychological, and social problems.[43] Motherhood, in the eyes of 1920s and 1930s era experts, was one of those problems. It was the Gilbreths who applied Taylor's ideas of efficiency and scientific management to the home and to motherhood.

During the 1910s, wife and husband team Lillian and Frank Gilbreth, the pioneers of motion study, analyzed workers' movements, filming the details of workers' tasks and their body postures while recording the time. This approach became known as the motion study technique, which Taylor incorporated in his book. The Gilbreths concluded that all tasks were made up of a maximum of 16 basic elements, each of which they named a "Therblig" (Gilbreth nearly spelled backwards).[44] Taylor developed the stopwatch time study, which combined with the Gilbreths' motion study methods, later became the field of time and motion study. Labor unions then and now rejected Taylorism as a kind of de-skilling and speedup that harms workers' autonomy and well-being, but benefits managers.[45] The Gilbreths and Taylor ultimately split in 1914 over their differing views on workers' rights, but their research and ideas about time efficiency had great influence on each other.

Lillian Gilbreth, an industrial psychologist who became a management consultant, applied the ideas of motion study and waste elimination to motherhood. She was an expert extolling the virtues of time efficiency in the home, yet in an era in which domesticity and domestic labor were increasingly devalued, Gilbreth valued mothers' time and recognized the immense labor and skills involved in running a household. Recipient of a Ph.D. in psychology from Brown University and mother to eleven children, Gilbreth applied tools drawn from industrial settings to the home. She publicized these ideas most notably in two books, *The Home-Maker and Her Job* (1927) and *Living With Our Children* (1928). Aiming to reduce wasted movements for women working "the finest job in the world," Gilbreth suggested, for example, that housewives ask their children to unwind a ball of string while following them as they cleared the kitchen table, in order to learn the most efficient way to complete the task.[46] Gilbreth is most remembered today as the long-suffering mother in the 1948 book (and 1950 film) *Cheaper By The Dozen*, written by two of her children (Frank Jr. and Ernestine), which tells the story of 12 children growing up with parents who are efficiency experts.[47] Although her temporal thrift philosophy did share commonalities with Catharine Beecher's ideas, Gilbreth was also an advocate for working mothers: "part of her motivation for having so many children," Lancaster writes, "was to prove a point—that educated women need not abandon family life." Becoming known as "The First Lady of Engineering," Gilbreth helped make the idea of middle-class, professional mothers less threatening: "Gilbreth faced, and to some extent solved, one of the central dilemmas of modern American women, namely how to combine family and work." The fact that Gilbreth was widowed at a fairly young age with many children to support in part spurred her on to a long career as a management consultant, household efficiency expert, and designer of model efficiency kitchens for private firms. Her ideas have shaped the ways we think about time and domesticity: "[w]hether we realize it or not," Gilbreth's biographer Jane Lancaster writes, "she influenced the way we work, the way we arrange our houses, and our attitude toward time."[48]

Gilbreth created her time management philosophy for the home with the goal of giving harried mothers extra time to fill, as they desired. Unlike Taylorism, which focused on productivity so that managers could reap the benefits of greater worker output and management profit, Gilbreth encouraged efficient mothers (who were their own managers) to turn to other pursuits when their household work was done. Time saved by working efficiently could be spent in leisure pursuits, hobbies, volunteer work, or part-time employment, "all activities that promoted women's psychological satisfaction, added variety to their days, and made them happier."[49] Gilbreth's approach to motherhood and housework emphasized the value of mothers' time. She detailed the ways she and her husband had given their efficiency methods a trial run at home before applying them to industry, highlighting the worth of (mothers') time that could be spent in other pursuits than household labor. She explained to members of the New York National Federation of Business and Professional Women's Clubs in 1930:

> We considered our time too valuable to be devoted to actual labor in the home. We were executives. So we worked out a plan for the running of our house, adopting charts and a maintenance and follow-up system as

it is used in factories. When one of the children took a bath or brushed his teeth he made a cross on a chart. Household tasks were divided between the children. We had just three rows of hooks, one marked "Jobs to be done," one marked "Jobs being done" and a third marked "Jobs completed" with tags which were moved from hook to hook to indicate the progress of the task.[50]

While this statement implied that some people's time was more valuable than others (i.e., managers' time matters more than laborers' time), Gilbreth was one of the few writers on time and domesticity in these years who believed that mothers' time was valuable.

The earlier ideas of maternalism had valued the private virtues and skills of domesticity, which antimaternalists attacked. In her work, Lillian Gilbreth redefined women's domesticity and raised the status of homemakers by treating them as specialized experts who did important work.[51] Her example suggests that if women claimed "expertness" for themselves as mothers and harnessed the authority that comes with expertness, they could elevate scientific motherhood and domesticity in a way that gave them status and authority. In her first book on the home, *The Home-Maker and Her Job*, Gilbreth defined the home as a place for women's self-expression, as well as a setting for mental and physical rest. By practicing household engineering, utilizing technology, and being alert to wasted time, mothers and wives could open up time to use in new ways. Gilbreth believed that a more rested homemaker (the term she used) would be a better mother. Like other specialists writing on motherhood in the 1920s, she emphasized the mother's role in nurturing the individuality of children, but she parted ways with other experts in her connection of efficiency to mothers' rest, and her equation of a rested mother with a high-quality mother. She advocated that both children and husbands share housework (fifty–fifty homemaking in her words), and "condemned women's unselfish, sacrificial mentality and insisted instead that they create time for pursuing their own interests."[52] Although she faced some press criticism for her views, for the most part the media understood the appeal that Gilbreth's personal story had for readers, and capitalized on it. Graham wrote, "Reporters would shock the public by disclosing that Gilbreth had eleven children (often presenting a picture of the brood as evidence) and then revealing that she made time for her career by using scientific management in her own home."[53]

Although not explicitly a feminist, Gilbreth's writings on the career–family dilemma joined that of avowed feminists like Doris Stevens and Lorine Pruette, who in the 1920s were decrying "the second shift" that working mothers faced, and the superwomen that American society expected mothers to be.[54] Gilbreth drew on her authority as a mother of 11 to turn otherwise debased features of femininity into assets. By making women's domestic work visible—through motion studies for example—she was giving it value. Gilbreth modeled a potential counter effect to who claims "expertness": the possibility that—in the right hands—rather than delegitimizing women, women could control the narrative of motherhood in ways that empowered them. Yet, Gilbreth's efficiency solutions required mothers to be proficient, well organized, and to waste no time, setting a high bar for mothers to meet. Her focus on the home and the idea of modernization, including consumption of innovations like electric refrigerators, automatic washing machines, vacuum cleaners, and convenience foods resonated for middle-class mothers, but must have felt less accessible to working-class or poor mothers. "[Gilbreth's] resolution of the conflicts between motherhood and science," Laurel Graham concluded, "reinforced women's hope that modernizing their homes would make them into more capable mothers."[55]

By the 1930s, the messages about time discipline and scientific motherhood had spread across the nation. Historian Lynn Weiner observed that social work, child guidance, preschool education, and medicine had by then institutionalized professionals' authority on motherhood, and stipulated the ways that mothers of all types were to care for their children, and conceptualize and organize time in the home.[56] In popular articles and childcare books, writers, journalists, and psychologists took up parent education, and disseminated Watson's "routinized child" prescriptions widely. Many mothers took note. In Wyoming County, New York, in the mid-1930s, the Mary Jemison Study Club for Mothers put on a series of skits to educate their husbands about Watson's edicts in his *Infant Care* pamphlets. Re-enacting a scene in which a child requires elaborate rituals before going to sleep at night, the mother reads to the father from a childcare manual:

> A well-regulated routine life for a child is absolutely essential to his physical and mental welfare. Regular habits can be formed only if the child learns from experience that he is to do the *same thing* every day at the *same hour*.[57]

Psychologist and early childhood educator Ada Hart Artlitt argued that the home should be governed not by "mother-love," but rather by the "kitchen time-piece."[58] Store-bought products and medicalized childbirth replaced the earlier, more natural approach to maternity.

> Scientific motherhood came to favor the bottle over breast-feeding, medicated hospital birth over natural home birth, and rigidly scheduled days and nights over a more fluid approach to time. ... Rationality and order—then important in such other arenas of American culture as business, home economics, and education—informed proper mothering as well. Standards of efficiency, time, and measurement were to control a baby's day as well as a factory's routine.[59]

In a literal translation of this emphasis on closely scheduled and measured time from the factory to the home, during the 1930s the Children's Bureau, part of the United States Department of Labor, published "Child's Daily Time Cards." These cards, printed to look like the time cards that employees had stamped when they entered and exited factories (to record for the supervisor hours worked), stipulated schedules for children's daily activities. Instructing mothers to "HANG THIS WHERE YOU CAN SEE IT EVERY DAY," the Time Card for 19-month to two-year-olds began at 7:00 a.m. with instructions for "Toilet. Bath. Dress. Brush teeth. (Bath may be given at 8:30 a.m. if more convenient.)" The Time Card stipulated that breakfast be served at 7:30 ("Cooked cereal with milk and a little sugar; coddled, soft-boiled, or poached egg; crisp bacon occasionally; boiled whole milk") followed by cod-liver oil and half an orange. The time between 7:30 a.m. and 8:30 a.m. was to be spent on Toilet and Play. The strict schedule continued to mark one to two hour intervals throughout the day (and how that time should be organized for the child), ending at 6:00 p.m. when it was time for "Toilet. Bed, lights out, windows open, door shut." Thus, the U.S. government equated children in their second year of life with workers in a factory. An addendum at the bottom of the Time Card instructed mothers that, while they had some autonomy to rearrange their child's schedule, they did not have much. "This plan may be varied to suit the family schedule, but one like this should be arranged and kept to closely," the U.S. Children's Bureau advised. "Whatever plan is used, meals should be at the same time every day."[60] Such synchronization was, ideally, to extend to the family and the household as a whole (and what to do with a toddler who threw a tantrum, refused to get dressed, or hated cereal or bedtime was left to the mother's discretion).

As the moving letters that poor mothers wrote to the Children's Bureau in the 1910s and 1920s demonstrate, hardworking mothers' lack of time and physical exhaustion often prevented them from being able to get or keep their children on schedules, although they tried. They internalized the antimaternalist message that it is the mother's fault that she does not have enough time; it is not the culture's problem or the Institution's problem. Their letters also demonstrate the ways that a shortage of resources, including government programs to support mothers, affected the quality of their lives.

One 1920 letter written by an overwhelmed Seattle mother to Children's Bureau head Julia Lathrop illustrates a mother doing her best to be "modern" and "scientific" in her approach to childcare, while at the same time expressing fatigue, and sorrow at the passage of time. Because such documents are rare, I quote the letter at length.

> I am a *busy* mother of three dear babies—aged 3 years, 20 months and 3 months. I am obliged to do all my work and we have not the conveniences and modern utilities that I wish we could afford. I am up-to-date in the care of my babies, reading and following the best literature on the care of babies. The help I need is in planning my work—a work

schedule or something to aid me in the daily routine. I do the very best I can. I am busy all day and all evening but my work is never done—I am tired enough to drop when night comes and in the morning look with dread upon the day ahead of me. I want to play with my babies, I want to have time to love them and laugh with them. I have wanted babies for years and now, when Im [sic] so tired and with unfinished work every where I turn, I could scream at their constant prattle. I love them until it hurts and know that, when they are out of their babyhood, I can never forgive myself for not making more of these precious years.

Is there not some way that I can do all these scientific and hygienic duties for babies, keep our house up in proper fashion and still have time to rock and play with my babies? What of all my housework and baby-care could best be left undone? I do not ask time for myself but it would be nice to have a short period during the evening in which to read as I feel that I am growing narrow with no thoughts other than my household.

Although Mary Mills West, herself a widowed mother of five, demonstrated compassion in her response and advised "cutting down to the mere essentials in your cooking and cleaning," she still advocated time discipline and scheduling, advising this mother to systematize her children's hours "and run their meals, naps, hours of play, and night sleep on a regular schedule."[61] The mother who wrote the letter recognized the fleeting and precious nature of her time with her children when they were still young, and the cruel truth that her own physical tiredness did not allow her to fully enjoy them. Despite Lillian Gilbreth's contention that women's happiness and mental health would improve if they had more time to spend on themselves, it is clear that the modern approach to time efficiency in the home was not accessible to some mothers. While this mother—whose voice could represent the voices and emotions of many mothers—felt that the demands of scientific motherhood kept her from enjoying her babies, her paradoxical hope was that time regulation would, in some way, help her.

Dangerous, Disorganized Mothers

The economic, social, and political uncertainty triggered by the Great Depression spread a narrative of the family in crisis, and the government hailed wives and mothers as leaders in enabling besieged families to survive.[62] At the same time, the nation fretted over the masculinity of unemployed men and expressed disapproval of working wives, whose wages were essential to family survival. Franklin D. Roosevelt's New Deal legislation led to the expansion of the welfare state. While some women grew more politically active and professionally successful in the 1930s, public attacks on women increased, and the federal government passed legislation discriminating against wage-earning wives.[63] Antimaternalism was on the rise, as the expert community and the American public increasingly criticized mothers' damaging effects on the family.

Experts increasingly implicated disorganization, whether in children's routines or family structure, in family difficulties, and they most often blamed wives and mothers for these problems. Social scientists' criticisms of the "disordered" family, which largely centered on the black family but also included immigrant families, still fingered white, native-born women in whose households, for example, they found feminine men who lacked authority. So-called matriarchs were especially threatening: "[w]omen assuming masculine prerogatives," Feldstein notes, "were particularly 'disorganizing.'"[64] These admonitions against wage-earning women and "dominant" mothers became more strident in the crisis years of the Depression, as did critiques about disorder, as an army of sociologists and social workers descended upon homes to analyze the American family in a time of crisis.[65] In *Caste and Class in a Southern Town* (1937), white social psychologist John Dollard considered white–black relations in a Jim Crow "Southerntown." Although intended as an expose of the risks the southern caste system presented to both blacks and whites, Dollard's use of concepts like prudence, order, and organization reflect the culture's anxiety about the perceived loss of these in the American family, the African American family in particular, and in mothers' care of their children. Dollard also characterized the feminine, or femininity, as disordered: "Like studies of white families," Feldstein writes, "*Caste and Class* associated rationality, independence, and wage earning with masculinity." Dollard described the homes of white town inhabitants as "well-painted ... and neat," an illustration that a "sense of discipline and order is more apparent." His contrasting description of homes in "nigger town" was of small, poorly constructed houses, overgrown lawns, and a general sense of disorder and backwardness: "Behind the houses the frequent privies testify to the fact that these people are not wholly included in our modern technology."[66]

Ignoring the effects of racism and poverty, Dollard connected disorder with a lack of schedules and time discipline, stating that only "those who have correct working habits involving abstinence and foresight" could receive "economic justice." He darkly warned that those who "do not have these habits, and the lower-class Negroes do not, would have to be trained by force to have them."[67] Economically independent, wage-earning black women led to a "weak, mother-centered family" which was, in Dollard's estimation, a disorganized family. Similarly, in his 1939 text *The Negro Family in the United States*, black sociologist E. Franklin Frazier described disorganized families most often headed by dominant black mothers.[68] In these analyses, mothers—black mothers in particular—were blamed for the "disorganized" family—the family that lacked time discipline and order. Dollard and Frazier anticipated the infamous 1965 report "The Negro Family: The Case for National Action," written by the then-Assistant Secretary of Labor Daniel Patrick Moynihan. Known simply as "The Moynihan Report," this devastating analysis described racial inequality in terms of family structure, pointing to disorganization, absent black fathers, and matriarchal black mothers as the causes of dysfunction in the American black family.[69] "The Moynihan Report" influenced American public policy on the family for half a century. It was an intensely antimaternalist document.

African American parent education organizations that interacted with white institutions faced racism and stereotyped views, which included critical references to disordered families and black mothers' use of time. The School of Household Administration at the University of Cincinnati trained African American women in child study and parent education. These black educators began mothers' study groups—some with up to 70 members—in conjunction with Cincinnati women's clubs, day nurseries, kindergartens, and health centers. By 1930, two years after its founding, more than eleven hundred African American women had joined the School of Household Administration's child study groups. Attendance continued to increase even after the start of the Depression. In a 1939 letter, one of the white program administrators wrote:

> We have found it necessary to have the Negro project supervised by a white worker inasmuch as this both adds to the esteem in which the project is regarded by the Negro people and assures that the classes will be met on time and conducted for the required period.[70]

Similarly, the director of a Cincinnati kindergarten complained that the African American mothers were always late for meetings and often fell asleep during lectures (not considering that this might reflect fatigue after days of combining waged labor with unwaged care and mothering work).[71] These attitudes reflected early ideas drawn from the racialization of American motherhood, including the nineteenth and early twentieth century depictions of the modern, white American mother in contrast to the superstitious or unhygienic ethnic or black mother.[72] They also drew on ideas of scientific motherhood, which stipulated that experts knew better than mothers the best way to raise children.

Like their critiques of African American mothers' undisciplined use of time, white, native-born social workers and parent educators condemned immigrant mothers' failures to adhere to rigid parenting schedules and to use time well. They applied their own middle-class standards to working-class mothers. Advocating a scientific understanding of children's nature and needs, they insisted that children should be disciplined from infancy and forced to adhere to scheduled feedings, strictly observed. Mothers who picked up babies who had been fed and cleaned were accused of spoiling their children. In contrast, many immigrant mothers allowed their babies to dictate the feeding schedule, and initiated discipline at later ages.[73] Advocate of scientific motherhood Elsa Herzfeld was horrified by what she perceived as the irregularity of immigrant breastfeeding habits, which today we call feeding on demand. After visiting early twentieth-century immigrant homes she reproachfully observed:

> The babies were nursed irregularly. If the mother was working or "goes out for the day," she nurses the baby at meal times and during the night. Irregular, artificial feedings supplement the nursing. In the case of a non-wage-earning mother, the nursings are equally irregular. The child is nursed when it cries or whenever the mother thinks it necessary, day or night. The clock is not consulted.[74]

Early twentieth-century apostles of scientific housekeeping, like home economist Mabel Kittredge, applied time as a tool of control in the model tenement movement, which she led. Kittredge believed that the problem with "old-fashioned housework," which immigrant women preferred, was that it was too dependent on outdated customs where "the sense of time, so important to the highly civilized, does not exist" and home life "is too dependent upon the work of one woman [so that it] cannot attain anything like a strict sense of regularity." As Ewen noted, the purpose of the model tenement movement—which Kittredge began with "housekeeping centers" and model flats at New York's Lower East Side's Henry Street Settlement—was in

> bringing order out of disorder ... to instill a clock-like regularity and discipline to tenement living through the re-education of the mother. The imposition of the clock would allow women to develop a daily schedule, and consistent repetition would inculcate habits that would promote order and efficiency; by adopting an assembly line approach, [immigrant] mothers could become model workers.[75]

In this philosophy, adherence to clock time became an instrument used to both shape and determine the immigrant mother's level of assimilation.[76]

The assumption that mothers required training in time discipline and its importance in childcare was often off the mark. Educators discovered that some rural mothers already adhered to schedules for their babies and children, necessitated by the demands of their own—and their children's—physical labor on farms. A child-study club leader tried to deliver a lesson to a group of farmwomen from East Concord, New York, on ways to discipline and regulate children's eating and sleeping habits, but the questions she posed puzzled rural mothers. She reported back to the Cornell Home Bureau (which sponsored parenting clubs from the late 1920s through 1945) that

> In the country it seems [children] eat everything—have schedules—go to bed early and the children have to help out a great deal as the mothers are so busy—many outdoors a better part of the day. The whole family is so busy from hard work that they retire very early.[77]

Some rural mothers were not afraid to challenge, or ignore, the experts. In her study of Tennessee tenant farm mothers in the 1930s, sociologist Margaret Jarman Hagood found that it was unusual for mothers to nurse their babies on a schedule: "The notion was new to some and incomprehensible to a few."[78] A group of farmwomen in a mothers' study group in St. Lawrence County, New York, disagreed with childhood experts that children should play sequestered from adults:

> Our group believed that a child should have some privacy but should not be completely isolated as was stated in the book. Most of the mothers agreed that they would rather have their children near them so they could work and watch them too.[79]

Immigrant women could not organize their days according to strict schedules; instead, they decided for themselves what tasks to do at what time of day. Following their own sense of order, they defined their own domestic rhythms.[80]

Other immigrant mothers embraced the tenets of scientific motherhood, viewing them as modern and superior. As one Jewish mother interviewed in the 1980s about raising children in the 1930s and 1940s remarked, "Just because your mother and your grandmother did it I didn't think that was the best thing. I was a modern mother and the modern way was to go to a specialist."[81] These mothers sought out professionals rather than relatives for advice: "I never took my mother-in-law's remedies," another stated.

> She came from the other side. I mean, after all, we're American. We're not from the little shtetla. ... I [had] the biggest man [doctor] in the city when Phyllis was born ... I wanted to know what we do today. Not what we did thirty, forty years ago.[82]

As sociologist Jacquelyn Litt concluded from her interviews of Jewish-American mothers (some of them immigrants) of this era, they were happy to follow the advice of male physicians because to do so was reassuring and "help[ed] them secure their positions as good, American mothers."[83]

Recognizing time discipline and scientific motherhood as tools of control, African American mothers were more reluctant than white mothers to embrace their tenets. While some middle-class African American mothers employed scientific motherhood, working-class African Americans found themselves estranged from the medicalized approach of the Northern system, which replaced the home births and "granny midwives" of the South with hospitals, and white doctors and nurses.[84] Participants in the Great Migration which took American blacks in historic numbers from the rural South to the urban North, African American mothers of this generation had real cause to distrust white medical professionals. They were hesitant to abandon the tradition of extended relationships of caretaking they had employed in the South, the idea that "it takes a village" to raise a child.[85] Some clear-sightedly linked scientific motherhood to the consumer culture—evidenced by the rise of mass advertising—that was sweeping the nation. One African American single mother reflecting on her struggles to raise a healthy child during the 1930s described both relying on the advice of her mother and grandmother, and turning to store-bought products: "You get modern, I guess. I mean you go and buy, you don't make, you don't bother with all these remedies. You go and buy."[86] Another African American woman signaled her respect for the maternal knowledge of previous generations, as well as confidence in her own knowledge:

> [W]hy go to the doctor and ask them everything? You got a mind of your own. ... I mean, you have to use your own judgment sometime about your own kids. You feel better to ask your mother [or] ... somebody in neighborhood, you know, who—had more kids, instead...And if somebody had about three or four kids, they know a little bit more than what my mother knew because they had more kids than she did. ... When I was raising my kids I was in the country, you couldn't run to the doctor, you know, every time they got sick.[87]

Litt concluded from her interviews with working-class Philadelphia African American mothers who raised children in the 1920s, 1930s, and 1940s that social networks were the critical elements informing their approach to childcare. These mothers continued to largely rely on the advice of family and friends in raising their children, rather than on medical and scientific authority.[88]

Some early twentieth-century mothers were uncomfortable with the idea that mothers were overly obsessed with their children and recognized the misogyny embedded in this belief. The group secretary's minutes from a 1932 Cornell mothers' group meeting read: "The comment oftenest voiced is 'Have these writers had experience with children?' The methods are so different from our former knowledge of dealing with children that some are slow to accept them."[89] Another mother acerbically stated to psychologist John Watson after one of his moralizing lectures before a group of mothers: "Thank God, my children are grown—and that I had a chance to enjoy them before I met you."[90]

Poor mothers of all backgrounds found themselves without the luxury of time to focus on their children's psychic development and physical schedules. Writer Tillie Olsen beautifully captured the dilemma of a Depression-era white, working-class mother in her novella "I Stand Here Ironing." When asked by a teacher to explore the reasons for her teenage daughter's emotional difficulties she responded:

> And when is there time to remember, to sift, to weigh, to estimate, to total? I will start and there will be an interruption and I will have to

gather it all together again. Or I will become engulfed with all I did or did not do, with what should have been and what cannot be helped.[91]

Another early twentieth-century mother, exhausted by the daily rounds of motherhood, when asked whether she was having meaningful experiences with her children replied: "It may be that I am having interesting experiences with [my] children, but I cannot tell you what they are. I do not see them. I am too busy with their care to see their development."[92] An overworked Kansas mother lamented in a 1921 letter to the Children's Bureau:

> Oh! If I could only rest a while, but I don't see any chance. I have had my children so fast and have had so much to do I am worn out. There are seven in the family now and I am only 26. What will I be like in ten years more, if I live?[93]

Alice Walker described her hardworking African American mother, who in the 1930s labored beside her husband in the fields and whose days began before sunrise and did not end until late at night: "There was never a moment for her to sit down, undisturbed, to unravel her own private thoughts, never a time free from interruption—by work and the noisy inquiries of her many children."[94] For the most part, poor and working-class mothers in the 1920s and 1930s felt that experts did not understand their circumstances, or the quandaries they faced. An African American Nashville mother interviewed in 1933 said of parent education groups:

> I don't need nobody to tell me anything. All I need is a place to leave my William when I go to work. I used to go to that Mothers' Club, but schucks, it ain't nothing. White folks just naturally can't tell you nothing about raising children.[95]

Mothers' Boys: Antimaternalism and the Damaging Mother

In response to national and global events during the 1930s and 1940s, the parent education movement modified its theories about childhood and motherhood. The economic crisis, followed by war, caused the expert community to retool its message. A more flexible approach to parenting, influenced by psychoanalysis, replaced the strict regimentation of scientific motherhood. The near-exclusive focus of attention on the child in 1920s parent education gave way in 1930s groups and publications to more attention on the family. Professionals encouraged fathers to strengthen their familial influence, in part to offset what they perceived as maternal intensity and control. Popular articles and books criticized the old-fashioned self-sacrificing mother as domineering and damaging to her children.

These decades in the United States witnessed the unleashing of an astonishing barrage of antimaternalism, catalyzed by Philip Wylie's 1942 *Generation* of *Vipers*. In books like Wylie's and psychologist David Levy's *Maternal Overprotection* (1943), the childhood expert community increasingly pointed their fingers at mothers, whom they characterized as overprotective and even devouring. Historian Rebecca Jo Plant has offered a convincing interpretation of why *Generation of Vipers* hit such a nerve in the United States. She argues that Wylie's momism critique was the culminating expression of an interwar assault on the late-Victorian matriarch and the idea of moral motherhood.[96] It also took aim at the feminist advances women had made, convinced that women wanted to "have their cake and eat it too" by demanding equal rights while still expecting gender-based privileges. It was the same argument that anti-ERA forces had mustered in the 1920s. Summoning this modern scenario for his readers, Wylie attempted to deliver a final blow to "the battered, yet remarkably enduring, ideology of moral motherhood."[97] The kind of caricature Wylie created of (middle-class) mothers—lazy, parasitical, idle, consumerist—represented a denunciation of the importance of domestic labor, women's community involvement, and caregiving. Wylie attacked clubwomen, female volunteers, housewives, consumers of popular culture, and mothers who cultivated warm bonds with their sons. The feminist response was mixed: both Simone de Beauvoir and Betty Friedan quoted from Wylie's text in their own books, interpreting his argument as a revelation about the ways sexual inequality in the public arena forced women to seek power in the private one.[98] Maternalist historian Mary Beard, who had a long history in progressive social movements and in her own 1946 book *Woman As Force in History* argued that women as mothers and community caretakers had made innumerable contributions to civilization, recognized this for the assault on wives and mothers that it was: "If [the homemaker] does not regain her own sense of … her inherited power, she will be the kind of material on which Hitler and other dictators of our age have preyed for their designs," she warned, adding, "And in our society we allow a man like Philip Wylie to make 'Mom' just a 'jerk.'"[99]

By the mid-1940s, Plant maintains, antimaternalism had gone mainstream: "Critics argued that what appeared like self-sacrificing mother love could in fact be narcissistic, possessive, and pathogenic."[100] In the post-World War II years "[M]om-bashing," as Ruth Feldstein noted, "became a national pastime."[101] In December 1945, *Look* magazine excerpted Wylie's momism chapter, and a deluge of middle-class mothers wrote letters in response. One mother of six who had lost a son during the war, rejoined:

> You talk of old fat women with nothing to do I wish you could just follow me thru one week you would probably be helpless for the rest of your life. I not only cook, sew, wash, iron, sweep, and clean but find time for church activities and Red Cross work also cookies for U.S.O. and keep a sleeping room available for the U.S.O. Travelers Aid for service men wives or mothers. I have 2 sons in High School and I for one should not have to defend the mothers of this generation who have not

only given of their time and energy in the cause of war and peace but have given their sons and their very hearts.[102]

This woman was invoking the earlier American idea of patriotic motherhood, which held that loyal mothers were to produce citizen-soldiers, and equated mothers' sacrifices to their sacrifice of their sons to the state. Less than three decades earlier, socialist Kate Richards O'Hare had been imprisoned for challenging patriotic motherhood, arguing in a 1917 anti-war speech in Bowman, North Dakota, that it epitomized the corruption of (working-class) motherhood that occurred under capitalism and militarism. She proclaimed that patriotic motherhood reduced women to "brood sows" who reproduced soldiers—"American fertilizer"—who in turn killed for, or were killed by, the state.[103] Twenty-eight years later, the United States had come full-circle, no longer believing there was a connection between motherhood and politics, or motherhood and sacrifice, unless it was a psychically unhealthy one.

In a 1945 *Ladies' Home Journal* article, journalist Amram Scheinfeld took up the question that psychiatrist Edward Strecker had raised in his influential article of that year: "Are American Moms a Menace?" Strecker, professor of psychiatry and consultant to the Army and Navy, would definitively answer that question in his 1951 *Their Mothers' Sons: The Psychiatrist Examines an American Problem*. Strecker believed that "moms" were responsible for "psychoneurotics" in the armed forces. By either over-attention or domination during the formative years mothers, he argued, kept their sons from maturing emotionally. Strecker described "moms" as sweet, doting and self-sacrificing, or as the polar opposite: stern, capable, and domineering: "Both these moms," Strecker wrote, "are busily engaged finding in their children ego satisfactions for life's thrwartings and frustrations." He blamed mothers for "exact[ing] in payment the emotional lives of their children."[104] These antimaternalist ideas would, as we shall see, show up in multiple forms in the 1940s, 1950s, and beyond.

Mid-century antimaternalists like Strecker and Scheinfeld constructed American mothers as influential, damaging forces, threatening not only the masculinity of their husbands, but that of their sons as well. Scheinfeld heartily agreed that American moms were a menace, and traced this danger to overly powerful mothers and excessive maternal influence in the home. He highlighted the value of homes in which "there is a balanced situation, with a sensible mother in her proper place." But "danger looms when the father's influence is weakened or missing," and the mother becomes a "mom, either of the overbearing type, who squashes her son, or the indulgent kind, who pampers and spoils him with saccharine over-attention." He cited the research of child psychiatrist Dr. David M. Levy, who in the 1940s was publishing on maternal overprotection.[105] In this work, Levy indicted mothers who breastfed or bottle-fed children too long; who "frequently kissed and fondled their sons, in some cases sharing the mother's bed up to the boy's adolescence." These "overprotected" situations, he noted, were those in which the father was "weak-willed or submissive" (often because he was a "mothers' boy" himself) and left the handling of the child to the mother. Scheinfeld asserted that mothers displaced both their unfulfilled sexual needs and professional ambitions on their sons:

> Frequently her oversolicitousness and undue attachment to her sons result from her inadequate sex life, which may cause her to seek in a son a love substitute. Again, if her own ambitions have been suppressed, she may strive to achieve success through her son, driving him beyond his powers.

"So it is that mother's boys abound," he concluded, "among the social misfits, ne'er-do-wells, criminals, alcoholics, and homosexuals."[106]

In a complete reversal of the earlier American idea of patriotic motherhood, antimaternalists cast mothers as a menace to the country, and to their sons' abilities to perform on the battlefield. Scheinfeld described the "growing domination by American mothers of the "mom" type as an "immediate menace to our security." An information education officer in the Army Air Force theorized that the insidious reliance of the American man on "'Mom' and her pies" had "killed as many men as a thousand German machine guns."[107] Scheinfeld offered a list of ten "Don'ts for Doting Mothers" (IF YOU WANT YOUR BOYS TO DEVELOP NORMALLY). He advised against bed sharing, exclusively female atmospheres, overly long breast or bottle feeding, excessive fondling and kissing, pushing sons too hard, whining that he is neglecting you, being jealous of his girlfriends, and—especially for widows or divorced mothers—"don't try to turn your son into a substitution for your husband, or make him feel that he will be an ingrate if he marries and has a home of his own."[108] Such offensive attacks on mothers made their way into the arts and popular culture. A 1956 best-selling book, *The Crack in the Picture Window*, described suburban America as a matriarchal society and the typical husband as "a woman-based, inadequate, money-terrified neuter" and the typical wife "a nagging slob."[109]

Ironically, by the 1940s and 1950s, experts praised women of color as more instinctual mothers who inflicted less damage on their children than did white women.[110] Yet even civil rights leaders who celebrated black "mamas" and the key roles they played in the rising movement still joined whites in criticizing black matriarchs for raising sons who were either too meek or too violent.[111] As the war progressed, government propaganda urged women to take war jobs, but the psychological literature argued that mothers who worked outside the home damaged their children. While the trend toward combining labor force participation with mothering continued to accelerate in the post-World War II years, wage-earning mothers—among whose ranks African American mothers had always found themselves—were still suspect. Black single mothers faced limitations in access to federal and state financial assistance, as well as other benefits.[112] Women and mothers of all races received conflicting social messages, which posed a conundrum. There was no winning.

Even feminists made American mothers feel devalued. In 1963, Betty Friedan published *The Feminine Mystique*, in which she challenged the widely held 1950s belief that "fulfillment as a woman had only one definition for American women after 1949—the housewife-mother."[113] In her explosive book, which many credit with playing a pivotal role in the launching of the revitalized American women's movement, Friedan asserted that housewives in the early 1960s were unhappy—"suffering from the problem that has no name"—and longing and equipped for more than lives as full-time mothers and housewives. Historians have argued that, like de Beauvoir before her, Friedan reproduced the antimaternalist critique that circulated widely in postwar popular culture and expert literature.[114] She also spoke predominantly to white, middle-class women. As the slew of letters Friedan's critics wrote her after *The Feminine Mystique's* publication reveal, rather than feeling greater self-worth in their maternal and domestic roles, after reading Friedan's book some mothers and wives felt demoralized and inadequate.[115] One reader of *The Feminine Mystique* underlined her own maternal time investment and her frustration about the revised expectations for ideal mothers, some of them coming from the feminist movement:

> I was brought up to believe that a woman was herself when she made a home for her husband and children. That was considered quite an achievement and women were looked up to because they were Mothers and wives not scientists, chemists, doctors, lawyers or astronauts. Please, won't someone come to the defense of the women who put in twelve hours a day trying to be good Mothers and wives, so they won't feel that in years to come they too may be replaced by another time saving appliance.[116]

In 1964, La Leche League founder and mother of seven Marion Tompson brought her three-and-a-half months old son, whom she was nursing, with her to hear Betty Friedan speak at a meeting of the Maternal and Child Health Association in Springfield, Illinois. After listening to Friedan's message that women should measure their self-worth by getting a job, Tompson stood up and explained that just seeing her son breastfeeding, happy, and healthy, and knowing how she had contributed to this was all the justification she needed to feel important as a woman. She later recalled:

> With that, Ms. Friedan walked over to me, drew herself up, and said, "You are building up your self-esteem at the expense of your baby!" Imagine! I realized then that we were the product of two very different life experiences, and she might never understand why I enjoyed and valued being a mother.[117]

Here Friedan was channeling the ideas of Dr. David Levy and other male antimaternalists of the time.[118]

By the mid-1930s some experts had begun to criticize time discipline and its application to motherhood. While in the 1920s Dr. Arnold Gesell had popularized developmental schedules for children, by the 1930s he rejected the parallel between child-rearing and factory production, counseling mothers, "Don't watch the clock, watch the child."[119] Scientific motherhood also succumbed to broader forces of political and international change, including the rise of fascism and the outbreak of World War II.

Thus, in a complete reversal, experts now criticized mothers who practiced the scientific parenting strategies that had been heavily promoted in the 1920s and 1930s. Pediatricians disseminated revised guidelines for feeding children on demand, and advocated that mothers now utilize child-centered parenting practices. Specialists increasingly pointed to mothers as the linchpins in producing happy and productive, or unhappy and damaged, citizens. A few pundits and experts still equated motherhood with women's patriotic contributions to the nation. Pediatrician Edith Johnson illustrated this in a 1944 radio speech from New York's Baby Institute: "In a world at war, mothers still sing to their babies. The proper care and training, the development of our children, is as essential to true and final victory as the warfare on our fighting fronts."[120] The concept of democracy, for which the United States was fighting in Europe, became increasingly important in conceptions of family life, including parent–child relations. Experts linked democratic child-rearing practices to the maintenance of democracy in the United States.

Social scientists implicated authoritarian child-rearing practices with the rise of fascism in Germany, and some extremists even compared overbearing, rigid mothers to Nazis. The domination of "Mom" was linked to metaphorical male castration and at the critics' most extreme, to Hitler's domination of Europe.[121]

By the postwar period and into the Cold War years American mothers, armed with Dr. Benjamin Spock's incredibly popular 1946 *The Common Sense Book of Baby and Child Care*, themselves began to reject the time disciplined mothering of the 1920s and 1930s. Spock-influenced mothers did not, however, reject maternal reliance on medical authority, but embraced it even more as they expanded their families, moved to the suburbs, and raised their children. Seeking "normalcy" after the end of a second world war, the nation turned to family building and conformity, and did so, as Vandenberg-Daves emphasized, "in perhaps the century's most rigidly enforced definitions of masculinity and femininity."[122] The 1950s, characterized by sharply rising fertility and marriage rates, was accompanied by a pronatalist ideology that encouraged large families.[123] An era of rapid suburbanization and geographic mobility, the 1950s found many middle-class mothers isolated from extended family and close-knit communities.

Spock's book represented a publishing phenomenon: within ten months it had sold 6,478 copies in hardcover and 541,460 copies in paperback. Within three years, paperback sales soared to a million copies a year. By 1998, *The Common Sense Book of Baby and Child Care* had been translated into 39 languages and had sold over 50 million copies.[124] Spock's colloquial writing style, his merging of mothers' experiences (in the first edition, his wife Anne's) with medical expertise, and his rejection of behaviorism and its inflexible schedules all contributed to the fervent reception the book enjoyed. But the publishing juggernaut also represented men and medical authorities continuing to tell women how to mother, and mothers' needs and desires for such advice.

In rejecting behaviorism, Spock like others was influenced by the spread of Freudian psychoanalysis into child development theory in the United States in the 1930s and 1940s. Rather than imposing the parent's will on the child, mothers should now follow the child's needs and natural schedule. Rima Apple described this radical departure from earlier approaches:

> Mothers were no longer strict disciplinarians; in the intense mothering of Spock's book, they were supportive nurturers. They must not rush their children prematurely into weaning, eating solid foods, tub bathing, or toilet training and the like. Rather, modern mothers carefully observed their children and followed their lead.[125]

Spock was not the first pediatrician to condemn time discipline applied to motherhood. Dorothy Whipple, a mother and physician, published *Our American Babies: The Art of Baby Care* in 1943, three years before Spock's book. Looking back on her medical training during the 1920s, the highpoint of behaviorism, Whipple recalled being taught that, after birth, babies should be conditioned in germ-free environments where "an infant's needs were attended to with stop-watch regularity by a well-trained attendant." When she tried to apply these practices to her own children at home, she found it impossible:

> [t]o go away from my own crying baby, and stay within earshot for an hour or more before the clock said I could give him milk I knew he wanted, that, I confess, I found to be a different matter.[126]

As a pediatrician, Whipple did not reject schedules outright, but recommended that babies set their own schedules, and that mothers should realize that the baby "is a better guide than the clock upon the wall." Paraphrasing Gesell's advice Whipple concluded, "It is better for the child ... that mothers watch the baby carefully and follow the baby's clock."[127] Her own maternal emotions and instinct led her to reject a time-focused approach to care: the bestowing of maternal authority on a machine, the clock, backed up by the advice of male experts.

The Alternative Birth Movement and Maternal Control

The 1950s laid the foundation for a redefinition of scientific motherhood. Some experts criticized Spock's relaxed approach to baby care and even blamed him for rebellious 1950s and 1960s-era youth-led social movements. These experts associated Spock with what they considered permissive child-rearing of the post-World War II era, which they believed resulted in "youth who criticized their elders, who challenged authority, and who caused dissension throughout the nation."[128] Critics also assailed Spock for his gingerly suggestion in the 1946 edition of *Baby and Child Care* that dad might "occasionally" change a diaper, offer the baby a bottle, or even make the formula on Sunday. Illuminating the rigid notions of masculinity and femininity that characterized the post-World War II years, a respected sociologist of the time warned that a helpful father might be assumed of "having a little too much fat on the inner thigh."[129]

Other physicians condemned Spock and connected his advocacy of child-centered motherhood with the potential destruction of American democracy. Conservative fear-mongers seized on the fact that Spock himself joined the anti-war movement, and was a political liberal. In *Bringing Up Babies: A Family Doctor's Practical Approach to Child Care* (1962), Dr. Walter Sackett Jr. warned that lenient mothering could ultimately lead to a socialist nation. Writing at the height of the Cold War he cautioned, "If we teach our offspring to expect everything to be provided on demand, we must admit the possibility of sowing the seeds of socialism."[130] Yet as Vandenberg-Daves has noted, by the 1960s experts who had previously drawn their authority from science and masculinity "now stood more uncertainly on their pedestals. In addition to the creation of the atomic bomb, the hyperrationalism of the first half of the century seemed partly responsible for atrocities like Hitler's "final solution."[131] The countercultural ideas of rebellious youth and hippy culture endorsed a return to the natural, and this extended to pregnancy and childbirth.

By the 1950s, childbirth had become medicalized. By the middle of the decade, 95 percent of all births in the United States took place in hospitals. In comparison, in 1940 only 50 percent of births had occurred in hospitals, and fewer than 5 percent in 1900. Forceps, twilight sleep, and medical intervention increasingly characterized American births.[132] Maternal mortality decreased dramatically in the 1940s, causing Americans to question the earlier assumption that in childbearing women confronted both pain and peril. Physicians and nurses used new mothers' hospital stays to indoctrinate them in the rules and routines of modern motherhood. While white, middle-class women were given access to pain relief in childbirth—sometimes against their wishes—poor and women of color at times faced physicians who believed they were impervious to pain, and were reluctant to give them the pain relief they needed or required.[133]

As the 1950s turned into the 1960s, advocates of alternative mothering, whether African American and immigrant mothers who continued to rely on extended family and kin networks for child-rearing help and advice, or white, middle-class mothers who now supported natural childbirth and breastfeeding, either explicitly or implicitly criticized the experts' admonitions about the ways mothers should use time. They offered different models, possibilities for how mothers could experience the embodied parts of maternity, including pregnancy, labor and childbirth, and breastfeeding. Feminist writers, including Adrienne Rich, condemned the patriarchal nature of motherhood in the United States and the narrow parameters of what constituted "good" mothering in the 1950s and 1960s. The feminist movement joined forces with the women's health movement and alternative birth movement in the 1960s and 1970s, and Rich is one symbol of that coming together.[134] Some constituents of the feminist movement pushed back against male-centric models of motherwork and mothering.

Alternative approaches to childbirth and women's health that began to spread in the 1940s and beyond gave women a greater voice in their own experiences of pregnancy, birth, and healthcare, and challenged rigid approaches to time. Movements such as Grantly Dick-Read's "childbirth without fear" and Lamaze's "prepared childbirth" brought the ideas of European medical practitioners to the United States.[135] Both men stressed the importance of women's active, cognizant participation in the birth process, and the importance of allowing the natural rhythm of birth and the woman's body to dictate the process, rather than a medicalized and clock-driven approach. Later female advocates of ecofeminism and natural childbirth believed that to diminish the capacity and power of a woman's body would lead mothers to "become marked by manmade clocks and the truths of scientific experts."[136] While the white, middle-class women who led the natural childbirth movement of the 1940s and 1950s rejected the association between maternity and suffering—along with the idea that childbearing involved a civic element—the movement did not attract a diverse constituency. "Natural" childbirth seemed an inaccessible luxury for women seeking access to vital prenatal and maternal health care: "[n]either the critique of medicalized childbirth," Plant writes, "nor the celebration of 'natural motherhood' held much appeal for women struggling to obtain basic medical care."[137] The natural childbirth community increasingly used nurse midwives, as mothers looked to the approaches of earlier generations and their birthing methods, rather than to the future and a relentless march forward to routinized and medicalized birth. Rima Apple has described "the genesis of a redefinition of scientific motherhood" in the 1950s, and argues that the redefinition included a challenging of the experts' ideas about time discipline and motherhood.[138]

Advocates of midwifery and natural childbirth called for new and different ways of measuring time in labor. Physicians often diagnosed especially long labors as "false" labor in order to "normalize" events so they conformed to the medical model and expert-generated tables of what was statistically normal in childbirth. In contrast, midwives attending home births often saw labors start and stop, and believed that labor could reverse itself; they trusted "that 'progress' is not an inevitable direction."[139] Home birth midwives in the 1950s and 1960s assumed that social and emotional factors could influence a woman's labor and began to reassess the medical definitions of labor itself. In hospitals, long labors often led to medical interventions including the breaking of the membranes, hormones to stimulate more advanced labor, or cesarean sections. In examining the history of childbirth in the United States, Wendy Simonds and her co-authors describe a kind of "speed-up" of hospital labors over time. Examining various editions of the classic textbook *Williams Obstetrics*, they noted that the reported length of labor dropped from an average first stage of labor in first births of 12.5 hours in 1948 to 10.5 in 1980, and from 7.3 hours for second and subsequent births in 1948 down to only 5 hours by the 1980 edition.

> The rush is largely institutional: births in hospitals need to be meshed together to form an overarching institutional tempo. Predictability is important; timing matters, as staff moves from birth to birth, as women are moved from place to place. … "Active management," managing labor by the clock with interventions as necessary to speed it up, is part of the medical ethos. Although they may often have to watch the clock the obstetricians have set for them, it is not part of the midwifery approach.[140]

In her book-length poem *Natural Birth*, African American writer Toi Derricotte described living with a white Michigan family in 1962 who invited her, an unwed pregnant teenager, into their home. She found herself overwhelmed by the sterility and temporal rigidity of their domestic, routinized household and of the hospital when it was her time to give birth. "why is everything so quiet? Why does the man come home/from school everyday at 3:30 and read the paper? Why a different casserole on the table every night and everyone eats one portion and one portion only?" She describes the couple's "quiet ticking bedroom" and wonders,

> how will *my* house ever run on silence, when in me there is such noise, such hatred for peeling apples, canning, and waking to feed baby, and alarm clocks in the soul, and in the skin of baby, in the rind of oranges, apples, peels in the garbage, and paper saved because it is cheaper to save and wrap and wash and use everything again.

She describes the hospital as "another world, ordered and white, [where] the night moved by on wheels." She noticed the newness of the bed, the room, the quiet, the hospital gown they put me in, the sheets rolled up hard and starched and white and everything white except the clock on the wall in red and black and the nurse's back as she moved out of the room without speaking, everything conspired to make me feel afraid/ how long, how much will I suffer?[141]

Supporters of alternative approaches to pregnancy and childbirth also pointed to a dramatic increase in the practice of bottle feeding infants, another outcome of scientific motherhood. More than 80 percent of American mothers breastfed their newborns in 1920; by 1972 this percentage had plummeted to 22. Modern, scientific motherhood valued the artificial over the natural: "Like maternal instinct, the maternal breast lost its stature in the age of modernity," Vandenberg-Daves notes.[142] Proponents of scientific motherhood were uncomfortable with the variable quantities of breast milk, which did not easily lend itself to exact measurement or fixed schedules. In the 1940s, doctors recommended that breastfeeding mothers use a scale to weigh the baby before and after each feeding session, which required an intensely laborious tracking process for mothers who were already time-strapped. Gesell, Ing, and Ames (1943) advocated pre- and post-weighing and instructed breastfeeding mothers to record the weight difference so they could know how much milk their babies were ingesting. They also coached mothers on the precise amount of time their babies should be allowed to nurse. Wendy Simonds and her co-authors described this tallying of time: "When the baby was finally put to the breast, another clock began ticking: the baby's time at breast was limited to the arbitrary number of minutes that doctors thought it ought to take the baby to empty the breast."[143]

In its advocating of measurement and tracking, scientific motherhood aimed to clean up the messy embodiment of mothering. Martin Manalansan has written about measurement as an antidote to messiness: "the procedures, techniques, and concepts of measurement," he writes, "obscure the inherent messiness and always tainted qualities of social life outside pristine norms."[144] Messiness, as Manalansan noted, works against the discourses of measuring, accounting, and auditing that have been and are connected to management practices and institutional policies. These discourses are also about control: who has it, and how that control or power is wielded. Motherhood itself (and the embodied processes that make it possible) is inherently messy, and who should be in charge of regulating these processes is contested. It is for this reason, Jacquelyn Rose reminds us, that most bodily experiences of women, including menstruation, pregnancy, and menopause, have been viewed as disorders or debilitations: "too much blood and guts, bodies either too wet or too dry, bodies that inconveniently blur the boundaries between inside and out."[145]

Mid-twentieth century female lactation advocates rejected the concept of measurement, whether of breast milk or of time. They embraced the messiness of unmeasured bodily fluids (breast milk), feeding on demand, and a flexible weaning rhythm set by the mother and the baby. Promoters of breastfeeding in the 1940s and 1950s created a motherhood reform community and connected scientific motherhood to their critiques of modern industrial life. They spurned experts like Frederic Butler, who in his 1943 edition of the popular *Infants and Children* argued for mothers nursing for no more than seven months, and advocated a strictly regimented feeding schedule of every four hours: 6 a.m., 10 a.m., 2 p.m., 6 p.m., 10 p.m., and 2 a.m.[146] This temporal regulation of breastfeeding was connected to the institutional tempo of the hospital.

> Physicians thought in terms of scheduling feedings not just because of the widespread importance of the clock in industrial societies, but specifically because their contacts with newborns were in hospital nurseries, where feedings are scheduled according to bureaucratic demands: eight-hour shifts do not lend themselves to three-hour feedings. Was the four-hour recommendation just a coincidence?[147]

The 1956 founding of the La Leche League, a voluntary association of mostly white, Catholic women promoting breastfeeding and a maternalist vision of motherhood, was a response to this cultural change, and to Dr. Butler's kind of Foucaultian time discipline. The League argued that breastfeeding offered important advantages for the baby and the mother and society, since breastfeeding produced loving, trusting children and adults. La Leche leaders encouraged mothers to set the parameters of how time would be used in their households. The League advocated prolonged breastfeeding and believed the mother and the child, not the doctor, should determine its duration. Historian Lynn Weiner demonstrated the ways that mid-twentieth century advocates of breastfeeding rejected dominant American ideas about measurement and order, time discipline, and motherhood: "[t]he idea that the child, her needs interpreted by the mother, should set the schedule for feedings and later for weaning distinguished the league from physicians who favored a breast-feeding regimen regulated by external norms of time."[148] Instead of letting the clock, the calendar, or the doctor determine the time for eating and weaning, La Leche mothers made those decisions, based on their children's and their own needs. In so doing mothers exhibited agency by taking back temporal control from the experts to decide the best way to nurture, and feed, their babies.

Yet, twenty-first century mothers still experience the clock watching and temporal stress that alternative birth and lactation movement activists rejected in the mid-twentieth century.[149] One breastfeeding mother interviewed in 2005 described her initial efforts at feeding her infant daughter:

> It was like propping up pillows, sitting up, OK nose, navel, knees; putting her to me; putting it in her mouth; suck, suck, suck. Watching the clock, which you know, you just can't do, I mean, now I know, I don't

even look at the clock, she knows when she's done. But before, it was like, OK; oh, it's only been twenty minutes. Have I had milk letdown? Is she dimpling? Is her bottom lip pulled out? Can she still breathe? ... I mean, it was like a nightmare.[150]

Time Binds and Antimaternalism

Elizabeth Freeman has shown the ways that experts and cultural spokespeople applied industrial capitalism to women's labor inside the home. There it began to take the form of "a rationalized, coordinated, and synchronized labor process." Freeman has argued that the concept of "Time Binds" has been used to regulate bodies: "[b]y 'time binds,' I mean something beyond the obvious point that people find themselves with less time than they need," she writes.

> Instead, I mean that naked flesh is bound into socially meaningful embodiment through temporal regulation: binding is what turns mere existence into a form of mastery in a process I'll refer to as *chrononormativity*, or the use of time to organize individual human bodies toward maximum productivity.[151]

In an effort to control and organize mothers, experts and proponents of scientific motherhood in the early twentieth century applied temporal regulation to motherhood. Considering domesticity as "a particular tempo, a way of living time rather than merely a relationship to the space of the home," during the 1920s and 1930s authorities pronounced the efficient and clock scheduled use of time as *the* best way to live time.[152] Maximum productivity became a goal that specialists applied to motherhood, and in this calculation, they equated the home with the factory, and children with products. By the 1940s and 1950s, larger world events like the rise of Hitler (who used the factory model to exterminate human beings) and the hyper disciplined German state, along with the Cold War with its attendant distrust of communist efficiency, led to a rethinking of the efficiency model. A rising women's health movement and mothering reform community also helped weaken scientific motherhood. Yet the idea of a well-organized and economical use of time as a marker of American character persists in this country. Although the prescriptions from the experts kept changing over the 40 years examined in this book, the experts' belief in their infallibility and duty to inform ignorant mothers on the best way to raise their children, and to use time, did not.

As the motherhood ideal changed over the years between 1920 and 1960, many American mothers sought to achieve this abstract image, despite the fact that the ideal itself stemmed from antimaternalism, and was largely created and publicized by men. In its disregard for mothers' knowledge and emotions, and its insistence on the superiority of experts and time efficiency, scientific motherhood was antimaternalist. It led to a shrinking of mothers' networks, a decline in resources, and an increase in the responsibilities and expectations placed upon mothers. Antimaternalism denied women time as a resource. At the same time that the experts were telling mothers how to manage their time, they expressed an increased expectation of what they believed mothers should produce and accomplish in that time. Advocates of scientific mothering urged mothers to put their children on strict schedules so that they, effectively, produced "products" for the capitalistic and militaristic state. Antimaternalism tried to diminish maternal power by attacking it, pathologizing it, and using clock time and schedules to control it. Antimaternalists aimed to not only take away women's time, but to take away what mothers do best: loving and taking care of their children. It was dehumanizing, aiming to force women to, robotlike, live by regimented schedules that went against the natural rhythms of children and the temporalities of care. Antimaternalism sought to remake women into impersonal automatons and ignored the realities of mothers' lives and desires.

Antimaternalism and the temporal regulation of motherhood connect American mothers across wide swaths of time. Decades before the alternative childbirth movement and the reflections of poets like Derricotte and Rich who wrote about the embodiment of maternity and the emotions of mothers, poor mothers in the 1930s gave birth, suckled, and cared for their children in harrowing circumstances. In the depths of the greatest economic depression the country had ever known, American cultural messaging still told mothers of all races, classes, and ethnic backgrounds the best ways to utilize time in their mothering. These hard-pressed mothers found strict schedules and domestic order often impossible to realize, although they often tried. We turn to their lives and images in the next chapter.

Notes

1 Quoted in Jodi Vandenberg-Daves, *Modern Motherhood: An American History* (New Brunswick, NJ, and London: Rutgers University Press, 2014), 97–98.
2 John B. Watson, *Psychological Care of Infant and Child* (New York: W.W. Norton, 1928); Watson, "The Weakness of Women," in Elaine Showalter, ed., *These Modern Women: Autobiographical Essays from the Twenties* (Old Westbury, NY: Feminist Press, 1979), 142.
3 Quoted in Vandenberg-Daves, *Modern Motherhood*, 78.
4 Vandenberg-Daves, *Modern Motherhood*, 97.
5 Julia Grant, *Raising Baby by the Book: The Education of American Mothers* (New Haven, CT, and London: Yale University Press, 1998), 85–86.
6 Quoted in Rima D. Apple, *Perfect Motherhood: Science and Childrearing in America* (New Brunswick, NJ, and London: Rutgers University Press, 2006), 2.
7 Rebecca Jo Plant, *Mom: The Transformation of Motherhood in Modern America* (Chicago, IL, and London: The University of Chicago Press, 2010), 87. See all of Chapter 3.
8 Plant, *Mom*, 88.
9 Laurel D. Graham, "Domesticating Efficiency: Lillian Gilbreth's Scientific Management of Homemakers, 1924–1930," *Signs*, Vol. 24, No. 3 (Spring, 1999): 633–675. See 646.

Alarm Clocks in the Soul 49

10 Quoted in Michael O'Malley, *Keeping Watch: A History of American Time* (New York: Viking Penguin, 1990), 42.
11 Quoted in O'Malley, *Keeping Watch*, 50.
12 Quoted in Thomas Allen, "Clockwork Nation: Modern Time, Moral Perfection and American Identity in Catharine Beecher and Henry Thoreau," *Journal of American Studies*, Vol. 39, No. 1 (2005): 65–86. See 68.
13 Quoted in O'Malley, *Keeping Watch*, 50.
14 O'Malley, *Keeping Watch*, 180.
15 Allen, "Clockwork Nation," 75.
16 Elizabeth Freeman, *Time Binds: Queer Temporalities, Queer Histories* (Durham, NC, and London: Duke University Press, 2010), 39.
17 Dana Luciano, *Arranging Grief: Sacred Time and the Body in Nineteenth-Century America* (New York: New York University Press, 2007), 5.
18 JaneMaree Maher, "Accumulating Care: Mothers Beyond the Conflicting Temporalities of Caring and Work," *Time & Society*, Vol. 18, Nos. 2/3 (September 1, 2009): 231–245. See 234.
19 Karen Davies, *Women, Time and the Weaving of the Strands of Everyday Life* (Aldershot, England, and Brookfield, VT: Gower Publishing Co., 1990), 38. Karl Marx wrote that in the factory system, the ways that employers equated labor power to time changed the ways that commoditized human beings understood time. Employers buy time from their employees: time, money, and productivity became connected. In this interpretation, time itself becomes a commodity. See Karl Marx, *Das Kapital*, or. pub. 1867.
20 Henry J. Rutz, "A Politics of Time Introduction: The Idea of a Politics of Time," in Henry J. Rutz, ed., *The Politics of Time* (Washington, D.C.: American Ethnological Society Monograph, 1992).
21 Freeman, *Time Binds: Queer Temporalities, Queer Histories*, 3. As an example she points to the ways that the advent of wage work "entailed a violent retemporalization of bodies once tuned to the seasonal rhythms of agricultural labor."
22 Michel Foucault, *Discipline and Punish: The Birth of the Prison* (New York: Vintage Books, 1995), 2nd ed.
23 Davies, *Women, Time, and the Weaving*, 37.
24 Joan Tronto, "Time's Place," *Feminist Theory*, Vol. 4, No. 2 (August 2003): 119–138. See 123.
25 Davies, *Women, Time and the Weaving*, 126.
26 Penelope Deutscher, "Repetition Facility: Beauvoir on Women's Time," *Australian Feminist Studies*, Vol. 21, No. 51 (November 2006): 327–342.
27 Quoted in Deutscher, "Repetition Facility," 330–331.
28 Quoted in Deutscher, "Repetition Facility," 332, 328.
29 Quoted in Deutscher, "Repetition Facility," 328.
30 "A Woman on Women: Review of *The Second Sex* by Simone de Beauvoir," *The Crisis*, June/July 1953, 383+.
31 Deutscher, "Repetition Facility," 329.
32 Davies, *Women, Time and the Weaving*, 239.
33 Maher, "Accumulating Care," 238.
34 Maher, "Accumulating Care," 238.
35 Quoted in Maggie Nelson, *The Argonauts* (Minneapolis, MN: Graywolf Press, 2015), 140.
36 Quoted in E.P. Thompson, "Time, Work-Discipline and Industrial Capitalism," *Past & Present*, No. 38 (December 1967): 56-97. Quote on 79.
37 Eviatar Zerubavel, "Private Time and Public Time: The Temporal Structure of Social Accessibility and Professional Commitments," *Social Forces*, Vol. 58, No. 1 (September 1979): 38–58.
38 Davies, *Women, Time and the Weaving*, 37.

39 Maher, "Accumulating Care," 239.
40 Steven Harper and Fariss-Terry Mousa, "Time and Motion Studies," Oxford Bibliographies Online, http://www.oxfordbibliographies.com/view/document/obo-9780199846740/obo-9780199846740-0027.xml, downloaded August 1, 2016.
41 Quoted in O'Malley, *Keeping Watch*, 164; Samuel Haber, *Efficiency and Uplift: Scientific Management in the Progressive Era, 1890-1920* (reprint ed. Chicago: University of Chicago Press 1973), ix. Orig. pub. 1964.
42 Frederick Winslow Taylor, *The Principles of Scientific Management* (New York: Harper, 1911).
43 Graham, "Domesticating Efficiency," 638.
44 O'Malley, *Keeping Watch*, 235.
45 "Time and Motion Study," Encyclopedia.com. http://www.encyclopedia.com/topic/time_and_motion_study.aspx, downloaded August 1, 2016.
46 Lillian Gilbreth, *The Home-Maker and Her Job* (New York: D. Appleton, 1927); *Living with Our Children* (New York: W.W. Norton, 1928).
47 Jane Lancaster, *Making Time: A Life Beyond "Cheaper by the Dozen"* (Lebanon, NH: Northeastern University Press, 2004), 1. See also Julie Des Jardins, *Lillian Gilbreth: Redefining Domesticity* (Boulder, CO: Westview Press, 2013).
48 Lancaster, *Making Time*, 3, 2.
49 Graham, "Domesticating Efficiency," 654. Gilbreth made these arguments in *The Home-Maker and Her Job*.
50 Quoted in Graham, "Domesticating Efficiency," 641.
51 Des Jardins, *Lillian Gilbreth*, 152.
52 Graham, "Domesticating Efficiency," 655, 658.
53 Graham, "Domesticating Efficiency," 655.
54 See Mary K. Trigg, *Feminism as Life's Work: Four Modern American Women through Two World Wars* (New Brunswick, NJ, and London: Rutgers University Press, 2014).
55 Graham, "Domesticating Efficiency," 662–663.
56 Lynn W. Weiner, "Reconstructing Motherhood: The La Leche League in Postwar America," in Rima D. Apple and Janet Lynne Golden, eds., *Mothers and Motherhood: Readings in American History* (Charlottesville, VA: The University of Virginia Press, 1997), 362–388.
57 Quoted in Grant, *Raising Baby by the Book*, 144. These ideas are still with us today, and some desperate middle-class parents hire sleep coaches to help them train their children in sleep schedules.
58 Quoted in Plant, *Mom*, 93.
59 Weiner, "Reconstructing Motherhood," 368.
60 I am indebted to Rima Apple for publishing a photograph of these Time Cards. See Apple, *Perfect Motherhood*, 65. The source is Division of Child Hygiene, Minnesota Department of Health.
61 Molly Ladd-Taylor, ed., *Raising a Baby the Government Way: Mothers' Letters to the Children's Bureau, 1915–1932* (New Brunswick, NJ, and London: Rutgers University Press, 1986), 129–131. Mary Mills West was the author of the popular and widely circulated Children's Bureau pamphlet *Infant Care*.
62 Ruth Feldstein, *Motherhood in Black and White: Race and Sex in American Liberalism, 1930–1965* (Ithaca, NY, and London: Cornell University Press, 2000), 12, and all of chapter 1.
63 Feldstein, *Motherhood in Black and White*, 15. See also Jeanne Westin, *Making Do: How Women Survived the '30s* (New York: Follet, 1976); Susan Ware, *Holding Their Own: American Women in the 1930s* (Charlottesville, VA: The University of Virginia, 1982).
64 Feldstein, *Motherhood in Black and White*, 23–24.

65 Mirra Komarosvky's *The Unemployed Man and His Family* (New York: The Dryden Press, 1940) is one example of this genre.
66 Quoted in Feldstein, *Motherhood in Black and White*, 26.
67 Quoted in Feldstein, *Motherhood in Black and White*, 26–27.
68 E. Franklin Frazier, *The Negro Family in the United States* (Chicago, IL: The University of Chicago Press, 1939).
69 Daniel Geary, "The Moynihan Report: An Annotated Edition," *The Nation*, September 14, 2015. https://www.theatlantic.com/politics/archive/2015/09/the-moynihan-report-an-annotated-edition/404632/ downloaded November 30, 2020.
70 Quoted in Grant, *Raising Baby by the Book*, 110–111.
71 Grant, *Raising Baby by the Book*, 89.
72 Plant, *Mom*, 13.
73 Grant, *Raising Baby by the Book*, 76; Elizabeth Ewen, *Immigrant Women in the Land of Dollars: Life and Culture on the Lower East Side, 1890–1925* (New York: Monthly Review Press, 1985), 136.
74 Elsa Herzfeld, "Superstitions and Customs of Tenement Women," *Charities and the Commons* 14 (1905), 985. Quoted in Ewen, *Immigrant Women in the Land of Dollars*, 135.
75 Quoted in Ewen, *Immigrant Women in the Land of Dollars*, 160. See Mabel Kittredge, *Practical Homemaking: A Textbook for Young Housekeepers* (New York: The Century Company, 1914); *Housekeeping Notes: How to Furnish and Keep House in a Tenement Flat* (Boston, MA: Whitcomb and Barrows, 1911).
76 Ewen, *Immigrant Women in the Land of Dollars*, 136.
77 Quoted in Grant, *Raising Baby by the Book*, 145.
78 Margaret Jarman Hagood, *Mothers of the South: Portraiture of the White Tenant Farm Woman* (Chapel Hill, NC: University of North Carolina Press, 1939), 137–138.
79 Quoted in Grant, *Raising Baby by the Book*, 155.
80 Ewen, *Immigrant Women in the Land of Dollars*, 161.
81 Jacquelyn S. Litt, *Medicalized Motherhood: Perspectives from the Lives of African-American and Jewish Women* (New Brunswick, NJ, and London: Rutgers University Press, 2000), 52.
82 Litt, *Medicalized Motherhood*, 55.
83 Litt, *Medicalized Motherhood*, 66.
84 Although four out of five white Mississippi mothers had physicians deliver their babies between 1916 and 1918, 88 percent of blacks in those years had midwives. Ladd-Taylor, *Raising a Baby*, 15.
85 Apple, *Perfect Motherhood*, 88–89.
86 Quoted in Apple, *Perfect Motherhood*, 89.
87 Quoted in Vandenberg-Daves, *Modern Motherhood*, 93.
88 Litt, *Medicalized Motherhood*, 71, 79, 90, 133.
89 Quoted in Grant, *Raising Baby by the Book*, 153.
90 Quoted in Vandenberg-Daves, *Modern Motherhood*, 98.
91 Quoted in Grant, *Raising Baby by the Book*, 80.
92 Quoted in Grant, *Raising Baby by the Book*, 80–81.
93 Ladd-Taylor, *Raising a Baby the Government Way*, 132.
94 Alice Walker, "In Search of Our Mothers' Gardens," in Angelyn Mitchell, ed., *Within the Circle: An Anthology of African American Literary Criticism from the Harlem Renaissance to the Present* (Durham, NC, and London: Duke University Press, 1994), 401–409. Quote from 406.
95 Quoted in Grant, *Raising Baby by the Book*, 80.
96 Plant, *Mom*, 22 but see all of Chapter 3, "Debunking the All-American Mom: Philip Wylie's Momism Critique," 19–85.

97 Plant, *Mom*, 22.
98 Plant, *Mom*, 30.
99 Nancy F. Cott, ed., *Mary Ritter Beard: A Woman Making History: Mary Ritter Beard through Her Letters* (New Haven, CT: Yale University Press, 1991), 269.
100 Plant, *Mom*, 8.
101 Feldstein, *Motherhood in Black and White*, 2.
102 Quoted in Plant, *Mom*, 37.
103 Kathleen Kennedy, "Casting an Evil Eye on the Youth of the Nation: Motherhood and Political Subversion in the Wartime Prosecution of Kate Richards O'Hare, 1917–1924," *American Studies*, Vol. 39, No. 3 (Fall 1989): 105–129. O'Hare was tried under wartime laws, convicted of sedition, and sentenced to five years in prison. She served 13 months, until President Woodrow Wilson commuted her sentence in May 1920.
104 Quoted in Amram Scheinfeld, "Are American Moms a Menace?" *Ladies' Home Journal*, November 1945. Reprinted in Nancy A. Walker, ed., *Women's Magazines 1940–1960: Gender Roles and the Popular Press* (Boston, MA, and New York: Bedford/St. Martin's Press, 1998), 108–114. See 108.
105 David M. Levy, "Maternal Overprotection," *Psychiatry: Interpersonal and Biological Processes*, Vol. 4, No. 3 (1941): 393–438; David M. Levy, *Maternal Overprotection* (New York: Columbia University Press, 1943).
106 Quoted in Scheinfeld, "Are American Moms a Menace?," 109, 111.
107 Stephanie Coontz, "When We Hated Mom," *The New York Times*, May 7, 2011.
108 Scheinfeld, "Are American Moms a Menace?," 113–114.
109 Coontz, "When We Hated Mom."
110 Plant, *Mom*, 8, 14.
111 Vandenberg-Daves, *Modern Motherhood*, 179–180.
112 Vandenberg-Daves, *Modern Motherhood*, 200–202.
113 Betty Friedan, *The Feminine Mystique* (New York: Dell Publishing Company, 1963), 38.
114 Plant, *Mom*, 146–177; Deutscher, "Repetition Facility."
115 Plant, *Mom*, 160–174.
116 Quoted in Plant, *Mom*, 167.
117 "Passionate Journey of LLLI Founder," originally published October 2016. https://www.llli.org/passionate-journey-of-llli-founder/ downloaded January 7, 2021.
118 Sometimes the most vociferous antimaternalists had antagonistic relationships with their own mothers. Both John Watson and Betty Friedan were known to have hated their mothers.
119 Quoted in Vandenberg-Daves, *Modern Motherhood*, 98.
120 Quoted in Grant, *Raising Baby by the Book*, 182.
121 Vandenberg-Daves, *Modern Motherhood*; Grant, *Raising Baby by the Book*, 183.
122 Vandenberg-Daves, *Modern Motherhood*, 173.
123 See Weiner, "Reconstructing Motherhood," 370, 363, and Elaine Tyler May, *Homeward Bound: American Families in the Cold War Era* (New York: Basic Books, 1999).
124 Apple, *Perfect Motherhood*, 117.
125 Apple, *Perfect Motherhood*, 118–119.
126 Quoted in Apple, *Perfect Motherhood*, 116. Dorothy V. Whipple, *Our American Babies: The Art of Baby Care* (New York: M. Barrows, 1943), viii.
127 Quoted in Apple, *Perfect Motherhood*, 117.
128 Apple, *Perfect Motherhood*, 107.

129 Coontz, "When We Hated Mom."
130 Quoted in Apple, *Perfect Motherhood*, 119.
131 Vandenberg-Daves, *Modern Motherhood*, 211.
132 Weiner, "Reconstructing Motherhood," 369.
133 Plant, *Mom*, 129, 136.
134 Adrienne Rich, *Of Woman Born*. See also Boston Women's Health Book Collective, *Our Bodies, Ourselves* (Boston, MA: New England Free Press, 1971); Boston Women's Health Book Collective, *Ourselves and Our Children* (New York: Random House, 1978).
135 Grantly Dick-Read's 1944 *Childbirth without Fear* was a bestseller, and his ideas circulated widely in popular women's magazines of the time. The French obstetrician Fernand Lamaze developed his technique of deep breathing during childbirth—now called "the Lamaze method"—after studying the Soviet "psychoprophylactic" method.
136 Irene Diamond, *Fertile Ground: Women, Earth, and the Limits of Control* (Boston, MA: Beacon Press, 1994), 25.
137 Plant, *Mom*, 139.
138 See Apple, *Perfect Motherhood*, 125; 133–134. On the history of childbirth and alternative approaches see Irene Lusztig, *The Motherhood Archives* (Women Make Movies, 2013).
139 Wendy Simonds, Barbara Katz Rothman, and Bari Meltzer Norman, *Laboring On: Birth in Transition in the United States* (New York and London: Routledge, 2007), 64.
140 Simonds et al., *Laboring On*, 66–67.
141 Toi Derricotte, "From 'Natural Birth,'" *The Iowa Review*, Vol. 12, No. 2/3 (Spring-Summer, 1981): 63–68.
142 Vandenberg-Daves, *Modern Motherhood*, 82.
143 Simonds et al., *Laboring On*, 83.
144 Martin F. Manalansan IV, "Messy Mismeasures: Exploring the Wilderness of Queer Migrant Lives," *The South Atlantic Quarterly*, Vol. 117, No. 3 (July 2018): 491–506. Quote from 491.
145 Jacqueline Rose, *Mothers: An Essay on Love and Cruelty* (New York: Farrar, Straus and Giroux, 2018), 23.
146 Weiner, "Reconstructing Motherhood," 372.
147 Simonds et al., *Laboring On*, 84.
148 Weiner, "Reconstructing Motherhood," 372.
149 For an interesting rhetorical history of contemporary infant-feeding controversies and how they have been shaped by past events, attitudes, and beliefs see Amy Koerber, *Breast or Bottle?: Contemporary Controversies in Infant-Feeding Policy and Practice* (Columbia, SC: The University of South Carolina Press, 2013).
150 Quoted in Cindy A. Stearns, "The Work of Breastfeeding," *Women's Studies Quarterly*, Vol. 37, Nos. 3 & 4 (Fall/Winter 2009): 63–80.
151 Freeman, *Time Binds*, 39, 3.
152 Freeman, *Time Binds*, 39.

Reference List

"A Woman on Women: Review of *The Second Sex* by Simone de Beauvoir." *The Crisis*, June/July 1953, 383+.

Allen, Thomas. "Clockwork Nation: Modern Time, Moral Perfection and American Identity in Catharine Beecher and Henry Thoreau." *Journal of American Studies*, Vol. 39, No. 1 (2005): 65–86.

Apple, Rima D. *Perfect Motherhood: Science and Childrearing in America*. New Brunswick, NJ and London: Rutgers University Press, 2006.

Coontz, Stephanie. "When We Hated Mom." *The New York Times*, May 7, 2011.

Cott, Nancy F., ed. *Mary Ritter Beard: A Woman Making History: Mary Ritter Beard through Her Letters*. New Haven, CT: Yale University Press, 1991.

Daly, Kerry J. *Families & Time: Keeping Pace in a Hurried Culture*. Thousand Oaks, CA and London: Sage Publications, 1996.

Davies, Karen. *Women, Time and the Weaving of the Strands of Everyday Life*. Aldershot, Hampshire: Gower Publishing Co., 1990.

Derricotte, Toi. "From 'Natural Birth." *The Iowa Review*, Vol. 12, No. 2/3 (Spring–Summer, 1981): 63–68.

Des Jardins, Julie. *Lillian Gilbreth: Redefining Domesticity*. Boulder, CO: Westview Press, 2013.

Deutscher, Penelope. "Repetition Facility: Beauvoir on Women's Time." *Australian Feminist Studies*, Vol. 21, No. 51 (November 2006): 327–342.

Ewen, Elizabeth. *Immigrant Women in the Land of Dollars: Life and Culture on the Lower East Side, 1890–1925*. New York: Monthly Review Press, 1985.

Feldstein, Ruth. *Motherhood in Black and White: Race and Sex in American Liberalism, 1930–1965*. Ithaca, NY: Cornell University Press, 2000.

Foucault, Michel. *Discipline and Punish: The Birth of the Prison*. 2nd ed. New York: Vintage Books, 1995.

Freeman, Elizabeth. *Time Binds: Queer Temporalities, Queer Histories*. Durham, NC and London: Duke University Press, 2010.

Geary, Daniel. "The Moynihan Report: An Annotated Edition." *The Nation*, September 14, 2015.

Graham, Laurel D. "Domesticating Efficiency: Lillian Gilbreth's Scientific Management of Homemakers, 1924–1930." *Signs*, Vol. 24, No. 3 (Spring, 1999): 633–675.

Grant, Julia. *Raising Baby by the Book: The Education of American Mothers*. New Haven, CT: Yale University Press, 1998.

Hagood, Margaret Jarman. *Mothers of the South: Portraiture of the White Tenant Farm Woman*. New York & London: W. W. Norton & Co., 1977. Originally pub. 1939.

Kennedy, Kathleen. "Casting an Evil Eye on the Youth of the Nation: Motherhood and Political Subversion in the Wartime Prosecution of Kate Richards O'Hare, 1917–1924." *American Studies*, Vol. 39, No. 3 (Fall 1989): 105–129.

Ladd-Taylor, Molly, ed. *Raising a Baby the Government Way: Mothers' Letters to the Children's Bureau, 1915–1932*. New Brunswick, NJ and London: Rutgers University Press, 1986.

Lancaster, Jane. *Making Time: A Life Beyond "Cheaper by the Dozen."* Lebanon, NH: Northeastern University Press, 2004.

Levy, David M. "Maternal Overprotection." *Psychiatry: Interpersonal and Biological Processes*, Vol. 4, No. 3 (1941): 393–438.

Levy, David M. *Maternal Overprotection*. New York: Columbia University Press, 1943.

Luciano, Dana. *Arranging Grief: Sacred Time and the Body in Nineteenth-Century America*. New York: New York University Press, 2007.

Maher, JaneMaree. "Accumulating Care: Mothers Beyond the Conflicting Temporalities of Caring and Work." *Time & Society*, Vol. 18, Nos. 2/3 (September 1, 2009): 231–245.

Manalansan IV, Martin F. "Messy Mismeasures: Exploring the Wilderness of Queer Migrant Lives." *The South Atlantic Quarterly*, Vol. 117, No. 3 (July 2018): 491–506.

Nelson, Maggie. *The Argonauts*. Minneapolis, MN: Graywolf Press, 2015.

O'Malley, Michael. *Keeping Watch: A History of American Time*. New York: Viking Penguin, 1990.

Rich, Adrienne Rich. *Of Woman Born: Motherhood as Experience and Institution*. New York and London: W.W. Norton & Company, 1986 Or. pub. 1976.

Rose, Jacqueline. *Mothers: An Essay on Love and Cruelty*. New York: Farrar, Straus and Giroux, 2018.

Scheinfeld, Amram. "Are American Moms a Menace?" *Ladies' Home Journal*, November 1945. Reprinted in Walker, Nancy A, ed. *Women's Magazines 1940–1960: Gender Roles and the Popular Press*. Boston and New York: Bedford/St. Martin's Press, 1998, 108–114.

Simonds, Wendy, Barbara Katz Rothman, and Bari Meltzer Norman. *Laboring On: Birth in Transition in the United States*. New York and London: Routledge, 2007.

Stearns, Cindy A. "The Work of Breastfeeding." *Women's Studies Quarterly*, Vol. 37, Nos. 3 & 4 (Fall/Winter 2009): 63–80.

Taylor, Frederick Winslow. *The Principles of Scientific Management*. New York: Harper, 1911.

Thompson, E.P. "Time, Work-Discipline and Industrial Capitalism." *Past & Present*, No. 38 (December 1967): 56-97.

Vandenberg-Daves, Jodi. *Modern Motherhood: An American History*. New Brunswick, NJ and London: Rutgers University Press, 2014.

Walker, Alice. "In Search of Our Mothers' Gardens." In Angelyn Mitchell, ed., *Within the Circle: An Anthology of African American Literary Criticism from the Harlem Renaissance to the Present*. Durham, NC and London: Duke University Press, 1994, 401–409.

Watson, John B. "The Weakness of Women." In Elaine Showalter, ed., *These Modern Women: Autobiographical Essays from the Twenties*. Old Westbury, NY: Feminist Press, 1979, 142.

Watson, John B. Watson. *Psychological Care of Infant and Child*. New York: W.W. Norton, 1928.

Weiner, Lynn W. "Reconstructing Motherhood: The La Leche League in Postwar America." In Rima D. Apple and Janet Lynne Golden, eds., *Mothers and Motherhood: Readings in American History*. Charlottesville, VA: The University of Virginia Press, 1997, 362–388.

Zerubavel, Eviatar. "Private Time and Public Time: The Temporal Structure of Social Accessibility and Professional Commitments." *Social Forces*, Vol. 58, No. 1 (September 1979): 38–58.

2 A Promaternal Narrative and Archive
Dorothea Lange's Photographs of Rural Mothers

During the Depression, when capitalism appeared on the verge of collapse and many rural American families had to take to the road to survive, working-class families found the middle-class model of clockwork rationality and time discipline especially difficult to achieve. The ideal of using time well, of orchestrated schedules of family life and domestic ritual became impossible to fulfill in hardscrabble lives of rural poverty and itinerancy.[1] Domesticity and ordering and maintaining a home were exceedingly challenging for wives and mothers who had to make do with lean-to-shacks and tents, and scavenged food. Scientific motherhood and its orderly precepts were likewise challenging to realize. Dorothea Lange's photographs of rural migratory mothers and their children in the 1930s illuminate the multiple ways that working-class mothers tried to create order in circumstances that were far from ideal. Their private sphere was often outside, their families on the road. Their domesticity had a different organizing logic and use of time than the middle-class ideal, and survival and making ends meet was most often the goal. Lange's collective photographs of rural mothers in the challenging decade represent a promaternal narrative and archive that is at odds with antimaternal narratives of the time. Her photographs demonstrate the power of imagery to serve as a counter-narrative to antimaternalism and the dehumanization it implies.

The poor rural mothers whom Lange photographed in the 1930s present a different cumulative image of motherhood than dominant American portrayals. These prevailing, judgmental voices warned of mothers who loved their children too much; suggested that the mother–child bond was loosening; and that motherhood no longer included sacrifice.[2] Lange's images suggest a dramatically different truth: these mothers' bonds with their children appeared intense; they were willing to and did make physical and emotional sacrifices to help their children realize their futures. In this chapter I analyze the photographs Lange took of rural, itinerant mothers in the years between 1935 and 1939 as a promaternal narrative and archive. I also examine Lange's own conflicted emotions and experiences of motherhood, which shaped the visual construction of motherhood that she created in the pictures she took of mothers and their children in these years.

DOI: 10.4324/9781003334712-3

Dorothea Lange was one of the photographers and chroniclers of the Great Depression. Born in 1895 into a middle-class family in Hoboken, New Jersey, Lange lived in San Francisco for most of her adult life. Lange's mother was one of six children from a professional German immigrant family, and she had two children—Dorothea and a son, Martin, born six years later. Lange's father left the family in 1907, when Dorothea was 12, and to support the family, her mother went to work at the New York Public Library. She later became an investigator for the juvenile court system, providing her daughter with a role model in social work and social service. Dorothea had polio as a child, which as an adult left her self-conscious about a limp in one leg.

As a teenager and against her mother's wishes, Lange was drawn to photography and found New York City apprenticeships, including one with noted Columbia University photographer Clarence White. Lange did not attend college and left home at 23. She moved to San Francisco where she found a job in a photograph-supply house and then established her own studio. From 1918 to 1935 she worked as a portrait photographer. She met influential west coast painter Maynard Dixon in San Francisco, whom she married in 1920 when she was 25. Recently divorced and father of a teenaged daughter, he was 20 years older than Lange. They had two sons together, the first in 1925 when Dorothea was 30, and the second in 1928 when she was 33.[3] Lange and Dixon moved in bohemian, socially liberal circles.[4]

The onset of the depression inspired Lange to begin a new kind of photography, one that sought to capture the human suffering brought on by the economic crisis. In 1933 she began to take documentary photographs full time. Wanting to affect change, Lange put her faith in the emotional immediacy of photographic images. Describing what drove her to shoot the 1933 May Day demonstrations of the unemployed at San Francisco's Civic Center she stated:

> I will set myself a big problem. I will go down there, I will photograph this thing, I will come back, and develop it. I will print it and I will mount it and I will do this to see if I can grab a hunk of lightening.[5]

In 1936 she ended her marriage to Dixon and married Paul Taylor, an agricultural economist at the University of California, Berkeley, who had seen her photographs and employed her for the California State Emergency Relief Administration the previous year. A pioneer in the investigation of California's migrant labor conditions, Taylor had persuaded Lange to join his research team as a field photographer. He reinforced her belief in the power of the image, which he believed added an essential dimension to his academic documentation of rural poverty and the plight of migrant workers. When Lange and Taylor wed, he had temporary custody of his three children and Lange had permanent custody of her two young sons.[6] The spring of 1936, when Lange took her most celebrated photograph, was a period of renewed energy and optimism for her.[7] Newly married to Taylor, believing this marriage would create family stability and give her time for her own work, she focused on her government assignments with vigor.

Many have called Dorothea Lange's 1936 photograph *Migrant Mother* the most famous image of the Depression.[8] According to one account, *Migrant Mother* is the most reproduced photograph in the world.[9] *Migrant Mother* has most often been interpreted as a reassuring symbol of maternal love and American endurance. Viewed from a different perspective, it is an image of a mother taken by a mother, and it—along with the many other photographs Lange took of depression-era mothers—offers us insights into the lives and emotions of poor rural mothers in a hard-pressed decade, and into Lange herself. Lange's mothers reject scientific motherhood and time discipline in their portrayal of the more complicated temporalities of maternal care. Symbolic of fortitude and maternal strength, these images insist upon the essential nature of the work of mothers, while they capture the emotional ambivalence of motherhood, which was also Lange's own. They also demonstrate the enormity of stress migratory mothers experienced, and the nearly impossible expectations placed upon them in their roles as primary caretakers and financial contributors to, or supporters of, their families. Lange documents the pressures migratory mothers felt to meet these expectations with little to no support from the government, their families, or their communities.

Lange came upon Louise Thompson, whose image she captured in *Migrant Mother*, at a brief stop at a camp of migrant pea pickers near Nipomo, California, at the end of a long March day. Lange found the 32-year-old woman sitting under an improvised tent with her children. Native American and eventually mother to 11, Thompson had been born on a Cherokee reservation in Oklahoma, raised on a farm, and married at 17. Later the family moved to California, where her husband worked in sawmills and fields until he died in 1931, leaving her with five children, and pregnant with a sixth. In 1936, Thompson was a fieldworker and in a relationship with James Hill, with whom she had four more children. When Lange came upon Thompson, Hill and the boys were off in an effort to get the family car fixed.[10] Lange took several exposures of the scene. The famous fifth one depicts a destitute mother with two tousle-haired children on either shoulder, faces turned away from the camera. A grubby-faced baby is asleep on her lap, and the mother's right hand is raised to her face, gazing into the distance with a look that viewers have interpreted as apprehension and worry, strength and endurance—the same attributes Americans would need to make it through the depression. "*Migrant Mother* surrendered herself to Lange's expert direction," Curtis wrote, "striking a pose that would burn itself into the memory of American culture."[11] Lange described her technique for constructing the *Migrant Mother* photographs:

I was following instinct, not reason. I drove into that soggy camp and parked my car like a homing pigeon. I saw and approached the hungry and desperate mother, as if drawn by a magnet. I do not remember how I explained my presence to her, or my camera, but I do remember she asked me no questions. I made five exposures, working closer and closer from the same direction. I did not ask her name or her history. She told me her age, that she was thirty-two. She said that they had been living on frozen vegetables from the surrounding field and birds that the children had killed. She had just sold the tires from her car to buy food. Here she sat in a lean-to tent with her children huddled around her, and seemed to know that my picture might help her, and so she helped me. There was a sort of equality about it.[12]

Migrant Mother is only one of many photographs that Lange took of rural mothers and their children; even she objected that, in the public's fascination with *Migrant Mother*, so many of her other photographs were overlooked. A search of the U.S. Library of Congress database of Lange images, using the term "Lange mothers" pulls up 104 different photographs, and there are more[13] (Figure 2.1).

Figure 2.1 Dorothea Lange, *Migrant Mother*, March 1936

The Farm Security Administration Photographic Project (1935–1942) is now recognized as the most famous of America's documentary projects. Launched under the umbrella of the Resettlement Administration in 1935, which became the Farm Security Administration (FSA) in 1937, at its peak a team of about 20 men and women were led by the indomitable Roy Stryker to create a photographic archive of the impact of the Great Depression on the country, especially in rural America. FSA photographers fanned out across the nation, capturing the plight of southern sharecroppers, migrant farmworkers, and Dust Bowl refugees.[14] Stryker gave his photographers "shooting scripts," outlines that at first required them to focus on agricultural conditions, such as "picking, hauling, sorting, preparing, drying, canning, packaging, loading for shipping." As time went on, Stryker broadened this artistic directive to explore broader sociological questions addressing such things as experiences of community, time and work, and farmworkers' gathering places.[15] Stryker required his photographers to provide propaganda and evidence of the Roosevelt administration's largesse, asking them to produce images "of FSA houses, cabins, settlements, and fields, of the pressure cookers FSA gave out and their grateful recipients."[16] Although he did not explicitly direct Lange or his other photographers to take pictures of mothers (many of Lange's male colleagues did as well), Stryker did in one script request "the photographic study of the differences in the men's world and the women's world."[17] Photography historian Alan Trachtenberg described this FSA project as the greatest collaborative effort in the history of photography "to mobilize resources to create a cumulative picture of a place and time."[18] The agency distributed the eighty thousand photographs that resulted to newspapers and magazines, aiming at an urban, middle-class audience in hopes of building support for President Franklin D. Roosevelt's rural programs.[19]

According to her biographer, Lange's intentions in her photography were most strongly influenced by the historical era in which she lived, and in her desire for social change. Linda Gordon argues that the Depression "created a political opening for expanding and deepening American democracy," in that it created "a moment of idealism, imagination, and unity in America's hopes for the country." Lange seized that opening and, through her photographs, labored to push this democratic vision forward, to expand popular understanding of who Americans were. Her photographs of mothers are a small fraction of her entire oeuvre that includes images of

> Mormons, Jews, and evangelicals; farmers, share croppers, and migrant farmworkers; workers domestic and industrial, male and female; citizens and immigrants not only black and white but also Mexican, Filipino, Chinese, and Japanese, notably the 120,000 Japanese Americans locked in internment camps during World War II.[20]

Later in life Lange turned her attention abroad, and photographed primarily working people in Indonesia, Egypt, and Japan, portraying them with admiration for their labor, abilities, and pride. Gordon concludes that throughout her career Lange attempted to show her subjects as worthier than their conditions, always asserting that greater democracy was possible. Although she was not drawn to exploring her own emotional life through photography but rather to conditions in the external world, Lange did return to images that resonated for her, including children, nontraditional forms of family, and women's domestic efforts in the FSA camps.[21]

Dorothea Lange often opposed the official vision that Stryker expected his photographers to represent. Constantly struggling with her over editorial control of her negatives, Stryker fired Lange twice—in 1938 and again in 1939—reinstated her on a per diem basis, and dismissed her permanently in 1940. Despite the fact that the public and the media requested Lange's photographs more than those of any other FSA photographer, their clash had to do with Lange's unwillingness to endorse and represent an FSA policy she believed consolidated the erosion of farming traditions and local cultures and, although they were close, an at-times difficult relationship.[22] Because her photographs were so widely reproduced, in the new commercial photographic magazines *Life* and *Look* and other venues, some scholars have suggested that it was through Lange's eyes that Americans formed both contemporary impressions and later visual memories of the Depression, migrant labor in particular.[23]

While narratives about motherhood were changing in the 1930s, the exigencies of the depression caused some to return to earlier idealized notions of the maternal, linked to nature and the land. In interpreting early American literature, Annette Kolodny pointed to the symbolic relationship between "femaleness" and the land as source and origin in our national consciousness. She describes the metaphor of "primitive land" as "a woman, a womb of generation and a provider of sustenance," describing "the female principle of receptivity, repose and integral satisfaction inherent in 'mother earth' [as] one of our most cherished national fantasies." The Puritans, Kolodny suggested, viewed the agrarian world as a "'maternal garden' receiving and nurturing human children."[24] Adair argues that the "dream remembered" during the American Depression was one of mythic wholeness, a timeless connection to the fertile earth, a reunion with the feminized land.[25] Adair suggests: "the space of timelessness in nature ... has often been construed and fetishized as the feminine."[26] *Migrant Mother*, or maternal love and endurance, could save the pastoral American vision, circular time, and democracy itself. Dorothea Lange was not immune to this imagining of an idealized feminized past: her biographer described the nostalgia that characterized Lange's later work, concluding that it "was nostalgia for an imaginary past, of course."[27]

At the same time the literary and mythic American imagination has associated nature—and women—with chaos and unruliness, with anti-measurement. As we have seen, measurement is a form of control and power, connected to masculinity, progress, and linear time. Jane Flax has argued that Western intellectual traditions have connected the feminine to the disordered and unconscious: "the space outside of the conscious, ordered and moral subject in civilization has always connoted the feminine in the history of Western thought."[28] This is partly why motherhood and maternal power are so threatening, and it helps explain the patriarchal need to control the powerful mother through time discipline and dictates about proper motherhood. Martin Manalansan and others have shown how the modern West has used measurement to control spaces, through colonialism and capitalist expansion.[29] Those spaces included the maternal body and mind. Adrienne Rich pointed to the colonization of the mother when she wrote about patriarchal control of motherhood in *Of Woman Born*. Similarly, literary critic Vivyan Adair described the Joads, the family at the center of John Steinbeck's fabled novel *The Grapes of Wrath* (1939), invoking paradise lost when they "recall[ed] with nostalgia that they and their fathers before them had colonized, cultivated, impregnated, and controlled the land, the mother."[30]

A Promaternal Narrative and Archive

Lange took her photographs of migrant mothers in the years between 1935 and 1939, and they represent mothers from across the United States—who hailed from Oklahoma, Idaho, Minnesota, Arkansas, California, Oregon, New Jersey, Tennessee, North Carolina, Texas, Mississippi, and South Carolina. Many of the mothers depicted in Lange's photographs were living in FSA migratory labor camps, including the Kern resettlement camp and the Shafter camp, both in California. Her images portray mothers in a variety of family arrangements, including multigenerational families comprising grandmothers, mothers, and children. Many of the women had migrated—some over great distances—most often with their husbands and children, sometimes with extended family, sometimes as single mothers. Gordon notes Lange's gender politics as revealed in her photographs: an attraction to "lone parents with children," including tender images of fathers with children, and to other nontraditional family arrangements. Gordon attributes this to Lange's refusal to "accept the myth that the nuclear family was the only 'normal' family form."[31] Lange's images depict mothers who are resourceful, agentic, hardworking, strong, loving, resilient, protective, hopeful, creative, and industrious. Her photographs capture other emotions as well: fatigue, sorrow, resignation, and anger. They reflect the maintenance and nurturance that are at the heart of the temporalities of care. A July 1937 photograph shows a careworn white woman in a dress and apron sitting at a table covered with a checkered oilcloth, in a dim cabin interior, door open to a pastoral scene. Titled "Grandmother of fifty-six children, mother of fourteen, ten living. Near Chesnee, South Carolina," Lange connects this woman with fertility and family ties, as well as fatigue and maternal loss.[32] She also makes the point that even if her child dies, the mother always remains mother to that child.

Lange's images offer a powerful counter-narrative to the antimaternalism of the time. Some of them illuminate mothers without husbands, mothers who were agricultural laborers for the benefit of their children and the survival of their families. One June 1936 photograph of a Tulsa, Oklahoma refugee family who traveled over fifteen hundred miles to California to find work shows three young white children and their mother sitting in a field at the side of a road, beside their dilapidated jalopy. Boxes, a tire, a washbasin, and other domestic implements are tied with rope to the car's roof and rear. Lange's caption reads in part:

> Mother and three half-grown children; no father. "Anybody as wants to work can get by. But if a person loses their faith in the soil like so many of them back there in Oklahoma, then there ain't no hope for them. We're making it all right here, all but for the schooling, 'cause that boy of mine, he wants to go to the University."[33]

While this white single mother endorsed the American pastoral ideal of keeping faith in the soil, she also looked to the future. Her statement offers insight into her hopes for her son, her willingness to work, and her own optimism: "We're making it all right here," she declared. A 1935 portrait of a Madonna-like Mexican mother and her chubby baby, bare-chested and draped in a cotton blanket in her lap, shows the mother, hand to her neck and sitting in front of a large tree, gazing beatifically heavenward. A sentimental image tied to nature and maternal devotion and care, Lange's caption/title conveys that this immigrant mother, now in California, tells her children "that I would like to go to Mexico, but they tell me 'We don't want to go, we belong here.'"[34] Pushed or pulled into the future by her children, this mother and her family are building a new life in America. These mothers had hopes and dreams for their children. While "happiness" might have seemed too presumptuous a goal, they hoped for financial stability, education, homes, and better lives, and sacrificed to realize these goals. They often had to rely on their children's labor—along with their own—in the service of a better future[35] (Figure 2.2).

A 1939 Lange photograph shows a slim, white, overalls-clad mother standing with two young sons beside a small tent pitched at the side of a road, where the family car is parked. Lange's text informs the viewer that this is a fatherless migratory family, newly arrived in Yakima Valley, Washington, from Minnesota, and they are camping behind a gas station. "The mother," Lange writes, "is trying to support three boys by picking pears." A former waitress, she has just returned from the orchard, and at the end of a long August day when Lange snapped the photograph, the temperature hovered at 106 degrees. Agricultural labor is a family affair: this single mother's young son had spent the day with her working in the orchards. "The oldest boy, age ten," Lange wrote, "helped carry ladder from tree to tree."[36] A March 1937 photograph that Lange took

64 A Promaternal Narrative and Archive

Figure 2.2 Dorothea Lange, *Mexican Mother in California*, June 1935

near Guadalupe, California, is a portrait of a Japanese-American mother and her young daughter, both wearing dresses and large bonnets to shield their faces from the sun, posed touching in front of what appears to be a crate holding some kind of vegetable or fruit crop. Lange identifies both of them in her text as agricultural workers. The mother's face is warm and beneficent.[37]

Other Lange images of multicultural motherhood are equally positive in their portrayal of maternal love, across race and class. A July 1939 photograph depicts two African American tobacco tenant farming mothers, leaning on opposite sides of a cabin's doorway. The image projects order, along with maternal pride and affection. The two related mothers in Wake County, North Carolina, are wearing attractive dresses and earrings, and gazing down at two tidy African American children—a boy, leaning against the cabin/house, and a little girl of about two, neatly dressed and pressed up in the doorway. Both children look directly at the camera. The second mother is securely holding another small, barefooted child. Lange's caption for this warm, comforting, and domestic image tells us that this photograph only represents some of these African American mothers' children.[38] One scholar stated that Lange addressed the racism she observed by creating ennobling and enduring portraits: "[t]hese are people who seem like they

A Promaternal Narrative and Archive   65

Figure 2.3 Dorothea Lange, *Two Tobacco Tenant Mothers*, July 1939

are timeless, and Dorothea was always interested in capturing a sense of timelessness"[39] (Figure 2.3).

Like other FSA photographers (all of whom were white), Lange had to walk a fine line in her portrayal of racism and racial injustice. Racism saturated New Deal agencies, including the Department of Agriculture, the umbrella organization within which the FSA operated. FSA camps were whites-only: according to Gordon, people of color were aware of this and did not try to get into the camps.[40] Lange took many of her photographs of migratory mothers and their children in the federally supported camps, and these images simultaneously present a case for the construction and funding of the camps and elucidate the precarity of poor mothers' lives in an era of technological change and uprootedness. Department of Agriculture policy prohibited violation of southern racial norms and highlighting of racism in FSA photography: "No blacks and whites in social contact, no references to racial oppression, no images of racial inequality, or abuse of blacks were to be shown." Photographers who did depict racism met resistance and even threats of bodily harm.[41] Once a member of Stryker's staff deleted a phrase from a Lange caption that read: "Old Negro—*the kind the planters like* [italicized words removed.] He hoes, picks cotton, and is full of good humor."[42] Some Lange images do illuminate racial power relations, whites and blacks working together in the fields, children of different races playing together. One historian believed Lange's photographs suggest that poor blacks were neater than poor whites, and Lange did apparently believe that black women did more flower gardening and decorating than white women. She was intentional in her positive portrayals of African Americans: most of all, Lange hoped to accomplish social justice with her images and to reveal the truth, to chronicle her times. She believed a photographer should be "above all a promoter of consciousness."[43]

Some Lange pictures portrayed mothers who worked alongside their husbands in the fields and orchards, laboring to help the family make ends meet. A 1939 photograph reveals a white pregnant mother with a three-year-old daughter, living in an FSA camp in Merrill, Klamath County, Oregon. "During this year," Lange wrote, "she has worked with her husband in: strawberries (Helvetia, Oregon); cherries (Salem, Oregon); beans (West Stayton, Oregon); hops (Independence, Oregon). Is now in potato pickers' camp at the end of the season." In a rare interior photograph shot in what appears to be a tent, the seven months pregnant mother, eyes wide, mouth closed, looks straight into the camera. Dishes, silverware, cans of Campbell's soup, flour, napkins, and a saltshaker stand on the shelves behind her. A notebook with a full page of writing lies on another table within camera range; most likely they were Lange's field notes. The family is in dire economic straits. The young mother tells Lange: "We haven't got a cent now and we've lost our car because we helped some people out. It seems like it's taken every cent to eat off, that and traveling around."[44] Another 1939 Lange photograph portrays a stolid, older white woman wearing a flowered house dress, rumpled sweater, and bonnet, looking down—her face hidden from the camera—as she picks hop flowers, which were used to make beer. Lange wrote sparely: "Mother of family now migrants of Pacific coast. Were farm owners in 1936. Picking hops. Polk County, Oregon."[45]

Margaret Jarman Hagood, a social scientist and contemporary of Lange's, described in her 1939 book *Mothers of the South: Portraiture of the White Tenant Farm Woman*, the essential nature of rural wives' and mother's field work during the 1930s. Over 16 months, Hagood visited 254 homes in the Carolina Piedmont and in Georgia and Alabama, striving to learn more about the lives of white sharecropper mothers. In three-quarters of the families she visited, mothers routinely labored in the fields:

> The rule is to do as nearly full-time work as housekeeping and cooking permit during chopping, hoeing, and picking times on the cotton farm, or during most of the summer in the tobacco farm, with the fall spent largely in the striphouse. The number, age, and sex of children make for various modifications in the division of labor.[46]

Hagood learned from interviewing the mothers that if they did not have young children, they preferred field labor to housework, since it was finite and yielded a tangible product, as opposed to the amorphous, endless drudgery of housework. As one mother explained,

> In the field there's just one thing and you can finish it up; but here in the house there's cooking, cleaning, washing, milking, churning, mending, sewing, canning, and always the children—and you don't know what to turn to next.[47]

Like the struggling mothers who had written letters to the U.S. Children's Bureau a decade before, these rural mothers' domestic labor was endless.

Through her photographs, Lange paints a multitude of ways that, in addition to their field and domestic labors, diverse migrant mothers cared for their children. In her representations, hardworking mothers are holding, soothing, nursing, clutching, feeding, or gazing at their children. Her photographs of mothers in migrant camps include several of them bringing their children to well-baby clinics for check-ups. One trio of photographs of a Latina woman and her two children visiting the public health doctor in California's Imperial Valley shows the mother calmly holding each of her children in turn as the female physician listens to their hearts and lungs with her stethoscope, and checks their teeth. Lange's title for the February 1939 series reads "Calipatria, Imperial Valley. Visiting public health doctor conducts well-baby clinic in local school building adjacent to pea harvest. Many migratory mothers attend."[48] Lange's photographs show the migratory mothers' maternal skills and conscientiousness (emphasizing that it was the norm to take their children for medical care), a positive since children in the camps suffered from higher rates of diseases, including malnutrition.[49] These rural mothers were following the mandates of the experts who insisted that "good" mothers sought medical advice and supervision.[50] They kept their eyes on their family's survival and on the future, while performing the daily round of caregiving and nurturing tasks that mothering demands.

Some of Lange's images of mothers showcase anticonsumerist, collective efforts and female social networks rather than displaying mothers in isolated homes, struggling to raise their children and learn the skills of mothering on their own, or with the sole guidance of experts. These mothers came together cooperatively to share resources and knowledge. An earlier group of Lange photographs highlights mothers in migrant-camp-sponsored organizations, swaddled babies in their arms or young children at their sides, at events including a Halloween party and a mothers' club meeting. A series of photographs Lange took in November 1937 at the Arvin, California camp shows a gathering of six white mothers, one bottle feeding her baby (a nod to modern motherhood), in a simple, wooden-slat walled room, clustered around a Singer sewing machine table and a pot-bellied stove, symbols of domesticity. A bespectacled woman, gray hair pulled back in a bun, is leading the meeting and reading from a notebook and what appears to be a ledger. A stack of hymnals sits on the table in front of her.[51] One of the photographs shows the women praying—the caption "Meeting of the Mother's [sic] Club in Arvin camp for migrant workers, Farm Security Administration (FSA) camp in California, opens with prayer" beside it.[52] Another image presents the mothers with hymnbooks in hand. Although none of the women appear to be singing, Lange titled the photograph "Singing hymns before opening of meeting of Mothers' Club at Arvin Farm Security Administration (FSA) Camp for Migrants, California." Perhaps to address the charges of Godless communism that critics of the camps (and of Lange) had raised, here Lange demonstrated that religion was allowed, and indeed encouraged, at the camps. She pointed out that thriftiness and economy were encouraged as well. Two other pictures in the series show the female leader in front of the group, with Lange's caption: "The discussion this evening centers on the possibility of buying kerosene oil in large quantities and distributing it cooperatively in camp, to cut costs. Kerosene is used both for cooking and for lighting purposes." [53]

Lange's photographs also include illustrations of childcare centers in migrant camps where "trained teachers" (her term) supervised pre-school age children in nursery schools while their mothers worked in the fields. Despite their cheery captions, these images suggest that young children would be better off in the care of their mothers. One shows a solitary childcare worker framed in the doorway of a humble building under a "First Aid/Nursery sign," a young child in her arms and another at her side. Arrayed on the stoop and tumbling out of the front of the building are 16 additional toddlers and children, all seemingly under the age of five, cared for by this one provider.[54] A second photograph with the same caption (which begins "While the mothers are working in the fields …") offers a close-up of a plump, diapered baby sleeping on a blanket in a large box, young children crowded around overhead, staring down with curiosity at the sleeping child. There is no adult in the scene[55] (Figure 2.4).

In some of Lange's images maternal care included domestic economy and the ordering of time that scientific motherhood proponents advocated. Two 1939 photographs of a young mother of a six-week-old baby in a labor contractors' camp show a pretty white woman in a ruffled-neck dress sitting on a bed, gazing down at her clean baby, dressed in newborn clothes and hand-knitted booties, nestled in her arms. Despite the fact that mother and child are living in a tent, the photograph conveys domestic stability and mother–infant bonding. A blanket-covered wicker bassinet sits to one side of the bed; coffee, Arm and Hammer baking soda, and baby oil line a table on the other side. The second photo shows the infant's eyes wide open and alert, apparently returning the mother's loving gaze. There is a temporal order and domesticity to this woman's mothering. "Young migrant mother with six weeks old baby born in a hospital with aid of FSA medical and [sic] association for migratory workers," Lange wrote in her extended caption. "She lives in a labor contractors camp near Westley, California. 'I try to keep him

Figure 2.4 Dorothea Lange, *While the Mothers are Working in the Fields*, November 1936

eatin' and sleepin' regular like I got him out of the hospital.'"[56] This text invokes medicalized, modern childbirth and aimed to reassure Americans that the U.S. government (represented by the Farm Security Administration) believed that babies should be born in hospitals, not in tents and the other make-do housing provided in migrant labor camps, and supplied funding for hospital births. By 1940, nearly half of American births took place in hospitals, rather than in homes. This photograph and caption represent that modernizing trend.[57] Lange's text also gave voice to the new mother, who expressed pride in her ability to keep her infant on a schedule, in spite of their living conditions. She was doing her best to transplant the disciplined institutional time of the hospital maternity ward to the tenuousness of a makeshift tent (Figure 2.5).

Lange's biographer maintains that Lange's visual focus on domesticity and order in her photographs stemmed from her desire to humanize the poor and to fight against the equation of poverty with weak character.[58] Many of Lange's visual images project order, which she achieved with composition that centered her subjects; revealed neat, well-organized backgrounds; and portrayed women—despite obvious obstacles—performing domestic tasks like washing, cooking, sewing. Through her photographs she

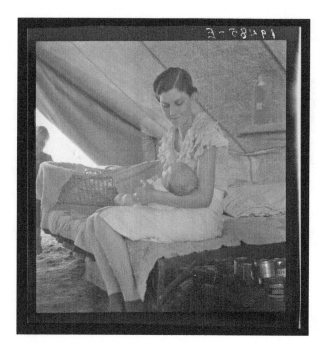

Figure 2.5 Dorothea Lange, *Young Migrant Mother with Six Weeks Old Baby*, April 1939

also expressed her respect for the traditionally female tasks of domesticity, caregiving, mothering, and for women themselves. "I hope through these pictures to express or to delineate or to reveal my love for women and their function," Lange stated in a 1964 interview. "Not only my love for women but my respect for their function."[59]

A striking series of 1939 images of one mother and child in Tulare County, California, illustrate maternal care and fortitude despite poverty and harrowing living conditions. This white mother of six lives in an FSA camp for migratory agricultural workers in Farmersville. Her children range in age from two to nineteen; the child in her arms, who appears about three years old, is ill, and they are waiting for the resident nurse to visit. One of the four photographs shows this mother and her child sitting on an iron-framed bed with the nurse who has arrived, in white uniform and cap, sitting beside them—interviewing the mother and examining the child. In each of the four images, the loving mother's arms encircle her daughter, whether in the doorway shot where older children can be seen in the darkened interior of a building that Lange identified as a steel shelter, or in the photographs of mother and child perched on the bed. In one picture, the mother patiently gazes down at her daughter. In another, both weary mother and bright-eyed daughter look to the side, and in the mother's eyes the viewer can read strength, perseverance, and love. The camera lingers on the mother's swollen, large-knuckled hands. Lange informs us that this mother and child have migrated with their family to California from Oklahoma. The mother has attended school up to the eighth grade. "They left their farming in Chicasha [sic] in the fall of 1936 to go to Arizona to pick cotton," Lange wrote. "They returned to Oklahoma to try again; failed and re-entered California February 27, 1938 to pick peas under a labor contractor. The father is chairman of camp council."[60] In none of these images does the mother appear worried that she loves her children too much, that either one of them needs "a mental weaning" from the other. This vulnerable child's need for her mother is clear (Figure 2.6).

The same year that Lange produced these pictures, she joined forces with Margaret Hagood, her colleague Harriet Herring, and the FSA photographer Marion Post Wolcott to create a comprehensive photographic study of life in the 13 counties of Piedmont, North Carolina, that Hagood had investigated in *Mothers of the South*. Lange's images, like Hagood's text, defied the stereotypes of "tobacco road" degenerates that Erskine Caldwell had fashioned in his 1932 novel about Georgia sharecroppers, and also served as a rebuttal to the antimaternalism of the time.[61] The care and attention to

Figure 2.6 Dorothea Lange, *Tulare County, Mother and Child*, May 1939

detail that Lange displayed in these photographs point to her respect for the essential dignity and skill of manual labor, in this case tobacco farming.[62] She extended that same respect to the nurturance and skill of maternal care, and the self-possession of migratory mothers.

Because a significant portion of the photographs produced by the Historical Section of the RA/FSA focused on women, some have argued that their presence attests to the success of gender symbols in both reassuring an anxious public, and conveying the need for relief. Wendy Kozol has written that the FSA photographs of women as mothers, wives, and victims of circumstance strengthened traditional ideas about gender relations and familial stability during the depression. She suggests that in depicting the archetypal role of mother, these "Madonnas of the Fields," surrounded as they are with their children, contributed to the FSA's gendered narrative of poverty and need.[63] Similarly, Jacqueline Ellis has critiqued the "reassuring symbols" in FSA photography, including images of mothers who remained strongly protective of their children, thus comforting a middle-class America that despite poverty, itinerancy, and homelessness, mothers would ensure that traditional family life would endure beyond the vicissitudes of the Depression.[64]

I argue instead that Lange's images of these mothers under duress go beyond reassurance and the depiction of traditional gender relations to offer a more complicated interpretation of motherhood. On the one hand, Lange's photographs portray the enduring nature of mother-love, and the joy and power that mothers experience—across race and class, despite incredible hardship, and sometimes without men. Many of the multiracial mothers Lange depicts are not in traditional families but are instead single mothers or members of multigenerational families. Lange portrayed mothers' labor as critical to the support of the family, their loving care as essential to family survival, and their lives characterized by backbreaking toil. Lange's photographs are positive images in an increasingly negative trajectory in American ideas about motherhood.[65] It is possible that Lange was self-consciously creating a promaternal narrative and archive that could refute the rising clamor of antimaternalism that was already circulating and that would explode in the 1940s United States.

At the same time Lange's photographs and captions also distill the ambivalence and conflicts of mothers—their stuckness, frustrations, anxiety, and terrifying responsibilities. Some of Lange's pictures capture mothers' loss and despair. A March 1937 photograph reveals a thin, young, white mother standing in a field, chopped chin-length hair bobby pinned away from her face, wearing a checkered dress, clutching a sweater underneath one elbow. Her eyes are downcast and she is biting the fingernails of one hand. Lange's caption informs the viewer that this young woman migrated from Oklahoma to California with her husband and two children, and her two-year-old died from exposure the previous winter. The Relief Administration is returning the family to Oklahoma.[66]

Although Lange did not specifically write about the emotions of migratory mothers in the 1930s, her photographs represent and illuminate them. Another series of snapshots taken in California in March 1937 show an eighteen-year-old mother and her toddler, sitting in the doorway of a tent. The interior of the tent is dark. In each of the three portraits, the mother—wearing jeans and a work shirt—is leaning forward on a ladder-backed chair, her soiled-faced child playing in the dirt (and in one scene eating it) at her feet. Reminiscent of Louise Thompson (the subject of *Migrant Mother*), whose photograph Lange had taken the previous year, this young mother looks directly at the camera in two shots, her folded hand to her mouth and a look of resignation, fatigue, and anger on her face. Although she is wearing a wedding ring, Lange's caption makes no mention of a husband, and reads simply, "Eighteen-year-old mother from Oklahoma, now a California migrant." In one of the photographs, the white mother is looking down tenderly at her son, her hand protectively near his fine, blond hair. The image captures a mother's ambivalence: simultaneously her face reflects irritation, acceptance, protection, and pride.[67] Another captioned photograph Lange took of this mother describes her as penniless and stranded in California.[68] Poet Adrienne Rich described the simultaneous "anger and tenderness" of motherhood, the rapidly shifting emotions that mothering can invoke. Rich wrote in her journal, as a middle-class, married, white American mother in 1960: "My children cause me the most exquisite suffering of which I have any experience. It is the suffering of ambivalence: the murderous alternation between bitter resentment and raw-edged nerves and blissful gratification and tenderness."[69] This ambivalence runs like a gossamer thread through the history of motherhood, including the history of rural mothers.

The Lives of Rural Mothers

Agrarian mothers and farm wives were isolated, often poor, and burdened by domestic responsibilities, economic obligations, and marriages that were frequently oppressive. At times they despaired at the impossibility of completing all the physical labor that was demanded of them in a single day. In Lange's photographs, the mothers often exhibit worried concern for the future, suggesting their inability to experience the kinds of magical "mother time" that idealized nineteenth-century depictions had suggested. Poor rural mothers had less access to birth control than urban or middle-class women, which intensified their worries about the future. One Kansas mother of two young boys one year apart with another child on the way wrote the U.S. Children's Bureau in 1928:

> I'm only in my twenties. We Rent a Farm & find it a hard row to hoe to provide food & clothe [sic] for us all. We can not meet expenses. My health is going down hill from hard work & Bearing babies. My husband works hard & worries, also has the Asthama [sic] so bad in

Winter I find My self doing a Man's Work. This is hard to be Mother, Wife, & especially the Outside Work.

Now what I want to know is Why can't We poor people be given Birth Control as well as Dr's ... I think it unfair Dr's. & Rich seek Birth Control & the poor can't seek nothing, only Poverty & more babies. —I'm willing to undergo anything after our next baby comes to make me steral [sic].[70]

In her study of agrarian wives and mothers in rural Nebraska between 1880 and 1940, Deborah Fink describes lives characterized by isolation, vulnerable dependence on husbands for survival and companionship, few female networks, and grinding labor. She concludes that the agrarian ideal failed because it was founded on a false belief in the moral superiority of rural life and a relentless subordination of women.[71] The celebration of farming and farmers as the heart of American society meshed poorly with the lives of many women who did much of the work of farming, but were overlooked.[72] Agrarianism, Fink argues, is a gendered ideology because it projects different principles for men and women. Women were not farmers, did not gain property ownership through their labor, and were assumed to be in charge of the home and to support and promote the industry of their husbands. "Women stirred inside the agrarian system and urban reformers took note of the hardships farm women faced," Fink noted. "Yet no one publicly questioned the assumptions that farm women would interpret their lives in terms of their duties as wives and mothers in service to the overarching good of the farm."[73]

Rural mothers in the 1930s faced intensified challenges. Higher standards of childcare and the dictates of scientific motherhood were jarringly at odds with the realities of the depressed rural economy. The issue of underage employment, addressed in the proposed federal Child Labor Amendment of 1924, brought the subject of children's work on farms, along with their toil in factories and industries, before the American public.[74] Fink's study of rural Boone County, Nebraska, in the 1930s showed an increasing rate of desertion by husbands. Women seldom sought divorce; economic necessity combined with cultural and religious traditions kept most mothers in marriages, even unhappy ones. Working-class women defined a good husband as a man who tried his best to provide for his family, prioritized his family over other commitments, and was not abusive.[75] Mothers, and women in general, had little say in social policy, and were economically dependent on men. They faced cultural norms that shaped a narrow parameter of what defined good mothering.

Rural women faced very real physical dangers in pregnancy and childbirth. Isolated on farms and in rural communities often many miles from physicians or family members, some lived in terror of pregnancy and childbirth. Mrs. A.P. of Wyoming wrote Children's Bureau Head Julia Lathrop in 1916:

I live sixty-five miles from a Dr. and my other babies (two) were very large at birth, one 12-lbs. the other 10 ½ lbs. I have been *very* badly torn each time, through the rectum the last time. My youngest child is 71/2 (and when I am delivered this time it will be past 81/2). I am 37 years old and I am so worried and filled with perfect horror at the prospects ahead. So many of my neighbors die at giving birth to their children.[76]

An eight-months pregnant mother, recently moved to California and describing herself as "a stranger in a strange land," wrote the Children's Bureau in 1921 asking for guidance on how to birth her own baby. "Can you give me any information on how to deliver the baby myself?" she queried.

[I]t will be impossible to go to the hospital or have a nurse or midwife here as we are only camping and living in a shack and tent. ... My only neighbors are the snakes, lizards, squirrels, and rats whose very presence has only made me so nervous that I jump a foot if I hear a leaf rustle in the wind.[77]

While itinerant rural mothers took both pride and joy in their children, they lived economically precarious existences that made it impossible for them to fulfill the middle-class ideals of motherhood as constructed at the time. Children were often overworked, poorly educated, and subjected to lives of transience. Rural mothers had little control over their fertility, worked in the fields until childbirth was near, and—torn between pride and trepidation—were ambivalent about the prospect of more children.[78] "The traditional pattern of the glory and the actual or imagined value of a large number of children pull in one direction," Margaret Hagood wrote in *Mothers of the South*, "while the desire to avoid the suffering of childbearing, the trouble of caring for another child, and the responsibility of another mouth to be fed and body to be clothed pull in the other."[79] Both women's and children's labor was vital to the success of family farms as well as itinerant agriculture. Like the task orientation that Karen Davies argued characterizes care work, farm work is also more amenable to overlapping temporalities than other kinds of work.[80] Farm mothers could more easily shift between care for their children, which has its own temporal rhythm, and planting and harvesting crops, which calls for a different cadence and use of time. Indeed, as Lange's photographs show, children often labored alongside their mothers in the Depression-era fields. Yet the limited sense of leisure that industrial workers might enjoy after the closing whistle blew was inaccessible to migrant mothers, whose work never ended. One tenant mother revealed to Hagood a miscarriage she suffered, "passing it" (the fetus) while walking home from the field one evening. She was wearing overalls and no one saw the blood. Because it was the busy season she returned to the fields the next morning, without visiting a doctor. She confided to Hagood that she had never been "the same inside" since.[81]

While children provided emotional gratification for rural women isolated on farms and in nuclear family households, they also burdened women with years of pregnancy, childbirth, nursing, childrearing, and economic obligation. Fink has argued that farm women as mothers were at the center of a contradiction, in that children's dependence and trust gave them, even if temporarily, power and authority. Children offered the hope of being taken care of in old age. They also gave working-class women a means by which to express their gender identity in the conventions that middle-class culture embraced: "motherhood told them," Fink wrote, "they were women."[82]

Sociologists Kathryn Edin and Maria Kefalas have investigated the question of why poor, single mothers in the twenty-first century United States put motherhood ahead of marriage. On the basis of interviews with 162 low-income unmarried mothers in Philadelphia, Edin and Kefalas concluded that the poor give a higher value to children than do members of the middle class, and that women with less than a high school education are much more likely to view motherhood as one of life's most fulfilling roles. With fewer options in work and education, poor women have less to lose and more to gain from becoming mothers. "The poor," Edin and Kefalas noted, "view childlessness as one of the greatest tragedies in life": motherhood, they conclude, offers a powerful place of meaning for poor women.[83] Their findings have resonance for the poor rural 1930s era mothers I consider in this chapter, as well as the African American and Irish-American Catholic mothers I will examine in following chapters. In the face of multiple challenges, these mothers took pride and comfort in, and exhibited tremendous strength and dedication to, their children.

Domesticity and the Sustenance of Life

Most of the mothers Lange photographed are outside, sitting or standing on the thresholds of houses, porches, or tents, or seen in or through doorways. This positioning captured their liminal status and in-betweenness. In some of these images, domesticity and household arts—home and hearth—are refashioned outside. One October 1939 photograph, "Mother of Migrant Family Sewing," depicts a sturdy looking, middle-aged white woman bent over a pair of overalls, which she is hand stitching. She is sitting on a stool or log on the banks of a river near Vale, Malheur County, Oregon. Household implements surround her, including a teakettle and cooking pots, a suitcase, a heap of dark-colored coats and pants to be mended. Ramshackle, leaning huts dot the land on the other side of the river. The woman is not looking at the camera but is frowning slightly, intently focused on her handiwork. She is wearing a flowered dress covered by a dark, heavy, shapeless coat. Her children are not in the photograph.[84] The image brings to mind historian E.P. Thompson's observation that if time-oriented labor characterized industrial capitalism, pre-industrial conventions passed into modern times in the rhythms of women's work and caring labor in the home.[85] This mother had made nature a temporary home, and persisted in keeping the family clothed and nurtured despite the hardship of their living conditions. One historian has suggested that it was through absences or lacunas that Lange conveyed a message about home and its meaning:

> She could photograph a shanty, and what she was really photographing was the house that wasn't there. She could photograph a doorframe, and what she was really photographing was the door that wasn't there. She could photograph the stovepipe and what she was really photographing was the hearth that wasn't there.[86]

In addition to portraying the elisions of their domestic circumstances, Lange's photographs of Depression-era mothers also capture the movement, flight, and transient nature of their peripatetic circumstances. A February 1939 photograph shows a statuesque white mother wearing a long, fur-trimmed coat, standing on the side of U.S. Highway 99 near Brawley, Imperial County, California. She holds her young daughter in her arms. They both look directly into the camera—the mother appears fatigued, sad, puzzled. Another child's shoulder is visible in the frame of the photograph. Lange writes that this is a homeless mother with the youngest of her seven children "walking the highway from Phoenix, Arizona where they picked cotton"—a distance of over 235 miles—and bound for San Diego. Their destination is 130 miles down the road, "where the father hopes to get on relief 'because he once lived there.'"[87] Two September 1939 photographs feature a white mother and her children in the passenger seat of a parked car. In both photographs, the mother, wearing round, wire-rimmed glasses, a warm, wool coat and holding a disheveled child clutching a bottle in her lap looks into the distance, appearing apprehensive, worried, burdened. A long shot shows the baby and the mother with a second child—barefoot and also untidy, a toddler wearing a heavy coat—perched on her shoulder and the back of her seat. The viewer is drawn to the mothers' hands, which are in her lap and around her child, fingers almost clasping, as if in prayer. No one is in the driver's seat, and the viewer can see another car through the open window, a child peering out the window, a dog in the backseat, and the family's covered possessions under a tarp on the roof. Lange titled these photographs "Mother and baby of family on the road. Tulelake, Siskiyou County, California," and "Mother and two children on the road."[88] They were published the same year that *Parents* magazine admonished American mothers to "add science to love and be a perfect mother," and represent the yawning gulf between maternal prescription and reality (Figure 2.7).

Several of Lange's photographs show mothers and children in cars or on the side of roads beside cars, and her captions underline the extreme difficulty of their circumstances. She wrote beside a 1938 image: "During the cotton strike, the father, a striking picker, has left his wife and child in the car while he applies to the Farm Security Administration for an emergency

Figure 2.7 Dorothea Lange, *Mother and Two Children on the Road*, September 1939

food grant. Shafter, California."[89] She captioned a 1936 photograph of a white mother and two children standing beside their car and what appears to be a shabby trailer where they are living: "Mother of five children from Oklahoma, now picking cotton in California, near Fresno."[90]

A better-known series of photographs Lange took of a migrant family on the road is dated November 1936 and represents a white mother, father, and child in arms, hitchhiking on California's U.S. Highway 99. In the first photograph, the neatly dressed father, hat on head and face downcast and not visible to the camera, holds a suitcase in either hand. The teenaged mother calmly looks downward; her shadow is long in the afternoon light. The straight ribbon of highway, dotted with utility poles, stretches beside them. In the second image the mother, child in her lap, is sitting on the suitcase on the side of the road, gazing into the distance. The child is crying. The slender father, face visible now, looks defeated into the expanse. The husband and wife are not looking at each other in either shot. The caption reads:

> Young family, penniless, hitchhiking on U.S. Highway 99 in California. The father, twenty-four, and the mother, seventeen, came from

Winston-Salem, North Carolina. Early in 1935, their baby was born in the Imperial Valley, California, where they were working as field laborers.[91]

The faith in linear time and the idea of time's essential productivity has broken down: the notion of progress, so central to modernity, is elusive in these images. The American belief in relocating in search of a better life is vacuous. There is no better life for these rural Americans on the move.

In their poetic 1939 *An American Exodus: A Record of Human Erosion in the Thirties*, Lange and her husband collaborated on a narrative that integrated images and text to tell this story of forced migration. Although this innovation in photo-textual storytelling did not receive the critical attention it deserves (it was eclipsed by the outbreak of World War II in Europe), the book symbolizes Lange and Taylor's unique partnership and remains a moving chronicle of rural poverty and the mass migration of displaced tenant farmers from the drought-ridden southern plains to California, the American exodus at the heart of the book. Some have called *An American Exodus* one of the most important photographic books of the twentieth century.[92] Between the middle of 1935 and May 1939, Taylor informs the reader, 300,000 Americans—an average of 6,000 a month—were counted entering California alone, by automobile. "More than nine-tenths are native American whites," he wrote. "A quarter had left Oklahoma and another quarter had left Texas, Arkansas, and Missouri."[93] "These people are not hand-picked failures," Taylor explained. "They are the human materials cruelly dislocated by the processes of human erosion. They have been scattered like the shavings from a clean-cutting plane, or like the dust of their farms, literally blown out." He describes these "American whites" trekking west, at the end of a long historical line that included Chinese, Japanese, Koreans, African Americans, "Hindustanis," Mexicans, and Filipinos, who followed crops and farmers to make their livings and survive.[94]

Californians labeled the white refugee farm families from the southern plains who migrated to California to escape the economic devastation of the depression and the environmental catastrophe of the dust bowl, "Okies." Although the drought refugees were not primarily from Oklahoma but from a number of plains states, the term "Okie" referred to their whiteness, which was in contrast to the equally suffering Mexican, Filipino, Japanese, Chinese, and Indian agricultural laborers. Like other New Deal progressives, Lange and Taylor believed they could not afford *not* to exploit racialized sympathy for the Okies as a means of advocating for improved treatment for all farmworkers. Their whiteness made their sufferings more shocking to the white American public, while their poverty and itinerancy—similar to Irish immigrants whom I will turn to in Chapter 4—brought their racial identity into question. The pejorative "Okie" label threatened their whiteness: "They were so 'low-grade'," Gordon notes, "that in the estimation of many white Californians, they seemed a different race."[95] NO MEXICANS

OR OKIES signs appeared in many locales. And indeed, they were refugees, their communities crushed, relocating for their very survival.[96]

The kinds of social prescriptions that linked good mothering to time discipline and orderly, synchronous homes become totally irrelevant in light of these American mothers, children, and families who had no permanent homes. Yet Lange's photographs affectingly demonstrate the grip that the idea of home and domesticity had on some of the mothers and families she chronicled. One photograph from Yakima, Washington, shows a little boy and his sister camped with their family along the banks of the Yakima River. The two of them, their seven siblings, and parents have migrated from California; a large roll of some material emerges from the upper left corner of the photograph and cuts straight across the image. The caption provides the clue to the unknown material: "Still carrying a roll of kitchen linoleum. Three years on the road." As scholar Anne Spirn remarked, "That rolled linoleum became memory of home, and dream of home."[97]

One of the most stirring themes in *An American Exodus* is the difficulty of creating homes while in constant motion. One migrant Taylor and Lange spoke with at the city dump in Bakersfield, California, in 1935 told them, "People has got to stop somewhere. Even a bird has got a nest." Another said, "What bothers us travellin' people most is we cain't get no place to stay still." These quotations are accompanied by a Lange photograph of an old white woman in a makeshift tent, face drawn and deeply lined, eyes squinted into the distance.[98] Historian Linda Gordon points to the multiple meanings of movement that *An American Exodus* captures, in its geographic tracing of migration from the eastern United States and the Great Plains to the west: "Images of highways show how 'on the road' bears a variety of meanings in American history, the movement and mobility so central to American culture, the automobile as a symbol of freedom and its transportation to a better life."[99] The life depicted in these photographs and accompanying texts seems hardly better, though. Lange included images she had taken in agricultural labor camps, squatter camps, and auto tent camps. Photographs depict men, women, and children at stoop labor in the fields: one shows a sleepy young girl in Kern County, California, in 1936, rubbing her eyes. The accompanying caption reads: "Oklahoma child with cotton sack ready to go into field with parents at 7 A.M."[100]

The words of the migrants themselves, along with the photographs, serve as the moral core of the story. Quotes from farmworkers and migrants line the front and back covers of the book in a democratic collage, arranged end to end so that cumulatively they represent a chorus of voices. This was Lange's and Taylor's intent: "So far as possible, we have let them [the living participants] speak to you face to face."[101]

In *Extreme Domesticity*, literary scholar Susan Fraiman sets out to map domesticity from the margins, to "contest received ideas about where and with whom domesticity lies."[102] She seeks to validate "those sequences of gestures," most often performed by women, which not only ensure domestic life, but sustain life itself. She describes the inferiorized categories associated with domesticity, all coded as "feminine": "These include the ordinary, familiar, and quotidian; the detailed, insignificant, and small in scale; the bodily and especially tactile; the emotional, subjective, and personal; the enclosed, introverted, and local; the dependent, relational, and maternal."[103] In a chapter that explores domesticity in the context of homelessness, Fraiman argues that domesticity is not absent for this population so much as it is broken and embattled. Like the itinerant mothers whom Lange photographed in the early twentieth century, the late twentieth-century homeless people depicted in the texts Fraiman interprets were anxious to reassemble the pieces of "home." For them, domestic spaces and domestic labor equated to "safety, sanity, and self-expression: survival in the most basic sense."[104] The devaluing of domesticity and the creation and maintenance of homes is another shape that antimaternalism takes.

Migration, as Sara Ahmed has noted, is a process of disorientation and reorientation that involves leaving one home and settling in another.[105] But for people constantly on the move, that reorientation is inaccessible, or delayed. As Fraiman has argued, "home," however invested in stability, is always vulnerable and provisional, never wholly fixed or singular. The domestic, she contends, is "a site of change and complexity" that is both variable and multiple, both a discursive construct and the product of "ongoing often unrecognized labor." Despite its instability, home has symbolic and emotional value; it "takes shape in answer to yearnings for some degree of predictability and continuity."[106] I read Lange's images of itinerant mothers setting up "home" on a riverbank, or in a tent, or in a car, as a form of agency and competence. Poor women, men, and children still seek access to the qualities that Freeman describes as domestic virtues: "privacy, safety, stability, coziness, quiet, beauty, intimacy, and routine."[107] The efforts of poor itinerant farm women to create these for their families, in whatever ways they could, is a way they strove for dignity, personhood, and sustenance for themselves and their families. The kind of domestic yearning that led the one family described earlier to travel three years with a rolled-up piece of linoleum both summons the past and references the future: "domesticity not wholly disappeared but ... dispersed across time, drawing on memories and fantasizing about the future." The men, women, and children that Lange documented in the 1930s carried bits of dwelling along with them: they were "traveling-in-dwelling, dwelling-in-traveling" people, occupying liminal spaces as they sought survival and more for their families.[108]

Photography and Truth

Lange consistently underlined her philosophy of using photography in the service of social investigation. She wrote, we use the camera as a tool of research. Upon a tripod of photographs, captions, and text we rest themes evolved out of long observations in the field. We adhere to the standards of documentary photography as we have conceived them.[109]

Photographs are not objective artifacts however, and the historian must use them with care. As James Curtis has noted, photographs are historical documents in their own right.[110] Photographs came to the United States in 1839; the first photographic image—a mirror-like image dubbed a daguerreotype (named after its inventor Louis Daguerre)—was a complicated and expensive undertaking. Ambrotypes and tintypes, the descendants of daguerreotypes, were widely circulated in middle-class culture by the time of the Civil War. Documentary photography, often consigned to journalism rather than art, arose during this period. "This consignment implied," Curtis notes, "that documentary photographers were mere recorders, skilled technicians to be sure, but passive observers of the social scene and definitely not artists." Late nineteenth-century urban photographers Jacob Riis and Lewis Himes focused their cameras on urban slums, establishing documentary photography as a tool of social reform. Historians trace the FSA Photographic Project to their influence.[111]

Curtis has described a documentary photographer as an historical actor bent upon communicating a message to an audience.[112] Some have criticized the practice of directing and posing subjects, which is occasionally done in documentary photography, although taking a series of pictures, and then selecting the best (as Lange did in *Migrant Mother*) is common in all photography. If, as Curtis states, documentary photographs are conscious acts of persuasion, we need to ask what it is that Lange was trying to say about motherhood in her photographs, and why. She was employed by the FSA—which had its own narratives it was working to construct—but she wandered from that narrative, which was why Stryker ultimately fired Lange. Like Riis and Himes, Lange was committed to the use of words (captions) to drive home the meaning of her images.[113] Yet Lange understood the impact of the visual image itself: "The camera is a powerful instrument for saying to the world: 'This is the way it is. Look at it. Look at it,'" she stated.[114]

The contemporary photographer Sally Mann has written about seeing, photography, and memory, arguing that once a photograph has been taken, we "see" reality, or we "see" the past, only through that image. We lose the memory of the actual moment; the captured image supplants it. As noted earlier, some Americans—even those who experienced and lived through it—carry Lange's photographs as their visual memory of the Great Depression. According to Mann, photography is "the malignant twin to imperfect memory."

> As far back as 1901 Emile Zola telegraphed the threat of this relatively new medium, remarking that you cannot claim to have really

seen something until you have photographed it. What Zola perhaps also knew or intuited was that once photographed, whatever you had "really seen" would never be seen by the eye of memory again. It would forever be cut from the continuum of being, a mere sliver, a slight, translucent paring from the fat life of time: elegiac, one-dimensional, immediately assuming the amber quality of nostalgia: an instantaneous memento mori.[115]

In Mann's estimation, while photography *seems* to preserve our past, it actually displaces and corrupts it, as it creates its own memories.

Yet simultaneously photography is one way of stopping or freezing time in mid-arc: of paring, slivering, or abducting time, in Mann's words. Noting that "all perception is selection," and that photographs necessarily exclude facets of the moment's complexity, Mann reminds us that photography is not reality. "Photographs economize the truth ... [T]hey are always moments more or less illusorily abducted from time's continuum." Thus, Lange's mothers and children are "figures on slippery paper slivered out of time," whose images and representations would have been lost to us otherwise.[116] How we read them depends on our own context and perception, on what we are looking for. How they were constructed and created depended on Lange's vision, emotions, and creative and political ambitions at that moment in time. Lange's goal as an artist was to lose the self and to become, as much as possible, only an observer. "One can get into a visual world, detaching yourself," she said in a filmed conversation near the end of her life. "It is a mental disengagement, so that you live for maybe two, three hours as completely as possible, a visual experience, where you feel that you have lost yourself, your identity. You are only an observer."[117]

Although Lange never explicitly stated what she hoped to convey in her photographs of mothers and their children, she did try to describe her methods and approach to her FSA photography in general. When asked in a 1964 oral history how she decided which pictures to take, she replied:

> When you were out in the field ... almost always alone, unknown, very often unprepared for, turned loose really ... You found your way ... We found our way in, slid in on the edges. We used our hunches, we lived, and it was hard, hard living. It wasn't easy, rather rough, not too far away from the people we [were] working with. ... And with the actual people, you worked with a certain common denominator. Now if they asked who you were, and they heard you were a representative of the government, who was interested in their difficulties, or in their condition, it's a very different thing from going in and saying, "I'm working for *Look* magazine, who wants to take pictures of you."[118]

When the interviewer asked Lange how she, a city dweller, was able to earn the trust of the rural people she photographed, she admitted that gaining trust could be a challenge, and described individuals who refused her permission to photograph, who were hostile, and the tactics she employed to try to earn their confidence.

Lange utilized research methods we would now call feminist, including self-disclosure, spending time with research subjects, and listening and not judging.[119] She described having "an invisible coat, that covers me," which she first created as "a lame little girl" walking down the streets of New York's Bowery. "I learned to be unseen at that age. And that has stayed with me all my working life," she confided to an interviewer. She drew on her own identity as a mother to forge connections with the mothers and children she photographed. "Before I ask questions," Lange observed,

> I tell them: who I am, why I'm there, how many children I have, how old my children are. I can then take out a notebook and write down exactly what I've been told, without ever feeling that I am imposing.[120]

She took her time.

> You know, so often it's just sticking around and being there, remaining there, not swooping in and swooping out in a cloud of dust; sitting down on the ground with people, letting the children look at your camera with their dirty, grimy little hands, and putting their fingers on the lens, and you let them, because you know that "if" you will behave in a generous manner, you're very apt to receive it, you know? ... I have asked for a drink of water and taken a long time to drink it, and I have told everything about myself long before I asked a question. "What are you doing here?" they'd say. "Why don't you go down and do this, that, and the other?" I've taken a long time, patiently, to explain, and as truthfully as I could.[121]

Lange's respect for her photographic subjects seems to have been genuine. Looking back over her career, she described her concern about invading privacy or overstepping boundaries, and her recognition of the times that she got it right. "I can only say I knew I was looking at something," she remarked. "Sometimes you have an inner sense that you have encompassed the thing ... . You know then that you are not taking anything away from anyone, their privacy, their dignity, their wholeness."[122] The white Southern photographer Sally Mann described a similar motivation for her series on black men:

> These pictures are not a voyeuristic inventory of my models' physical properties ... What I want to do is find out who those black men were that I encountered in my childhood, men that I never really saw, except through ... the perspective of a racist society.

Yet as Mann recognized, the temporary connection that is created between the photographer and her subject can be seen as a kind of performance art itself: "an intense period during which the relationship that obtains between sitter and photographer both informs and becomes the art."[123]

Many critics, including photographers, have described photography as inherently exploitative. Paula Rabinowitz identified the interrelationship between looking and power or between voyeurism and class consciousness in her examination of James Agee and Walker Evans's iconic textual-photographic montage of three southern 1930s tenant families, *Let Us Now Praise Famous Men*.[124] Rabinowitz concluded that the power of the gaze is both a sexual and class practice, and that "photographs are themselves objects of the gaze as well as purveyors of images."[125] Yet documentary photographers in the 1930s like Evans and Lange were in search of what they called "authenticity," and viewed the camera as a way to find truth. Agee, who wrote the prose for *Let Us Now Praise Famous Men*, put it this way: "the camera seems to me, next to unassisted and weaponless consciousness, the central instrument of our time." Even more effective than words, the camera can "perceive simply the cruel radiance of what is."[126] Unlike Dorothea Lange, Walker Evans refused to caption his photographs so that the images could speak for themselves, but in this case Agee's prose filled in the missing context. Some scholars object to adding interpretive language to photographs, concerned that the caption or text might become the most important part of the photograph.[127]

Sally Mann recognizes the potential for artistic misuse and the interrelationship between looking and power in her work, and in photography as an art form. "Exploitation lies at the root of every great portrait," she remarked, "and all of us know it. Even the simplest picture of another person is ethically complex, and the ambitious photographer, no matter how sincere, is compromised right from the git-go."[128] What a photographer can do, and Lange certainly tried, is to establish trust with her subjects and to, in Mann's words, "convince the total stranger before me that this work will be aesthetically resonant in some universal way and worth the risk he takes in making himself so vulnerable. It's a tricky moment," she continued. "Taking the picture is an invasive act, a one-sided exercise of power, the implications of which, which considered in historical perspective, are unsettling. Photography is always invasive, but these experiences are consensual and, in the best hours, transcendent."[129] That Lange's camera so frequently turned to mothers is no coincidence of course; she wanted to find out who these itinerant rural mothers were whether she was successful or not we can never fully know.

Exploitation became an issue surrounding the publication and dissemination of *Migrant Mother*, Lange's famous photograph of Florence Thompson. Linda Gordon notes that by 1955, when the Museum of Modern Art published the photograph in *Family of Man*, it had "traveled the world." Public property, *Migrant Mother* could be used for any purpose without fee. In 1957, Thompson and her family saw the photograph in *U.S. Camera* and wrote the magazine to complain, requesting that the publishing company

"Recall all the un-Sold Magazines." Thompson asked for Dorothea Lange's address so "That I may Inform her that should the picture appear in Any magazine again I and my Three Daughters shall be forced to Protect our rights." *U.S. Camera* sent the letter on to Lange, who was shaken that her photograph had "caused grief."[130] There were no grounds for a lawsuit, because the government—and thus the public—owned the photograph and Lange had earned no money from it. But Thompson's concerns over the appropriation of her image are understandable, and point to potential objections—about privacy and loss of pride, for example—the mothers and other down on their luck Americans whose images Lange captured in the 1930s might have harbored. As one migrant farmer told Lange, "I never have wrote back home and told my folks that we live in a tent. I've wrote that we live well and such as that but I never have wrote that we live in a tent."[131] In an extremely critical reading of Lange's life and artistic contributions, Jon Lauck describes Florence Thompson being humiliated by her experience with Lange. He notes that in the late 1970s, Thompson was living in a trailer park in California, still bitter and seeking compensation.[132]

Lauck's assessment was partially true. Seventeen years after Lange's own death from cancer, Florence Thompson lay critically ill in California with cancer, and the debilitation of a recent stroke. When interviewed by a reporter, Thompson's children pleaded for funds to defray their mother's weekly $1,400 medical costs (she had no health insurance). Within weeks after the article's publication, contributions totaled nearly thirty thousand dollars.[133] Gordon concludes, "In the end, Lange was able to help Thompson's family in a small way."[134]

Dorothea Lange did not emerge unchanged from her encounters with rural mothers and families in the Depression years. When her interviewer asked Lange the most significant thing she had learned about Americans, "or about man in general" in her travels the length and breadth of the country in the 1930s, she responded:

> Well, I many times encountered courage, real courage. Undeniable courage. I've heard it said that that was the highest quality of the human animal. There is no other. I've heard that. I think it was Mr. Freud. No, Mr. Jung. One or the other of early psychoanalysts. Alfred Adler or somebody. Well, I encountered that many times, in unexpected places. And I have learned to recognize it when I see it.[135]

Certainly, Lange's images of mothers depict strong and courageous women. Florence Thompson's headstone reads: "Migrant Mother. A legend of the strength of American motherhood."[136]

Dorothea Lange and Motherhood

There is an irony in Lange's *Migrant Mother* and her other moving depictions of resilient and nurturing mothers because for Lange, motherhood was fraught and conflicted. Dorothea Lange was a mother of two young sons and stepmother to three when she took the photographs of migrant mothers I analyze in this chapter.[137] Her own mothering practices and experiences of motherhood as Institution must have influenced the images of mothers she selected, and the emotions she sought to convey in these representations. Lange was a career woman and an artist who struggled to find time for her work. Married to painter Maynard Dixon from 1920 to 1935, Lange found her time given over to incessant domesticity and supporting her husband's artistic career. Recognizing the ways that access to time is gendered and that care has molded women's relation to time she stated:

> I could be of help to Maynard mostly by keeping everything smooth and being happy and making it an enjoyable time and taking care of the three children. I baked and cooked and you know when there's deep snow on the ground you're kept busy. The gloves, the galoshes, the wet clothes—you put them on and you take them off. And I used to drive him to where he was working, and drive him back those short winter days. In the summer time we had guests because we had a big place out of town there. I couldn't work then, really.[138]

In order to pursue her photography Lange sent her two young sons to boarding school, and to live with foster families. In her first oral history, conducted between October 1960 and late 1961, Lange described the decades-long sorrow she suffered because of this decision. "We put the boys in a day school in San Anselmo where they had arrangements for boarding pupils," she told the interviewer.

> John was only four and Dan was only seven and this was very, very hard for me to do. Even now when I speak of it I can feel the pain. I carry these things inside, and it hurts me in the same spot that it did then.[139]

According to several accounts, Lange also had two illegal abortions during these years, and traveled to Seattle to get them.[140]

In her later life and second marriage as in her years of young motherhood, Lange was torn between her desire to make life easy for her artistic, academic husbands and her own need to create. The first time Lange got the idea to craft simple, unaffected depictions of the men and women injured by the economic crisis was in her studio in San Francisco, when her children were away in boarding school. She remembered,

> Although my mind was over in San Anselmo most of the time and I didn't like to be separated from the children, it drove me to work, and I worked then as I would not have done, I am sure, if I had gone back

into my habitual life. There in my studio on Montgomery Street I was surrounded by evidences of the Depression.[141]

Determined to create something memorable because she felt that both she and her sons were paying a price for their separation, when Lange spotted a group of unemployed men gathering in the street outside her studio window, she ran down and snapped what would become one of her most important photographs, *White Angel Breadline* (1932).

The celebrated picture shows an unemployed man, in the middle of a crowd seeking relief, leaning on a wooden railing, his arms enclosing an empty tin cup. "The man's hands are clasped," Curtis writes, "so that he resembles a communicant at the alter rail." Recalling the decision to take this photograph Lange remarked, "You know there are moments such as these when time stands still, and all you do is hold your breath and hope it will wait for you."[142] The fact that she was separated from her children, and not fulfilling the motherhood ideal, powerfully motivated Lange. She told her interviewer,

> all I'm saying about that window is that it stays in my memory because I see it and I remember what has happened in my life through moments that I remember visually. I do say, however, that if the boys hadn't been taken from me by circumstances I might have said to myself, "I would do this, but I can't because..." as many women say to themselves over and over again, which is one reason why men have the advantage. I was driven by the fact that I was under personal turmoil to do something.[143]

In an oral history conducted near the end of her life when she was ill with esophageal cancer, Lange described feeling "somewhat of a failure" because she had been unable to dedicate the required hours and years of work to develop and advance the field of photojournalism. "I realize more and more what it takes to be a really good photographer," she stated. "You just go in over your head, not just up to your neck." Lange was never able to balance her passion for photography with her obligations to her family and other relationships. "I would disappoint my family very much if I devoted myself to photography," she continued.

> I'd have to step out. And as far as my husband is concerned, he would understand it, but he wouldn't know how to adjust to it, really, You might say, and I say to myself, that it isn't the amount of time it takes. But you know that tomorrow morning you have to see somebody who's coming from Asia, just for an hour, and tomorrow afternoon at five thirty you have to go to a cocktail party and a dinner in honor of someone—those things you have to do.[144]

Lange described "living the visual life" as a "pretty taxing proposition," and explained to an oral historian in 1964 that it was because "you can't fulfill all of your obligations quite so easily ... We're all hacked to pieces by our daily lives."[145]

Despite Lange's privileged class status, her reflections on time—and her own lack of it—summon an interpretation of gendered time and "mothers' time" that reflects its scarcity, and women's inability to control it. Lange did not have access to time as a resource in the ways that her husbands, who were fathers, did. Like the writer Tillie Olsen, who in *Silences* depicted the challenges motherhood poses for women who want and need to create art, Lange clearly understood what she termed "the difference between the role of the woman as artist and the man."[146] She stated:

> But what it takes to pursue my purposes is uninterrupted time, or time that you interrupt when you want to interrupt it. It means living an utterly different way of life, inexplicable to some people. My closest friends will call me in the middle of the morning and say, "Oh, are you busy? I'll just take a minute, but ... would you do me a great favor ... and, so on and so on." ...I'm not focusing this entirely on myself, I'm speaking of the difference between the role of the woman as artist and the man. There is a sharp difference, a gulf. The woman's position is immeasurably more complicated. There are not very many first class woman producers, not many. That is producers of outside things. They produce in other ways. Where they can do both, it's a conflict. I would like to try. I would like to have one year. I'd like to take one year, almost ask it of myself, "Could I have one year?" Just one, when I would not have to take into account anything but my own inner demands.[147]

Three decades later, Adrienne Rich would describe, as a mother of three young sons, her great need to create, to write poetry that was not about her children: "For me, poetry was where I lived as no-one's mother, where I existed as myself."[148]

Several years before Lange's divorce from her first husband, a San Francisco journalist interviewed her; although the author portrayed Dorothea as a bohemian and artist, Lange's comments to her (strikingly similar to those she would make 30 years later) illustrate how difficult it was for her to pursue her art and fulfill the culturally mandated roles of wife and mother. Asked how Lange and Dixon managed to represent "a shining exception to the proverbial 'tug of war' [that develops when] one artist marries another," Lange replied,

> Simple ... an artist's wife accepts the fact that she has to contend with many things that other wives do not. ... As Maynard's wife, it is my chief job to see that his life does not become too involved—that he has a clear field ... he needs a certain amount of freedom ... from the petty, personal things of life.

90 *A Promaternal Narrative and Archive*

The female journalist recognized the double burden Lange carried:

> Returning at night to the house on Russian Hill she would shut the door on her work, get dinner and devote the evening to her children. ... Her distinguished husband, it appeared, divided his evenings with the children and more work.[149]

Although Lange did not identify as a feminist, there were a group of women, including *The Nation* editor Freda Kirchwey, who were writing in the 1920s and 1930s about alternative, egalitarian models of marriage and motherhood.[150] Lange did not try to model either of her marriages on the companionate, feminist model; still it existed as an (admittedly difficult to achieve) ideal for women who, like their husbands, wanted to accomplish and create, and in order to do so needed equal access to time. The complicated temporalities of care—not just caring for children, but tending to husbands—held Lange back. While Dorothea sought to set her own working rhythm, her second husband Paul Taylor was happiest when she traveled with him to his research sites, which took a great deal of her time. Lange's first artist husband believed that his creative work came before hers. It is ironic and tragic that in her final interview Lange—who was ill with a terminal disease and literally running out of time—stated, "I would like to have one year."[151] Her adult son Dan Dixon recognized the battle Lange was fighting with time. In a film shot of Lange when she was assembling her photographs for a 1964 solo exhibit at New York's Museum of Modern Art (MOMA), he gently asked his mother: "How are you going to get it done in the time you have left? I don't trust the time. I really don't trust it." He was wise not to trust the time—Lange did not live to see the exhibit, but died three months before it was held posthumously.[152] Lange had a sharp sensibility for time's movement. At the end of her 1964 oral history, she stated:

> You know what today is? Today is the first day of Autumn. Have you felt it? Today it started. The summer ended this afternoon at two o'clock. All of a sudden. The air got still, a different smell, a kind of a funny, brooding quiet. Today it happened. I was out and I was just so aware of it. Can you feel it? And the cracks in my garden are wide. Today's the day.[153]

Some historians have faulted Lange for what they call her careerism, at-times prickly personality, and controlling nature, which had "apparent family consequences." Even James Curtis, largely sympathetic to Lange, wrote, "[a]lthough Lange apparently tried to create the stable home life that she had lacked as a child, she was unsuccessful."[154] He described violent arguments she had with her stepdaughter, her placing her two sons in foster care, affairs she allegedly had, and the abortions. Historian Jon Lauck insists that Lange's sons never forgave Lange for "placing them out" in boarding school and with foster families. It is unlikely that such criticisms would be made of a male artist, or a father.

Lange's poignant oral histories make clear the struggles she faced as a wife, mother, and artist. The tribute her son Dan made to Lange shortly after her death portrays a domestic, family-oriented woman whom he loved deeply.[155] In a film shot of Lange near the end of her life, it is evident that she and Dan were close. Dorothea, asking his opinion about which photographs she should include in the MOMA exhibit, says to her son: "I need to speak with you because you are one of those who, from time to time, have understood me—I'm happy to say—as well as anybody."[156] Even the daughter of Lange's stepdaughter, when interviewed in 2014 and asked about Lange's mothering abilities appeared forgiving, and mindful of the structural challenges Lange faced. Although she described Lange as "not very nurturing," she also recognized the double marital standard about access to time that her grandfather, artist Maynard Dixon, held. Even after the children were born, Maynard routinely went off on painting trips for months, leaving Dorothea at home as a single parent. "Maynard was free to continue his bohemian life," Lange's step-granddaughter recalled.

> Poor Dorothea was an artist, and was trying to do her work, and here she was stuck with all these children to take care of … young children, and a rebellious teenager [her mother]. With a charming husband [who] bounds in and out every couple of months.[157]

It is also clear from the comments of Lange's surviving family members and associates that the concept and creation of home was important to Lange, and she turned her artist's eye to that creation. One granddaughter remembers: "She was very particular of all of her belongings and of where things went. So I learned a tremendous amount from her, about how to create a space." Lange's son-in-law, when interviewed for the 2014 film that Lange's granddaughter, the filmmaker Dyanna Taylor filmed and directed, recalled: "The house was a product of that marriage … the rooms, the furniture, the light coming in, the living room, the silence, it was magical." Her son Dan recalled the small cabin on the California coast that Taylor and Lange bought later in life—and where Lange's family scattered her ashes after her death—as a place where "they [Lange and Taylor, and their visiting children and grandchildren] just let the time and the tides flow." "It had an enchanted feeling," he recalled. Some who knew Lange speculated that her physical and emotional traumas when photographing the relocation of Japanese Americans during the early 1940s stemmed from this deep need, and respect for, home. Her photographic assistant at the time recalled: "They [the relocated Japanese Americans] were ripped out of their homes … It was the tearing up of their homes that really got to [Lange]."[158] This same focus on the makeshift nature of itinerant rural mothers' temporary homes, or homelessness, was central to Lange's photographs of migratory mothers that I examine in this chapter.

According to her biographer, Lange "had the breath knocked out of her" when she first observed the living conditions of farmworkers, and she made it her mission to document those conditions for the nation to see. Portrayed above all as a photographer of democracy, Lange considered democracy an American ideal, one that she had an obligation to promote.[159] Her camera lens not only sought out laborers and the disadvantaged, it sought out mothers and their children, many of them hardworking and poor, who were also part of democracy. She left behind a rich cache of images that illuminate an important moment in the history of motherhood in the United States. Lange chronicled Depression-era rural mothers under duress, in flight, laboring in fields, seeking to create order and domestic spaces in temporary shelters or outdoors. Lange's mothers met these challenges with grit, dignity, grace, and maternal love. Her photographs remind us of the power of imagery to challenge antimaternalism.

Despite the power of the imagery produced by Lange and other FSA photographers, conflicts between FSA ideals and popular Depression-era ideas about the poor prevented the extended support to rural clients that Lange and her colleagues had envisioned and advocated for. The belief in poverty as an individual moral failure rather than interpreting its structural nature prevailed, and despite Lange's careful documentation of the efforts and successes of FSA clients, the idea persisted that accepting relief from the FSA meant "sign[ing] that you [were] not worth anything."[160] In the 1940s, with American involvement in World War II approaching and the fear of communism spreading, the American public lost faith in the programs of the Farm Security Administration. In 1943, the federal government disbanded the FSA photography project; in 1946, during the Truman presidency, the Farmers Home Administration replaced FSA itself.

How to interpret Lange's photographs of mothers and their children in the context of her own conflicted relationship to motherhood is challenging. Perhaps Lange captured images of the type of mother she wished she was but was unable to be—present, fiercely in support of her family, placing her children's survival and thriving ahead of her own, self-sacrificing, Madonna-like. She sincerely expressed her admiration for the social roles that women traditionally play, even if those roles did not always appeal to her. She was an imperfect woman and, like most of us, a less than perfect mother. According to her biographer, Lange refused to accept responsibility for placing her children in foster care and told friends that the children were at a friend's home, not admitting that she and Taylor paid strangers to board and care for them. "How did this behavior square with her acute sensibility to the suffering of poor children?" Gordon asks. "Perhaps the comparison made her own children's pain less significant," she concluded.[161]

The poor rural mothers Lange photographed in the 1930s did not have the time, resources, or inclinations to subscribe to the standards and expectations of motherhood promoted by larger cultural forces and institutions. Their suffering was perpetuated not by their inabilities to follow the "expert" advice but because the advice itself was (and is) part of a more extensive institutional and cultural system that fails to help and support mothers in this country. Lange documented all of this concretely in her photographs, which demonstrate the effects of poverty and overwork that itinerant farming mothers experienced in their roles as primary caretakers and financial contributors or supporters of their families. Lange also endured the impacts of antimaternalism herself: the unrealistic expectations placed upon mothers, the public tendency to criticize mothers, to find fault, and the lack of cultural and institutional support offered to mothers. Despite the increasing demands placed upon the maternal role, time is one of many resources denied to mothers. Time deprivation as a result of antimaternalism prevented these rural mothers (and Lange herself) from achieving the motherhood ideal.

An intensely domestic woman who took pride in orchestrating family rituals and creating restful and artistic homes, Lange's camera also lingered on rural women's domestic efforts and suggested that domesticity had value, that it could sustain human life. Lange's photographs illustrated rural women's mental and physical strength and gave dignity to the act of mothering. She understood the liminal nature of the lives of migratory mothers to some degree, because she too was constantly on the move, driving across the country non-stop with little time to create her own home and domestic space. A city dweller who lovingly documented rural America, some of Lange's images transmit the mythic American vision that connected the fertile earth with the feminized and maternal. Her photographs of mothers nursing their babies in open, outdoor spaces and pursuing domestic arts beside a river and in other natural settings firmly connect the maternal with nature.

Lange's images offer a powerful counter-narrative to the antimaternalism of the time. Right when the tides of public opinion were turning against American mothers, Dorothea Lange disseminated images that circled back to an earlier interpretation of mothers that cast them as the bedrock of the nation and the heart (and sometimes backbone and muscle) of the family. Her own complicated emotions as a mother must have mingled with her efforts to capture the emotions of mothers very different from herself. Both Lange's own example and her photographs with descriptive titles and captions add to our understanding of the emotional history of motherhood, and the effects that antimaternalism and its manifestations had on mothers. It is ironic (and satisfying) that, despite Lange's disbelief in her own artistic talent and the worth of the oeuvre she left behind, it is her work that endures. Neither her first husband, painter Maynard Dixon nor her second, scholar Paul Taylor, have come close to achieving the kind of posthumous fame that Dorothea Lange enjoys. That *Migrant Mother*—which more than any other photograph has come to symbolize an American conception of motherhood at its best—came from the camera of a woman who at times fled from motherhood also adds to our understanding of the kinds of ambivalence and struggles that mothers faced in the early to mid-twentieth century United States.

Notes

1. Thomas Allen, "Clockwork Nation: Modern Time, Moral Perfection and American Identity in Catharine Beecher and Henry Thoreau," *Journal of American Studies*, Vol. 39, No. 1 (2005): 65–86. See 66.
2. Rebecca Jo Plant, *Mom: The Transformation of Motherhood in Modern America* (Chicago, IL: University of Chicago Press, 2010), 87–88.
3. Biographical material drawn from James C. Curtis, "Dorothea Lange, Migrant Mother, and the Culture of the Great Depression," *Winterthur Portfolio*, Vol. 21, No. 1 (Spring 1986): 1–20.
4. See Linda Gordon, *Dorothea Lange: A Life beyond Limits* (New York: W.W. Norton, 2009).
5. Richard Dowd, *Oral History Interview with Dorothea Lange: 1964, May 22*. Archives of American Art, Smithsonian Museum. https://www.aaa.si.edu/collections/interviews/oral-history-interview-dorothea-lange-11757.
6. Linda Gordon, "Dorothea Lange: The Photographer as Agricultural Sociologist," *The Journal of American History*, Vol. 93, No. 3 (December 2006): 698–727; Curtis, "Dorothea Lange, Migrant Mother," 9.
7. Curtis, "Dorothea Lange, Migrant Mother," 9.
8. Dorothea Lange, "Migrant Mother," also titled "Destitute pea pickers in California. Mother of seven children. Age thirty-two. Nipomo, California," March 1936. Library of Congress, Prints & Photographs Division, FSA/OWI Collection, LC-Dig-fsa-8b29516].
9. Anne Whiston Spirn, *Daring to Look: Dorothea Lange's Photographs and Reports from the Field* (Chicago, IL, and London: University of Chicago Press, 2008), 15.
10. Gordon, *Dorothea Lange*, 235–236.
11. Curtis, "Dorothea Lange, Migrant Mother," 17.
12. Quoted in Jacqueline Ellis, *Silent Witnesses: Representations of Working-Class Women in the United States* (Bowling Green, OH: Bowling Green State University Popular Press, 1998), 41. Lange, "Migrant Mother."
13. Some of the 104 photographs are duplicates. Search done on April 22, 2016. Library of Congress, Prints and Photographs Online Catalog, http://www.loc.gov/pictures/.
14. James Curtis, "Making Sense of Documentary Photography," *History Matters: The U.S. Survey Course on the Web*, http://historymatters.gmu.edu/mse/Photos/, June 2003, p. 4 of online version.
15. See Gordon, *Dorothea Lange*, 200–208, especially 202. Apparently Stryker's "scripts" became more sociological after he met with sociologist Robert Lynd.
16. Gordon, *Dorothea Lange*, 204.
17. Wendy Kozol, "Madonnas of the Fields: Photography, Gender, and 1930s Farm Relief," *Genders*, No. 2 (Summer 1988): 2–23. See 9.
18. Quoted in Curtis, "Making Sense of Documentary Photography," 4.
19. Gordon, "Dorothea Lange: The Photographer," 700.
20. Gordon, *Dorothea Lange*, xiv.
21. Gordon, *Dorothea Lange*, xiv, xix.
22. Ellis, *Silent Witnesses*, 28–29. On Lange and Stryker's relationship see Gordon, *Dorothea Lange*, 287–300, 360, 417.
23. Ellis, *Silent Witnesses*, 29.
24. Annette Kolodny, *The Lay of the Land: Metaphor as Experience and History in American Life and Letters* (Chapel Hill, NC: University of North Carolina Press, 1975), 9.
25. Vivyan Adair, *From Good Ma to Welfare Queen: A Genealogy of the Poor Woman in American Literature, Photography, and Culture* (New York and London: Garland Publishing Co., 2000), 36.

26 Adair, *From Good Ma to Welfare Queen*, 37.
27 Gordon, *Dorothea Lange*, 367. See also Jon Lauck, "Dorothea Lange and the Limits of the Liberal Narrative: A Review Essay," Emporia State University, September 8, 2015, p. 26, https://esirc.emporia.edu/bitstream/handle/123456789/3374/Jon%20Lauck.pdf?sequence=1,18-19.
28 Cited in Adair, *From Good Ma to Welfare Queen*, 37.
29 Martin F. Manalansan IV, "Messy Mismeasures: Exploring the Wilderness of Queer Migrant Lives," *The South Atlantic Quarterly*, Vol. 117, No. 3 (July 2018): 491–506.
30 Adair, *From Good Ma to Welfare Queen*, 36.
31 Gordon, *Dorothea Lange*, 221.
32 Dorothea Lange, "Grandmother of Fifty-Six Children, Mother of Fourteen, Ten Living. Near Chesnee, South Carolina, July 1937." Library of Congress, Prints & Photographs Division, FSA/OWI Collection.
33 Dorothea Lange, "Depression refugee family from Tulsa, Oklahoma. Arrived in California June 1936. Mother and three half-grown children; no father. "Anybody as wants to work can get by. But if a person loses their faith in the soil like so many of them back there in Oklahoma, then there ain't no hope for them. We're making it all right here, all but for the schooling, 'cause that boy of mine, he wants to go to the University," November 1936. Library of Congress, Prints & Photographs Division, FSA/OWI Collection.
34 Dorothea Lange, "Mexican mother in California. "Sometimes I tell my children that I would like to go to Mexico, but they tell me 'We don't want to go, we belong here.'" (Note on Mexican labor situation in repatriation)," June 1935. Library of Congress, Prints & Photographs Division, FSA/OWI Collection, [LC-DIG-fsa-8b26837].
35 See Jacqueline Rose, "Mothers Superior," *Harper's Magazine*, May 2018. https://harpers.org/archive/2018/05/mother-superior/.
36 Dorothea Lange, "Fatherless migratory family camped behind gas station. The mother is trying to support three boys by picking pears. Just arrived from Minnesota, she used to work in a restaurant there. Oldest boy, age ten, helped carry ladder from tree to tree. Photograph made at end of day (temperature 106 degrees) when she returned from orchard. Yakima Valley, Washington," August 1939. Library of Congress, Prints & Photographs Division, FSA/OWI Collection.
37 Dorothea Lange, "Japanese mother and daughter, agricultural workers near Guadalupe, California," March 1937. Library of Congress, Prints & Photographs Division, FSA/OWI Collection.
38 Dorothea Lange, "Two tobacco tenant mothers (related) with part of their children. Wake County, North Carolina," July 1939. Library of Congress, Prints & Photographs Division, FSA/OWI Collection, [LC-DIG-fsa-8b33847].
39 Dyanna Taylor, *Dorothea Lange: Grab a Hunk of Lightening*. PBS American Masters Theater, 2014 documentary film.
40 Gordon, *Dorothea Lange*, 230.
41 Gordon, *Dorothea Lange*, 263, 264.
42 Gordon, *Dorothea Lange*, 264. The original caption in Lange's hand is in OM; the LoC caption is 017079-C.
43 Gordon, *Dorothea Lange*, 269, 256.
44 Dorothea Lange, "Young mother, aged twenty-two, has one little girl three years old. Merrill, Klamath County, Oregon. In mobile unit of FSA (Farm Security Administration) camp. New baby expected in December. During this year she has worked with her husband in: strawberries (Helvetia, Oregon); cherries (Salem, Oregon); beans (West Stayton, Oregon); hops (Independence, Oregon). Is now in potato pickers' camp at the end of that season. 'We haven't got a cent now and we've lost our car because we've helped some people out. It seems like it's taken every cent to eat off, that and traveling around,'"

96 A Promaternal Narrative and Archive

October 1939. Library of Congress, Prints & Photographs Division, FSA/OWI Collection.
45 Dorothea Lange, "Mother of family now migrants of Pacific coast. Were farm owners in Oklahoma until 1936. Picking hops. Polk Country, Oregon. See general caption number 45–1," August 1939. Library of Congress, Prints & Photographs Division, FSA/OWI Collection.
46 Margaret Jarman Hagood, *Mothers of the South: Portraiture of the White Tenant Farm Woman* (New York and London: W.W. Norton & Company, 1977), 86. The University of North Carolina Press originally published *Mothers of the South* in 1939.
47 Hagood, *Mothers of the South*, 90.
48 Dorothea Lange, "Calipatria, Imperial Valley. Visiting public health doctor conducts well-baby clinic in local school building adjacent to pea harvest. Many migratory mothers attend," February 1939. Library of Congress, Prints & Photographs Division, FSA/OWI Collection.
49 Gordon, *Dorothea Lange*, 162.
50 Rima D. Apple, *Perfect Motherhood: Science and Childrearing in America* (New Brunswick, NJ, and London: Rutgers University Press, 2006); Julia Grant, *Raising Baby by the Book: The Education of American Mothers* (New Haven, CT and London: Yale University Press, 1998).
51 Dorothea Lange, "Meeting of the Mothers' Club in Arvin camp for migrant workers, a Farm Security Administration (FSA) camp. The discussion this evening centers on the possibility of buying kerosene oil in large quantities and distributing it cooperatively in camp, to cut costs. Kerosene is used both for cooking and for lighting purposes," November 1938. Library of Congress, Prints & Photographs Division, FSA/OWI Collection.
52 Dorothea Lange, "Meeting of the Mothers' Club in Arvin camp for migrant workers, Farm Security Administration (FSA) camp in California, opens with prayer," November 1938. Library of Congress, Prints & Photographs Division, FSA/OWI Collection.
53 Dorothea Lange, "Singing hymns before opening of meeting of Mothers' Club at Arvin Farm Security Administration (FSA) camp for migrants, California," November 1938. The second image is "Hymn singing at meeting of Mothers' Club in Arvin migrant camp, California," November 1938. Both from Library of Congress, Prints & Photographs Division, FSA/OWI Collection.
54 Dorothea Lange, "While the mothers are working in the fields, the preschool children of migrant families are cared for in nursery school under trained teachers. Kern migrant camp, California," November 1936. Library of Congress, Prints & Photographs Division, FSA/OWI Collection, [LC-DIG-fsa-8b29870].
55 Dorothea Lange, "While the mothers are working in the fields…" The second image is LC-DIG-fsa-8a31316.
56 Dorothea Lange, "Young migrant mother with six weeks old baby born in a hospital with aid of Farm Society Administration (FSA) medical and association for migratory workers. She lives in a labor contractors camp near Westley, California. 'I try to keep him eatin' and sleepin' regular like I got him out of the hospital,'" April 1939. Library of Congress, Prints & Photographs Division, FSA/OWI Collection, [LC-DIG-fsa-8b33506].
57 Jodi Vandenberg-Daves, *Modern Motherhood: An American History* (New Brunswick, NJ and London: Rutgers University Press, 2014), 85.
58 Gordon, *Dorothea Lange*, 221–222.
59 Gordon, *Dorothea Lange*, 232. Original cite: Dorothy Lange KQED Audio Tapes, Oakland Museum of California, 1964–65. Twenty-six tapes of interviews with Lange by San Francisco station KQED are available online. Gordon

A Promaternal Narrative and Archive 97

believes that Lange had "a visceral love of homemaking," which moved her to focus on women's domestic efforts in the FSA camps.

60 Dorothea Lange, "Tulare County. Farm Security Administration camp (FSA) for migratory agricultural workers at Farmersville. Mother and child, come to California from Oklahoma. They have six children, aged two to nineteen years. The mother finished the eighth grade in school. They left their farming in Chicasha [sic] in the fall of 1936 to go to Arizona to pick cotton. They returned to Oklahoma to try again; failed and re-entered California February 27, 1938 to pick peas under a labor contractor. The father is chairman of camp council," May 1939. Library of Congress, Prints & Photographs Division, FSA/OWI Collection, [LC-DIG-fsa-8b33682].The other three photos of this series of mother and child include: "Tulare County, Farm Security Administration (FSA) camp. Migrant mother and child at doorway of steel shelter"; "Farm Security Administration (FSA) at Farmersville, California. Resident nurse interviews mother and examines sick baby"; and "Farm Security Administration (FSA) at Farmersville, California. Mother from Oklahoma, migrant, awaits visit of resident nurse for sick baby," Library of Congress, Prints & Photographs Division, FSA/OWI Collection.
61 Some of the images are published in Hagood, *Mothers of the South*, unnumbered centerpiece; Erskine Caldwell, *Tobacco Road* (New York: Grosset & Dunlap, 1932).
62 Gordon, *Dorothea Lange*, 274.
63 Kozol, "Madonnas of the Fields," 13.
64 Ellis, *Silent Witnesses*, 47.
65 See Stephanie Coontz, "When We Hated Mom," *The New York Times*, May 8, 2011; Molly Ladd-Taylor and Lauri Umansky, eds., *"Bad" Mothers: The Politics of Blame in Twentieth-Century America* (New York: New York University Press, 1998).
66 Dorothea Lange, "A mother in California who with her husband and her children will be returned to Oklahoma by the Relief Administration. The family had lost a two-year old baby during the winter as a result of exposure," March 1937. Library of Congress, Prints & Photographs Division, FSA/OWI Collection.
67 Dorothea Lange, "Eighteen year-old mother from Oklahoma, now a California migrant," March 1937. This title/caption includes all three portraits in this series. Library of Congress, Prints & Photographs Division, FSA/OWI Collection.
68 Dorothea Lange, "Young Oklahoma mother, age eighteen, penniless, stranded in California. Imperial Valley," March 1937. Library of Congress, Prints & Photographs Division, FSA/OWI Collection.
69 Adrienne Rich, *Of Woman Born: Motherhood as Experience and Institution* (New York and London: W.W. Norton, tenth anniversary edition, 1986), 21. Rich titled the first chapter "Anger and Tenderness."
70 Molly Ladd-Taylor, ed., *Raising a Baby the Government Way: Mothers' Letters to the Children's Bureau, 1915–1932* (New Brunswick, NJ and London: Rutgers University Press, 1986), 182–183.
71 See Sarah Larson, Review of Deborah Fink, *Agrarian Women*, in *The Annals of Iowa*, Vol. 52, No. 4 (Fall 1993): 476–479.
72 Deborah Fink, *Agrarian Women: Wives and Mothers in Rural Nebraska, 1880–1940* (Chapel Hill, NC: University of North Carolina Press, 1992), xv.
73 Fink, *Agrarian Women*, 29.
74 Fink, *Agrarian Women*, 166.
75 Vandenberg-Daves, *Modern Motherhood*, 163–164.
76 Mrs. A.P. to Miss Lathrop, Wyoming, October 19, 1916, in Ladd-Taylor, ed., *Raising a Baby*, 49.

98 A Promaternal Narrative and Archive

77 Mrs. S.D., California, Letter written to *The Ladies Home Journal*; Copy sent to the Children's Bureau September 19, 1921, in Ladd-Taylor, ed., *Raising a Baby*, 138–140.
78 Hagood, *Mothers of the South*, 108–120.
79 Hagood, *Mothers of the South*, 120.
80 Karen Davies, *Women, Time and the Weaving of the Strands of Everyday Life* (Aldershot, Hampshire, UK, and Brookfield, VT: Gower Publishing Co., 1990).
81 Hagood, *Mothers of the South*, 119–120.
82 Fink, *Agrarian Women*, 132.
83 Kathryn Edin and Maria Kefalas, *Promises I Can Keep: Why Poor Women Put Motherhood before Marriage* (Los Angeles, CA: UCLA Press, 2011), 203.
84 Dorothea Lange, "Mother of migrant family sewing. Near Vale, Malheur County, Oregon," October 1939. Library of Congress Prints and Photographs Division, FSA/OWI Collection.
85 E.P. Thompson, "Time, Work-Discipline and Industrialism Capitalism," *Past & Present*, No. 38 (December 1967): 56–97.
86 Taylor, *Dorothea Lange: Grab a Hunk of Lightening*.
87 Dorothea Lange, "On U.S. 99. Near Brawley, Imperial County. Homeless mother and youngest child of seven walking the highway from Phoenix, Arizona where they picked cotton. Bound for San Diego, where the father hopes to get on relief 'because he once lived there,'" February 1939. Library of Congress, Prints & Photographs Division, FSA/OWI Collection.
88 Dorothea Lange, "Mother and baby of family on the road, Tulelake, Siskiyou County, California. General caption number 65," September 1939; "Mother and two children on the road. Tulelake, Siskiyou County, California. General caption number 65." Library of Congress, Prints & Photographs Division, FSA/OWI Collection, [LC-DIG-fsa-8b34850].
89 Dorothea Lange, "During the cotton strike the father, a striking picker, has left his wife and child in the car while he applies to the Farm Security Administration for an emergency food grant. Shafter, California," November 1938. Library of Congress, Prints & Photographs Division, FSA/OWI Collection.
90 Dorothea Lange, "Mother of five children from Oklahoma, now picking cotton in California, near Fresno," November 1936. Library of Congress, Prints & Photographs Division, FSA/OWI Collection.
91 Both Lange photos share the following title: "Young family, penniless, hitchhiking on U.S. Highway 99 in California. The father, twenty-four, and the mother, seventeen, came from Winston-Salem, North Carolina. Early in 1935, their baby was born in the Imperial Valley, California, where they were working as field laborers." November 1936. Library of Congress, Prints & Photographs Division, FSA/OWI Collection.
92 Taylor, *Dorothea Lange: Grab a Hunk of Lightening*.
93 Dorothea Lange and Paul Schuster Taylor, *An American Exodus: A Record of Human Erosion in the Thirties* (New Haven, CT and London: Yale University Press, 1969), 110. Originally published in 1939.
94 Lange and Taylor, *An American Exodus*, 113.
95 Gordon, *Dorothea Lange*, 225–227.
96 Quoted in Gordon, *Dorothea Lange*, 225.
97 Taylor, *Dorothea Lange: Grab a Hunk of Lightening*.
98 Lange and Taylor, *An American Exodus*, 108–109.
99 Gordon, *Dorothea Lange*, 283.
100 Lange and Taylor, *An American Exodus*, 99.

101 Always careful not to put words into people's mouths, Lange and Taylor described their method: "Quotations which accompany photographs report what the persons photographed said, not what we think might be their unspoken thoughts." Lange and Taylor, *An American Exodus*, 15.
102 Susan Fraiman, *Extreme Domesticity: A View from the Margins* (New York: Columbia University Press, 2017), 5.
103 Fraiman, *Extreme Domesticity*, 17.
104 Fraiman, *Extreme Domesticity*, 23, 25.
105 Sara Ahmed, *Queer Phenomenology: Orientations; Objects; Others* (Durham, NC: Duke University Press, 2006), 9.
106 Fraiman, *Extreme Domesticity*, 119, 124.
107 Fraiman, *Extreme Domesticity*, 164.
108 Fraiman, *Extreme Domesticity*, 168, 192.
109 Lange and Taylor, *An American Exodus*, 15.
110 Curtis, "Making Sense of Documentary Photography," 2.
111 Curtis, "Making Sense of Documentary Photography," 2, 4.
112 Curtis, "Making Sense of Documentary Photography," 5.
113 Curtis, "Making Sense of Documentary Photography," 14.
114 Lange states this in *Dorothea Lange: Grab a Hunk of Lightening*.
115 Sally Mann, *Hold Still: A Memoir with Photographs* (New York: Little, Brown and Company, 2015), xiii.
116 Mann, *Hold Still*, 151.
117 Taylor, *Dorothea Lange: Grab a Hunk of Lightening*.
118 Doud, *Oral History Interview with Dorothea Lange*.
119 Shulamit Reinharz, *Feminist Methods in Social Research* (New York and London: Oxford University Press, 1992).
120 Taylor, *Dorothea Lange: Grab a Hunk of Lightening*.
121 Doud, *Oral History Interview with Dorothea Lange*.
122 Quoted in Gordon, *Dorothea Lange*, 116. But it is also true that the researcher has more power than the researched, and the photographer with camera in hand selects the shot, writes and edits the accompanying text, titles the picture, and chooses where and how to publish it. Although Lange would have liked to share her photographs with those whose images she captured, FSA policy forbade her. Later as an independent photographer she made sharing her photos with her subjects her policy.
123 Mann, *Hold Still*, 289.
124 Paula Rabinowitz, "Voyeurism and Class Consciousness: James Agee and Walker Evans, 'Let Us Now Praise Famous Men,'" *Cultural Critique*, No. 21 (Spring, 1992): 143–170. See 144. James Agee and Walker Evans, *Let Us Now Praise Famous Men* (New York: Houghton Mifflin, 1941).
125 Rabinowitz, "Voyeurism and Class Consciousness," 145, 146.
126 Quoted in Rabinowitz, "Voyeurism and Class Consciousness," 156, 157.
127 Rabinowitz, "Voyeurism and Class Consciousness," 162–163.
128 Mann, *Hold Still*, 292.
129 Mann, *Hold Still*, 292.
130 Gordon, *Dorothea Lange*, 241.
131 Quoted in Gordon, *Dorothea Lange*, 242.
132 Lauck, "Dorothea Lange and the Limits of the Liberal Narrative."
133 Curtis, "Dorothea Lange, Migrant Mother," 20.
134 Gordon, *Dorothea Lange*, 243.
135 Doud, *Oral History Interview with Dorothea Lange*.
136 Taylor, *Dorothea Lange: Grab a Hunk of Lightening*.
137 Lange actually had four stepchildren; the fourth was from her first marriage but was less in her life at the time.

100 *A Promaternal Narrative and Archive*

138 Suzanne Bassett Riess, *Dorothea Lange: The Making of a Documentary Photographer, Berkeley, 1968.* University of California, Bancroft Library/Berkeley Regional Oral History Office.
139 Riess, *Dorothea Lange: The Making of a Documentary Photographer, Berkeley, 1968.*
140 Milton Meltzer, *Dorothea Lange: A Photographer's Life* (Syracuse, NY: Syracuse University Press, 2000), 125–126; James C. Curtis, *Mind's Eye, Mind's Truth: FSA Photography Reconsidered* (Philadelphia, PA: Temple University Press, 1989), 53: Lauck, "Dorothea Lange and the Limits," p. 17.
141 Riess, *Dorothea Lange: The Making of a Documentary Photographer, Berkeley, 1968.*
142 Quoted in Curtis, "Dorothea Lange, Migrant Mother," 17.
143 Dorothea Lange Riess, *Dorothea Lange: The Making of a Documentary Photographer, Berkeley, 1968.*
144 Doud, *Oral History Interview with Dorothea Lange.*
145 Dorothea Lange, KQED Audio Tapes. Oakland Museum of California, 1964–1965. Tape 1.
146 Tillie Olsen, *Silences* (New York: The Feminist Press at the City of New York), 2003, originally published in 1978.
147 "Oral History Interview with Dorothea Lange: 1964 May 22."
148 Rich, *Of Woman Born*, 31.
149 Anne Sommer, "Their Other Halves, Mrs. Maynard Dixon," *San Francisco News*, February 11, 1932. Quoted in Gordon, *Dorothea Lange*, 107.
150 See Mary K. Trigg, *Feminism as Life's Work* (New Brunswick, NJ, and London: Rutgers University Press, 2014), 119–144; Elaine Showalter, ed., *These Modern Women: Autobiographical Essays from the Twenties* (New York: The Feminist Press, 1978).
151 Doud, *Oral History Interview with Dorothea Lange.*
152 Taylor, *Dorothea Lange: Grab a Hunk of Lightening.*
153 Riess, *Dorothea Lange: The Making of a Documentary Photographer, Berkeley, 1968.*
154 Curtis, "Dorothea Lange, Migrant Mother," 9.
155 Materials from Dorothea Lange's funeral, including the tribute from her son Daniel Rhodes Dixon, are included as an Appendix to Riess, *Dorothea Lange: The Making of a Documentary Photographer, Berkeley, 1968.*
156 Taylor, *Dorothea Lange: Grab a Hunk of Lightening.*
157 Taylor, *Dorothea Lange: Grab a Hunk of Lightening.*
158 All quotations are from Taylor, *Dorothea Lange: Grab a Hunk of Lightening.*
159 Gordon, *Dorothea Lange*, 162, 423–424.
160 Stephanie Whitney, "The Great Depression in Washington State," Civil Rights and Labor History Consortium, University of Washington, "Dorothea Lange in the Yakima Valley: Rural Poverty and Photography in the Depression," Part II. https://depts.washington.edu/depress/dorothea_lange_FSA_yakima.shtml.
161 Gordon, *Dorothea Lange*, 178.

Reference List

Adair, Vivyan. *From Good Ma to Welfare Queen: A Genealogy of the Poor Woman in American Literature, Photography, and Culture.* New York and London: Garland Publishing Co., 2000.

Agee, James Agee and Walker Evans. *Let Us Now Praise Famous Men.* Boston, MA and New York: Houghton Mifflin, 2001. Originally pub. 1939.

Allen, Thomas. "Clockwork Nation: Modern Time, Moral Perfection and American Identity in Catharine Beecher and Henry Thoreau." *Journal of American Studies*, Vol. 39, No. 1 (2005): 65–86.

Apple, Rima D. *Perfect Motherhood: Science and Childrearing in America.* New Brunswick, NJ and London: Rutgers University Press, 2006.

Curtis, James. "Making Sense of Documentary Photography." *History Matters: The U.S. Survey Course on the Web.* https://historymatters.gmu.edu/mse/Photos/, June 2003.

Curtis, James C. "Dorothea Lange, Migrant Mother, and the Culture of the Great Depression." *Winterthur Portfolio*, Vol. 21, No. 1 (Spring 1986): 1–20.

Curtis, James C. *Mind's Eye, Mind's Truth: FSA Photography Reconsidered.* Philadelphia, PA: Temple University Press, 1989.

Davies, Karen. *Women, Time and the Weaving of the Strands of Everyday Life.* Aldershot, Hampshire: Gower Publishing Co., 1990.

Doud, Richard. *Oral History Interview with Dorothea Lange: 1964 May 22.* Archives of American Art, Smithsonian Museum. https://www.aaa.si.edu/collections/interviews/oral-history-interview-dorothea-lange-11757.

Edin, Kathryn and Maria Kefalas. *Promises I Can Keep: Why Poor Women Put Motherhood Before Marriage.* Los Angeles, CA: UCLA Press, 2011.

Ellis, Jacqueline. *Silent Witnesses: Representations of Working-Class Women in the United States.* Bowling Green, OH: Bowling Green State University Popular Press, 1998.

Fink, Deborah. *Agrarian Women: Wives and Mothers in Rural Nebraska, 1880–1940.* Chapel Hill, NC: University of North Carolina Press, 1992.

Fraiman, Susan. *Extreme Domesticity: A View from the Margins.* New York: Columbia University Press, 2017.

Gordon, Linda. "Dorothea Lange: The Photographer as Agricultural Sociologist." *The Journal of American History*, Vol. 93, No. 3 (December 2006): 698–727.

Gordon, Linda. *Dorothea Lange: A Life Beyond Limits.* New York: W.W. Norton, 2009.

Grant, Julia. *Raising Baby by the Book: The Education of American Mothers.* New Haven, CT: Yale University Press, 1998.

Hagood, Margaret Jarman. *Mothers of the South: Portraiture of the White Tenant Farm Woman.* New York and London: W.W. Norton, 1977. Originally pub. 1939.

Kolodny, Annette. *The Lay of the Land: Metaphor as Experience and History in American Life and Letters.* Chapel Hill, NC: University of North Carolina Press, 1975.

Kozol, Wendy. "Madonnas of the Fields: Photography, Gender, and 1930s Farm Relief." *Genders*, No. 2 (Summer 1988): 2–23.

Ladd-Taylor, Molly, ed. *Raising a Baby the Government Way: Mothers' Letters to the Children's Bureau, 1915–1932.* New Brunswick, NJ and London: Rutgers University Press, 1986.

Lange, Dorothea. *KQED Audio Tapes.* Oakland Museum of California, 1964–1965. https://californiarevealed.org/islandora/object/cavpp%3A16390

Lange, Dorothea and Paul Schuster Taylor. *An American Exodus: A Record of Human Erosion in the Thirties.* New Haven, CT and London: Yale University Press, 1969.

Larson, Sarah. "Review of Deborah Fink, *Agrarian Women.*" *The Annals of Iowa*, Vol. 52, No. 4 (Fall 1993): 476–479.

Lauck, Jon. "Dorothea Lange and the Limits of the Liberal Narrative: A Review Essay." Emporia State University, September 8, 2015, p. 26, https://esirc.emporia.edu/bitstream/handle/123456789/3374/Jon%20Lauck.pdf?sequence=1,18-19.

Library of Congress. *Prints and Photographs Online Catalog.* http://www.loc.gov/pictures/.

Manalansan IV, Martin F. "Messy Mismeasures: Exploring the Wilderness of Queer Migrant Lives." *The South Atlantic Quarterly*, Vol. 117, No. 3 (July 2018): 491–506.

Mann, Sally. *Hold Still: A Memoir with Photographs.* New York: Little, Brown and Company, 2015.

Meltzer, Milton. *Dorothea Lange: A Photographer's Life.* Syracuse, NY: Syracuse University Press, 2000.

Olsen, Tillie. *Silences.* New York: The Feminist Press at the City of New York, 2003, originally published in 1978.

Plant, Rebecca Jo. *Mom: The Transformation of Motherhood in Modern America.* Chicago, IL: The University of Chicago Press, 2010.

Rabinowitz, Paula. "Voyeurism and Class Consciousness: James Agee and Walker Evans, "Let Us Now Praise Famous Men."" *Cultural Critique*, No. 21 (Spring, 1992): 143–170.

Rich, Adrienne Rich. *Of Woman Born: Motherhood as Experience and Institution.* New York and London: W.W. Norton & Company, 1986.

Riess, Suzanne Bassett. *Dorothea Lange: The Making of a Documentary Photographer, Berkeley, 1968.* University of California, Bancroft Library/Berkeley Regional Oral History Office. http://digitalassets.lib.berkeley.edu/roho/ucb/text/lange_dorothea__w.pdf

Rose, Jacqueline. "Mothers Superior." *Harper's Magazine*, May 2018.

Spirn, Anne Whiston. *Daring to Look: Dorothea Lange's Photographs and Reports from the Field.* Chicago, IL and London: University of Chicago Press, 2008.

Taylor, Dyanna. *Dorothea Lange: Grab a Hunk of Lightening.* PBS American Masters Theater, 2014 documentary film.

Thompson, E.P. "Time, Work-Discipline and Industrialism Capitalism." *Past & Present*, No. 38 (December 1967): 56-97.

Vandenberg-Daves, Jodi. *Modern Motherhood: An American History.* New Brunswick, NJ and London: Rutgers University Press, 2014.

3 Reclaiming Maternity
African American Mothers and Maternal Grief as a Counter-Narrative

While Kristeva points out that motherhood—in that it involves the eventual, inevitable separation between mother and child—always involves pain, African American mothers have been in greater danger of loss and maternal pain than white mothers. African American mothers carry within them the fear that they will not be able to adequately protect their children, or prepare them for a world that does not value them: "[B]lack women especially know fear—how to live despite it and how to metabolize it for our children so that they're not consumed by it."[1] In the 1920s, 1930s, 1940s, and 1950s black women brought children into the world who were in jeopardy of being lynched; dying early from highly contagious diseases that spread like light fire through urban communities; killed in a world war; or scapegoated because of racial and class discrimination in a changing America. Like the rural, itinerant mothers portrayed in the last chapter, the real circumstances of their lives could not have been further from antimaternalist depictions. African American mothers faced not only the consequences of poverty and a lack of institutional support; they also confronted the penalties and dangers of racism. The Great Migration that took blacks in record numbers from the rural South to the urban North, the economic collapse of the Great Depression, and the rise of the civil rights movement all elicited anxious, sometimes violent, responses from white Americans.[2] These violent responses took an especially heavy toll on African American mothers.

In a twentieth-century culture that increasingly disparaged the bonds between mothers and children, the historical legacy of slavery caused African Americans to place a high value on the relationships between mothers and their children, and the importance of this bond.[3] African American mothers rejected the antimaternalism of the early to mid-twentieth century and instead embraced a conception of motherhood that included self-sacrifice, a deepened understanding of self through maternal experience, and close emotional ties with their children. Hortense Spiller argued in her now-classic 1987 essay "Mama's Baby, Papa's Maybe" that enslavement eliminated the possibility of black motherhood because an enslaved woman's children belonged by law to her slave master. Hazel Carby stated that enslaved black women reproduced property, not citizens, thus eliminating

DOI: 10.4324/9781003334712-4

the possibility of black motherhood.[4] Under the dehumanizing institution of slavery, African American mothers did everything in their power to keep their children within their households and from being sold away from them at slave auctions. Some ran away from their masters to keep their children with them, placing themselves at great risk. Historian Deborah Gray White was one of the first to show the ways that enslaved mothers, despite their inhumane captivity, took risks and made choices to raise their children and keep them safe.[5] After Emancipation, many African American mothers made tremendous sacrifices in order to keep their children with them. In African culture, as well as African American culture, motherhood and children are highly valued. As Barbara Christian has noted, "There is no doubt that motherhood is for most African people symbolic of creativity and continuity."[6] In *Beloved* Toni Morrison portrayed the redemptive value that African American mothers place on their offspring: "The best thing she was, was her children. Whites might dirty *her* all right, but not her best thing, her beautiful, magical best thing—the part of her that was clean."[7] The antimaternalist message that relationships between mothers and their children were dangerous, dirty, smothering, sexual in nature, could not have resonated for black mothers who struggled to keep their children safe and by their sides.

Historically, African American mothers have been supportive of one another, and concerned about children collectively in the community rather than just the children in their own individual families. It has been the norm for other women in the community to help birth mothers raise their children. These "othermothers," in Patricia Hill Collins's words, "are women who assist blood mothers by sharing mothering responsibilities," and they have been central to the institution of black motherhood.[8] As Carol Stack concluded from three years of ethnographic research in a poor urban black community in the mid-1960's: "Close female kinsmen in The Flats do not expect a single person, the natural mother, to carry out by herself all of the behavior patterns which 'motherhood' entails."[9] Stack observed alliances of African Americans trading and exchanging goods, resources, and childcare and noted "the intensity of their acts of domestic cooperation ... among these persons, both kin and non-kin."[10] Othermothers and grandmothers provide nurturing, financial support, goods and services, childcare, role modeling, mentoring, and they maintain intergenerational and community connections.[11] Dani McClean described the othermothers in her upbringing when she recently wrote in *The Nation*:

> My grandmother, great-grandmother, aunts, and elders in the community supported my mother as she raised me. Their investment in me and in other children—some their blood relations, some not—demonstrated an ethic that we can all learn from. ... "I tell my daughter all the time: We don't live for the 'I.' We live for the we," Cat Brooks, an organizer in Oakland, told me.[12]

This ethic of living for the "We" has stimulated a more generalized ethic of care in black communities, where African American women feel responsible for all the community's children.[13] This ethic is the opposite of the isolated, experts-driven maternal models that scientific motherhood promulgated.

Although African American mothers performed and experienced their mothering within the changing ideas and prescriptions about American motherhood between 1920 and 1960, their circumstances were unique. Burdened with racism, greater likelihood of poverty, less access to resources, and a more pressing need to combine care work with waged labor, their experiences add another thread to the mosaic that is the history of motherhood in the United States. In considering time as a tool of control that is linked to antimaternalism, it is important to note that black mothers have had even less access to time as a resource than white mothers have, because of the structural disadvantages that they face. As historian Brittney Cooper has noted, time is political, and it is raced. "[I]f time had a race," Cooper stated, "it would be white. White people own time."[14] Citing Hegel's famous declaration that "[Africa] is no historical part of the world," she argues that white European philosophers placed Africans outside of history. This made it easier to disenfranchise and marginalize them. By treating time as if it does not have a political history, we ignore the ways that "progress" has often been tied to "the plunder of indigenous lands, the genocide of indigenous people and the stealing of Africans from their homeland." Black people, including the mothers I describe in this chapter, are often conceptualized as either outside of the bounds of time or as mired in the past. When whites accuse blacks who equate violence against African Americans with racism as being "stuck in the past," they are illustrating this tendency. Yet, "the past won't let us go," as Cooper insists.[15]

Black mothers have suffered virulent and violent antimaternalism. White Eurocentric culture has always typecast African American mothers in negative ways, as outliers to the maternal ideal. African American mothers have had to fight for their right to be mothers and they have been subject to state scrutiny and biopolitical surveillance.[16] In *Killing the Black Body*, Dorothy Roberts described the various ways that whites have curtailed the reproductive freedom of black American women:

> [C]onsidering this history—from slave masters' economic stake in bonded women's fertility to the racist strains of early birth control policy to sterilization abuse of Black women during the 1960s and 1970s to the current campaign to inject Norplant and Depo-Provera in the arms of Black teenagers and welfare mothers—paints a powerful picture of the link between race and reproductive freedom in America.[17]

For this reason, African American women often prefer the term reproductive justice to the language of choice.[18]

Ruth Feldstein has described the ways that scholars, popular writers, and the media categorized African American mothers in the years between

1920 and 1960. Stock descriptions included the strong black woman whose commitment to her family and ability to "get along" or "succeed" was suspect; the sexualized black mother who bore unnecessary and uncared-for children; and the working black mother who was an undeserving mother because she worked for wages and whose labor was marginalized through reference to its sketchy, indefinite nature.[19] White Americans considered African American women promiscuous by nature, incapable of sustaining respectable marriages and stable families in which to raise their children. In slavery, white owners had routinely raped African American women; categorizing black women as oversexed and promiscuous provided a convenient narrative to justify racist sins of the past.[20] In addition, white slaveholders had equated black women's reproductive capacities with procreating property, and income.[21] This painful history has informed black women's experiences of motherhood, as well as the white community's critiques of black mothers. It has also demonstrated the ways that institutionalized denial of reproductive freedom has uniquely shaped black women's history in the United States.

In addition, white culture has long derided African American women as "matriarchs" who pose a threat to their husbands and children. Critics of black mothers in the 1940s and 1950s focused on the psychological damage they could inflict. In *The Mark of Oppression* (1951), Abram Kardiner and Lionel Ovesey explored "the Personality of the American Negro," labeling in one case study the mother of "B.B." as "the real 'boss of the household.'" The result of such an overbearing mother? An adult son with an "infantile neediness" and "a struggle for the maternal breast."[22] This critique echoed broader American anxieties about maternal power and the danger of the mother being the more prominent member of the family. Describing the myth of the black matriarchy in 1970, Robert Staples wrote:

> In dealing with the question of the role of the black woman in the black struggle one must ultimately encounter the assertion that the black community is organized along matriarchal lines, that the domineering black female has been placed in a superordinate position in the family by the historical vicissitudes of slavery, and that her ascent to power has resulted in the psychological castration of the black male and produced a host of other negative results that include low educational achievement, personality disorders, juvenile delinquency, etc.[23]

Along with the stereotype of the black matriarch, an alternate portrayal of African American women has focused on their nurturance. Mainstream American discourse between 1890 and 1930 often cast black women as mammies, who were believed to love the white children in their care more than their own children.[24] The film *Gone With the Wind* venerated this stock character in the 1930s, but the concept had existed since the days of slavery. Distinguishing African American mothers as more "naturally" caring than white mothers fed into racial stereotypes, helped rationalize expectations that nonwhite women would care for the children of affluent white women, and symbolized the ways that mother-blaming after World War I swept across race and class.[25] The psychoanalyst Margaret Ribble, for instance, wrote in *The Rights of Infants* (1944) that old-school "Negro mammies of the South" more clearly intuited babies' needs than did well-educated white women.[26] When 1940s and 1950s-era psychiatrists labeled white mothers of autistic children "refrigerator mothers" because of what they considered their cold maternal rejection, analysts virtually never placed black women in this category.[27] Rebecca Plant has described the stereotyped ways that the expert community equated nurturance and maternal instinct with women of color, suggesting they believed that "aged 'mammies,' or mothers in developing countries who carried their babies in slings and fed them on demand—actually did a better job of caring for very young children than did educated white women."[28]

Some twentieth-century African Americans equated a mother's love with safety, a refuge from (white) urban modernity. John H. Owens's short poem "To Mother," published in 1930 in *The Crisis*, the publication of the National Association for the Advancement of Colored People (NAACP), illustrates this in a world-weary narrator who longs to return to the cherishing embrace of his mother. "Listen, O brown, kind mother, /I am weary and I would rest; / Put your old, warm arms about me, / Let me lie on your withered breast." He continues: "I am very sick of cities / Of faces cold and strange / I long for your sun-washed spaces / Blue skies and wind-swept range."[29] However, nurturing maternal love could not always protect brown and black children or adults from racial violence or other mortal threats. In this chapter I try to follow the commitment that historian Marisa Fuentes has made. As historians, we have a responsibility to do no harm, or do no additional harm. "How to recognize the violence and not reproduce it?" she has asked.[30] I have kept this important question in my mind as I have written this chapter.

Through an examination of an eclectic mix of artistic renditions of grieving African American mothers—in plays, short stories, photographs, and poetry created between 1920 and 1960, along with the real-life examples of Gold Star Mothers and Mamie Till Bradley—in this chapter I turn to consider maternal grief and resilience as a counter-narrative to antimaternalism. Sympathetic images of black maternal grief in these years—most coming out of the black community—highlighted maternal love, intense ties between mothers and children, and women's right to mother, all under attack in the antimaternalist and racist climate of the early to mid-twentieth century United States. The kinds of sacrifices that black women have historically made for their children stood in sharp relief to the evolving post-1920s American belief that motherhood no longer involved sacrifice, risk, or even labor. Black maternal grief and loss are still unacceptably endemic in the twenty-first-century United States. As anthropologist Cheryl Rodriguez stated, "[for Black mothers] loss—particularly the loss of a child—is a historic legacy."[31]

During these years, some African American mothers began to use their loss of their children, and their grief, to evoke social change. Although grief may seem like an intensely private experience and emotion, it can also be public and involve political identities and structures of feeling. Maternal grief sometimes leads to public motherhood, activism that helps mothers make sense of the deaths of their children and contributes to social justice.[32] Memory and remembrance can play a political role as well as a private function in healing grief. Memory keeping can be a political act. Black motherhood, then, is not only connected to intergenerational suffering, but also to survival, remembrance, and intergenerational ties.[33] African American mothers in the 1920–1960 decades responded to a destructive society that tried to unmother them by reclaiming maternal care. They considered domesticity and care as potent antidotes to a racist society, and their maternal care took multiple forms. Caring for black children in an uncaring society and maintaining nurturing homes in a hostile country are radical acts.

Lynching, Maternal Grief, and Agency

Death by lynching was a very real possibility for African Americans in the United States in the 1920s, especially in the South. Between 1890 and 1930, lynch mobs murdered more than thirty-two hundred African American men, women, and children.[34] Although lynchers primarily targeted men, they also murdered over 200 women, including eight months pregnant Mary Turner, whom a white Georgia mob killed in 1918 because she had threatened to seek warrants to prosecute those who had lynched her husband just days before.[35] Some scholars have argued that anti-black state violence has historically been masculinized, which actually continues and facilitates violence against black women.[36] Lynching, a vigilante practice in which white mobs seized, tortured, and killed their victims, was directed at African American men and women whom perpetrators perceived as having overstepped their place in the social hierarchy of the Jim Crow South. Nineteenth-century anti-lynching movement activists like Ida B. Wells-Barnett had clearly illuminated the terrors of white America's practice of lynching.[37] Yet decades later, white southerners continued to justify lynching as a necessary deterrent to protect white women from mythical black male rapists. Violent mobs in the U.S. unleashed a new wave of lynching after World War I and again in the 1930s. In the Tulsa Race Massacre of 1921, a white mob attacked residents, homes, and businesses in the largely African American Greenwood neighborhood of Tulsa, Oklahoma. Despite the fact that hundreds of blacks were killed and over 1,000 of their homes destroyed along with black-owned businesses, state officials and the white media largely covered up what was one of the deadliest riots in United States history.[38] Jazz singer Billie Holiday's "Strange Fruit," first recorded in 1939, protested American racism that was symbolized in the vicious lynching of African Americans. The powerful lyrics "Black bodies swingin' in the Southern breeze/Strange fruit hangin' from the poplar trees" depicted an America that considered black lives and bodies to be nothing more than "a fruit for the crows to pluck."[39]

The practice of lynching and the idealized representation of the Mammy came together in a legislative debate in the U.S. Congress in the early 1920s over the creation of a monument to the "black Mammy." Following on the heels of a failed effort in late 1922 to pass the nation's first and only federal law preventing lynching, Congress members responded to a proposal from the Washington, D.C. chapter of the United Daughters of the Confederacy to create the "Faithful Slave Mammies of the South" memorial.[40] Despite the nation's declaration of modernity in the 1920s, the call for a memorial to the Mammy demonstrates the ways that white Southerners hoped to keep black women grounded in the past, in this symbolic national representation of the days of slavery and the postbellum era. Southern nostalgia, fear of losing economic ground, and racism fueled much of this harkening back. In a more violent parallel, racists who threatened lynching tried to keep American black men (in particular) in a racial caste system of the past. Claiming ownership of time and the progress associated with it, white racist Americans expected black Americans to agree to continue to build the future of whites—through caring for their homes and children, tilling their land, and accepting subservient and anti-democratic treatment. Black Americans saw a different future for themselves.

African American journals and newspapers roundly condemned the proposal for a Mammy memorial in the nation's capital. Although the U.S. Senate approved the proposal in 1923, pressure from citizens and the black press prevented passage of the bill, which failed in the House. W.E.B. Du Bois took up the topic in *The Souls of Black Folk* (1927), referring to "the mammy" as "one of the most pitiful of the world's Christs ... an embodied sorrow." He argued that any dignity she had was eviscerated once the white children in her charge grew up and went on to lynch her sons.[41] *The Chicago Defender* juxtaposed the debate over lynching and the Mammy memorial in a cartoon titled "Mockery," which depicts a white Southerner presenting plans for the mammy statue to the dangling body of an African American lynching victim. The *Baltimore Afro-American* offered its own conception of the planned monument: a frowning Mammy settled atop a wash tub in place of a pedestal, her empty hand outstretched above the inscription: "In Grateful Memory to One We Never Paid a Cent of Wages During a Lifetime of Service."[42] According to historian Jodi Vandenberg-Daves, cartoons like these "were part of a broader attempt to reclaim African American maternity."[43]

Other leaders in the black community decried the ways in which the controversy over the Mammy monument obscured the real burdens of

African American mothers. Mary Church Terrell, president of the National Association of Colored Women, noted that

> no colored woman could look upon a statue of a black mammy with a dry eye when she remembered how often the slave woman's heart was torn with anguish, because the children ... were ruthlessly torn from her in infancy or in youth to be sold 'down the country,' where, in all human probability, she would never see them again.

Civil rights activist James Weldon Johnson declared, "It would be more worthy to erect a monument to the black mother, who, through sacrifice, hard work and heroism, battled to raise her own children and has thus far so well succeeded."[44] *The Crisis* editor Du Bois understood the dilemma black mothers faced in raising their children to feel loved and yet prepared to face the harsh world beyond the home: "It is, indeed, hard to be stern, cold and practical with the flesh of your flesh whom you are rearing for a sneering, cruel world. ... These are the reasons why we spoil our babies," he wrote in 1922.[45] Thus, in the years when behaviorist John Watson was admonishing (white) mothers not to love their children too much, African American mothers faced a racist culture that at times seemed bent on extinguishing their children.

African American authors of short stories and plays written in the 1920s and 1930s that focused on lynching depicted grieving mothers in one of two ways: so overcome with sorrow that they succumbed to death, or seizing agency to influence the future. In the short story "Two Americans," published in *The Crisis* in 1921 and written by *Philadelphia Press* literary editor Florence Lewis Bentley, the narrator's brother is lynched and the mother dies shortly afterward. A World War I story about terror, redemption, and forgiveness (a black soldier knowingly saves the life of a white soldier who has lynched his brother), when the mother discovers that the crowd is brutally assaulting Joe, her son, she cries out: "O My God! They got my boy!" The author continued, "And when she looked through the slats and seen him, she tumbled right down in a faint." The surviving son and his mother flee the South, taking a train North, but the son and narrator sadly reflects, "My mother didn't live long. Her heart was broken."[46] Similarly, in Robert W. Bagnall's 1922 short story "Lex Talionis"—one of the few short stories to focus on rape against African American women (and mothers of daughters)—the mother whose daughter died after being assaulted passes away one month later, "broken hearted."[47] In Georgia Douglass Johnson's 1925 one-act play, "A Sunday Morning in the South," the grandmother who is raising her nineteen-year-old grandson dies of a heart attack the instant she learns he has been lynched.[48]

Here, sorrow was embodied—the experience of grief was so connected to the body and so *felt* in the body that grief literally ended the life of the body. The grieving mothers and grandmothers in these short stories could not love their children too much, because their time with them might be cut short. To die of grief over loss of a child or a grandchild was the ultimate display of maternal love and sacrifice. These fictional depictions return to the pre-1920 association between maternity and suffering, the idea that motherhood involved cost, including the risk of death (primarily in childbirth, but here due to grief). They also reinforce the black community's belief in the purity of mother love and the connection between motherhood and self-sacrifice. They suggest that African Americans never accepted the antimaternalist assault on moral motherhood and the new maternal ideal of the early to mid-twentieth century. They also productively complicate the nature of black maternal mourning, challenging the pervasive image of the strong black mother, which denies her the right to be vulnerable.[49] As we know from contemporary accounts of maternal loss, mothers who lose children suffer psychological and physical trauma, which can be intergenerational. LaKisha Michelle Simmons has argued that black maternal loss reverberates through time: "To understand miscarriage and infant mortality," she writes, "we must understand the long history of loss in Black women's lives."[50] Some mothers are unable to survive the trauma and choose physical or mental detachment from life, or even suicide.[51]

Other fictional depictions of the 1920–1960 era highlight grieving mothers who survive, exhibit agency and resilience, and take action. Koritha Mitchell has argued that because she so often survives to grieve in the home from which her son is removed, the black mother bears witness. She is the observer that advocates of the racial status quo most want to silence, and through the figure of the mother, authors and readers access the conversation and conduct of those who lived with the "traumatizing shock of a commonly occurring violence."[52] As the eyewitness who survives, she is also able to remember the past, and redeem the past in the name of a new future.

Through the repugnant practice of lynching, the nation discouraged the affirmation of African American familial ties, and the moral authority of black motherhood. Americans increasingly tied the nuclear family to the country's progress and the allegiance of individuals and their capacity for propriety and personal discipline. By attacking the home space, whites "wanted to negate black citizenship in the most fundamental, painful way."[53] As historian Hannah Rosen has demonstrated, vigilantes often attacked black Americans in distinctly domestic ways, bringing racial violence near, or inside, their homes. These household intrusions "lasted at times for hours and involved prolonged interaction and dialogue between assailants and victims."[54] This forced occupants, in Mitchell's words, to "perform their powerlessness," as black husbands and fathers were impotent to prevent violence against their family members.[55]

Yet, African Americans recognized the political dimension of creating safe and nurturing private spaces and valued "those sequences of gestures" that ensured domestic life and the survival of the black family.[56] Some African American women activists viewed their management of domestic spaces as ways to emphasize the politics of respectability.[57] Others used homes as channels for creativity: Alice Walker's renowned essay "In Search of Our Mothers' Gardens" portrays her overworked mother's constant, riotous gardens as a metaphor for her need to create beauty in the midst of poverty for herself and her children, as an outlet for her artistry and imagination.[58]

Feminist theorist bell hooks described "homeplace" as "a site of resistance." Black women, who often worked outside the home tending white children or cleaning the homes of white families, strove to preserve enough of themselves to provide care and nurturance to their own families and communities. They created the homeplace that allowed African Americans to feel safe, and to cultivate their spirits. It was, hooks argues, an act of resistance.

> Historically, African-American people believed that the construction of a homeplace, however fragile and tenuous (the slave hut, the wooden shack), had a radical political dimension. Despite the brutal reality of racial apartheid, of domination, one's homeplace was the one site where one could freely confront the issue of humanization, where one could resist. Black women resisted by making homes where all black people could strive to be subjects, not objects, where we could be affirmed in our minds and hearts despite poverty, hardship, and deprivation, where we could restore to ourselves the dignity denied us on the outside in the public world.[59]

Thus, racial violence that entered the home was especially pernicious and destructive. "It is no accident that this homeplace," hooks writes,

> as fragile and as transitional as it may be, a makeshift shed, a small bit of earth where one rests, is always subject to violation and destruction. For when a people no longer have the space to construct homeplace, we cannot build a meaningful community resistance.[60]

Because racists wanted to obliterate the black home, white America often portrayed black mothers as anti-domestic. As we have seen, cultural critics and proponents of scientific motherhood connected orderly homes with ideal mothering. Even black sociologists like E. Franklin Frazier criticized dominating and disorganizing black "matriarchs" who, they believed, failed as mothers and homekeepers, thus weakening black families and hindering racial progress.[61] Lynching plays of the 1910s and 1920s, which echoed and inspired community conversation, portrayed African American mothers in a different light—as loving mothers, committed wives, and careful tenders of the home.

Lynching drama developed as a genre in the early twentieth century, and black women authors laid the foundation: Angelina Weld Grimke, Alice Dunbar-Nelson, Mary Burrill, and Georgia Douglas Johnson each penned lynching plays in these decades.[62] Defined as a play in which the threat or occurrence of a lynching, past or present, has major impact on the dramatic action, lynching plays were published in magazines for the black community so they could be performed in churches and schools or read aloud in homes.[63] Scholars consider them archival texts that embody African American artistic networks of exchange. Some were not published until decades after they were written. Black authors wrote lynching plays, often aiming to reach white audiences. In *Rachel*—considered the first play that pioneered the lynching drama— Angelina Weld Grimke hoped to appeal to white audiences and move white mothers to empathize with black mothers.[64] Lynching plays were one way for African Americans to participate in, and preserve evidence of, "embodied practices of black belonging." A form of artistic sustenance, these short plays showcased cohesive black community through their family-centered content and their one-act form, which contributed to communal literacy, as it allowed for informal production in private spheres.[65] Lynching plays can also be interpreted as an artistic response to the antimaternalism of the time.

Lynching Plays and Maternal Power

Georgia Douglas Johnson's South Street home in Washington, D.C., the nation's capital, served as a literary gathering place for black artists and writers in the 1920s. Beginning around 1922, the year before the Mammy memorial controversy, Johnson regularly held a literary salon in her living room, where guests gathered to share their writing, discuss books, and engage in political debate. A playwright and poet, Johnson authored three powerful anti-lynching plays: *Blue Blood* (1926), *Safe* (1929), and *Blue-Eyed Black Boy* (c 1930), which circulated privately and did not appear in print for years.[66] Some scholars analyzing the genre's content and meaning conclude that the depiction of the black mother/wife in anti-lynching dramas revolves around unsuccessful attempts to delay death, or to bargain for time: "Her roles as wife and mother," Mitchell writes, "are shaped by the desire to escape lynching while never being able to do so."[67] In this interpretation the mother/wife becomes the powerless protector of her most beloved—her children and husband—and in an effort to shield them, she hides the truth from them (the fact that she has been raped by a white man, for example). An alternate interpretation demonstrates the ways African American mothers utilize their power and agency, even in grief, in service to themselves and their families. A warden of secrets, in order to try to keep the family together and alive, the African American mothers elucidated in lynching plays offer an opposing narrative to the whore/Mammy binary that white society inculcated. They also rebut the stereotype of the negligent, absent black mother, and demonstrate the power of the pre-1920 ideal of motherhood. This ideal envisioned motherhood as a sacred estate and a full-time calling—one that involved physical suffering and self-sacrifice. This archetype was still alive in the black community, as these dramatic representations demonstrate.

114 *Reclaiming Maternity*

Johnson's 1929 play *Safe* wrenchingly exhibits the impossible dilemma black mothers, especially mothers of sons, found themselves in, and the ways that grief can inspire agency.[68] *Safe* retells the tragic real-life story of Sam Hosea. In 1893, the 21-year-old, under suspicion of killing his white boss, was captured and dragged out of his mother's cabin in Newman, Georgia. He was tied to a tree and burned alive. After his horrific murder, white newspapers portrayed him as a "monster in human form" (claiming that he had also raped his boss's wife) and an Atlanta shopkeeper displayed Hosea's knuckles in his store window.[69] *Safe* was Johnson's artistic response to this savagery.

Safe opens with a warm domestic scene, the home of Liza and John Pettigrew, whom Johnson identifies as wife and husband. Liza is pregnant with her first child, and is seated with her husband and mother, sewing small white garments for her expected baby. Her mother Mandy has come to help prepare for the baby's arrival. Liza's husband John is scanning the newspaper, and begins to read aloud about the arrest of Sam Hosea that morning for an altercation with his white boss over wages. The family is well aware of the danger: Mandy states, "that's mighty unhealthy sounding business for this part of the country. Hittin a white man, he better hadder made tracks far away from here I'm er thinking." They are also aware of the trauma that Hosea's mother must be experiencing. John states, "I reckon his ma is plum crazy if she's heered they got him." Hannah, a family friend, comes to the door to report the news: "they done formed a mob downtown and it mout be…hell to pay tonight!"[70]

The husband John ventures out to see what he can learn, and the women discuss the impossibility of dignified black manhood in the current racial caste system.[71] Liza comments: "What's little nigger boys born for anyhow? I sho hopes mine will be a girl." The frightened women hear a gunshot and a crowd approaching the house. "Ma, ma, do you think they got him—do you think they'll hang him?" Liza exclaims. After they turn off the lights, the three women hear 17-year-old Sam Hosea's voice above the melee: "Don't hang me, don't hang me! I don't want to die! Mother! Mother!" Heavily pregnant Liza runs to the door and looks out; her mother and friend drag her away. Shivering she cries, "Oh my God, did you hear that poor boy crying for his mother?"[72]

Doubled over in pain, Liza goes into labor and, as the male voices diminish outside, her friend Hannah goes to get a doctor. Mother urges daughter to rest but Liza cannot extinguish what she has heard, asking her mother, "Did you hear him cry for his mother? Did you?" Mandy responds, "Yes, honey chile, I heard him, but you mustn't think about that now. Fergit it. Remember your own little baby—you got him to think about. You got to born him safe!"[73]

"Wild-eyed," Liza goes into the bedroom. Her husband returns safely, the doctor arrives and goes to Liza who is in labor, while her husband joins his mother-in-law in the living room. They are concerned about how Liza's proximity to the violence will affect her and the baby. When they hear the newborn's healthy cry, they step forward but before they can enter the bedroom the doctor appears with a look of distress on his face. Anticipating the choice made by Sethe in Toni Morrison's *Beloved*, when Liza learns that her child is a boy, she strangles him. The doctor exclaimed:

> I turned my back a minute to wash in the basin. When I looked around again she had her hands about the baby's throat choking it. I tried to stop her, but its little tongue was already hanging from its mouth. It was dead! Then Liza began, she kept muttering over and over again, "Now he's safe—safe from the lynchers! Safe!"[74]

The new father collapses in a chair sobbing, Mandy goes to her daughter in the bedroom, and the doctor stands, "a picture of helplessness as he looks at them in their grief."[75]

Jacqueline Rose has suggested that in some historical moments, matricide might be the only way a mother can protect her child. In "lift[ing] the lid on America's suppressed history of slavery," in *Beloved* Toni Morrison was telling her white readers, Rose believes, "that in an inhumane world a mother can only be a mother in so far as history permits, which might mean killing your child."[76] In Johnson's *Safe*, the new mother seizes what agency she can to protect her newborn son and take control of his future, and her own. Unable to buy enough time to save their children, black mothers like Liza and Sethe were caught in impossible choices that would lead to unbearable grief in either outcome. Helpless to change the historical moment into which her child has been born, the only way that Liza (reminiscent of the slave Eliza in Harriet Beecher Stowe's antislavery novel *Uncle Tom's Cabin*, who escapes to the North with her five-year-old son after he was sold away from her) can keep her infant son safe from race hatred is by killing him. He was born into a world in which black survival was questionable at best. Cheryl Rodriguez has described the ways that racist violence especially impacts mothers: "[S]tate-sponsored violence targets and tortures Black mothers by denying them the possibility of raising their children in peace or, even more devastatingly, by denying mothers the right to see their children live and become adults."[77] Rather than accepting this fate and performing her powerlessness in this play, Liza seizes her power by snuffing out the life of her son before white racists can destroy him, thus protecting both of them.

Scholar Laura Dawkins places *Safe* in the context of other literary portrayals of black motherhood produced by women writers during the early decades of the twentieth century. Angelina Weld Grimke's short story *The Closing Door* (1919) and Shirley Graham's play *The Morning* (1940) also take up the topic of maternal infanticide. The mothers in these works, Dawkins writes, "can claim their children only through acts of violence."[78] Recognizing the tragic boundaries of their maternal power, they kill in the name of love, as Dawkins concludes: "the black mother's dead child functions as a trope for her mangled maternity, her 'unmothering' by a destructive society." Yet the murdering mother is also a figure of rebellion who rejects the ideal of the Mater Dolorosa—the sorrowing Madonna who gives up her fleshly ties to her child and relinquishes him into the world (and death). This revisionist narrative rereads Christian images of motherhood, and represents "a secular analogue in the domestic Madonna's culturally mandated obligation to deliver her children into society—to prepare them to leave her."[79]

Renouncing the maternal claim becomes impossible for the black mothers portrayed in lynching plays, who, in giving up their children to a racist society, surrender to their own and their children's suffering, and to a future that is shaped and defined by whites.[80] Mothers like *Safe's* Liza claim a different resolution, one that illuminates the profound bonds of motherhood. In sketching these feminine portraits, the African American writers draw upon Greek and Jewish mythology and the characters of Medea and Lilith, mythical mothers who attack or kill their own children.[81] In doing so they emphatically rejected Eurocentric models of motherhood, as well as antimaternalist messages cautioning mothers not to love their children too much. They also depict mothers seizing time to rewrite future racial tragedy.

The Power of Imagery to Challenge Antimaternalism

Black painters, photographers, and sculptors in these decades also took up the subject of African American motherhood and grief. Mothers of lynched sons inspired especially tragic representations of maternal grief, demonstrating the power of imagery to challenge antimaternalism (and the historical focus on loss of sons over daughters). One of the most striking images of the period portraying motherhood and sorrow was the sculpture "Mother and Son" (also called "Supplication"). Exhibited at the 1939 New York World's Fair and destroyed a year later in a shipping accident, "Mother and Son" is a powerful image that depicts a stricken African American mother on her knees cradling her dead son's body. Featured in a 1939 *The Crisis* issue, the caption reads, "The figure represents a mother gathering her lynched son into her arms." Created by perhaps the most successful African American sculptor of the twentieth century, Richmond Barthé, "Mother and Son" recalls Michelangelo's *Pieta*, which dates to 1498 and depicts the body of Jesus on the lap of his mother Mary after the crucifixion.[82]

Julia Kristeva has written, most extensively in "Stabat Mater," about the complexity of the figure of Mary in representations of motherhood. Trying to understand what it is about the Christian or virginal representation of the maternal that serves "to calm social anxiety and supply what the male lacks, but also to satisfy a woman," Kristeva turns to the avoidance of death.[83]

> The fate of the Virgin Mary is more radiant even than that of her son: not having been crucified, she has no tomb and does not die, and therefore

she has no need of resurrection. Mary does not die but rather—echoing Taoist and other oriental beliefs in which human bodies pass from one place to another in a never-ending cycle which is in itself an imitation of the process of childbirth—she passes over.[84]

While Mary represents "an ideal that no individual woman could possibly embody," Kristeva writes, "the Virgin also serve[s] as a mooring point for the humanization of the West, and in particular for the humanization of love."[85] Philosopher Fanny Soderback considers Mary as a complex and paradoxical figure, a symbol of maternal grief as well as the cycle of life. She connects Mary's emotional passage after her son's death with both maternal regeneration and mortality:

> [Mary's] life follows the very cyclicality of maternity—through transposition, she is born and reborn, offering continuity to the species and making possible new beginnings. Mothers *do* provide us with a sense of immortality (so long as regeneration takes place, we will live on in our children and grandchildren) ... but at the same time they function as reminders that we are engendered and hence will die, whether we want it or not.[86]

"Stabat Matar Dolorosa," which translates to "the sorrowful Mother was standing," was the title of a thirteenth-century Catholic hymn to the Virgin Mary. The translation of the original hymn reads in part:

At the Cross her station keeping,
Stood the mournful
Mother weeping,
Close to her Son to the last.

Through her heart,
His sorrow sharing,
All His bitter
Anguish bearing
Now at length the
Sword has passed.

O how sad and
Sore distressed
Was that Mother
...

Christ above in
Torment hangs,
She beneath

Beholds the pangs
Of her dying
Glorious Son.
...

Can the human
Heart refrain
From partaking in
Her pain,
In that Mother's
Pain untold?[87]
...

Jacqueline Rose has described suffering motherhood, or the representation of a mother bereft of her child, as a staple maternal image. She notes, however, that patriarchal culture does not want grieving mothers to place their grief within a larger social or political context:

> the mother must be noble and her agony redemptive. With the suffering of the whole world etched on her face, she carries and assuages the burden of human misery on behalf of everyone. What the pain of motherhood must never expose is a viciously unjust world in a complete mess.[88]

Mothers who connect their losses to social injustice break this cardinal rule. A poem written by Gloria Clyne, titled "Stabat Mater" and published in *The Crisis* in 1943, invokes the image of the white virgin mother, but equates a black mother's loss with gruesome racist violence. The poem portrays a grieving mother standing before her martyred son, but this son is a black American and a lynching victim. The author compares him to the crucified Christ, killed in an "American Calvary," referring to the site immediately outside of Jerusalem's walls where Christ was nailed to the cross and died. The short and potent poem reads:

The mother stood
And watched the tortured, half-burnt thing
That once had been her son,
This broken, bleeding thing,
Swing from a crueler tree
On an American Calvary.[89]

How do black mothers cope with the threat of violence, loss, and grief that is always with them? Some writers have conceptualized the idea of maternal loss as a legacy of black oppression, tracing it to the transatlantic slave trade that forced disconnection from the African continent.[90] Mothering while being black in America requires the understanding that racism always lurks and that, despite class status, all blacks are a potential target of racialized violence. Some black feminist theorists have objected to the stereotyped image of the strong black mother as "a shallow image that denies Black women the right to be vulnerable, despite its ubiquity."[91] Some have argued that linking black mothers to pain and terror, to grief and sorrow, and conceptualizing black motherhood as "the space of the crisis" is another kind of flattening and diminishment. Focusing on black maternal aesthetics in our contemporary moment Jennifer Nash writes:

> because the terrain of black maternal political life is so closely tethered to grief, crisis, and death ... part of my political and ethical interest is in disrupting the prevailing conceptions of black maternity that yoke it only to suffering, and in considering the aesthetic strategies black mothers have cultivated for powerfully staking claims to the universal.[92]

Anthropologist Dana-Ain Davis argues that "Radical Black mothering wants to trade sorrow; we do not need it to be our primary artifact."[93] Powerfully staking claims to the universal includes an embracing of the creativity, continuity, and joy that African American mothers have found in motherhood.

Yet, black maternal grief and loss were very real in the 1920–1960 era, and some artists turned to the depiction of black mothers' sorrow as a way to both highlight their suffering and rebut racist depictions. The archetypal 1952 photograph of Rosa Moore, captioned in *The Crisis* as "A MOTHER'S GRIEF," is a riveting image that illuminates the potential pain and exposure of motherhood. The son that Rosa Moore lost was Florida-born Harry Moore, her only child. The 46-year-old NAACP leader, described as quiet, soft-spoken, and self-effacing, was sleeping with his wife in their Florida home on Christmas night 1952, when a bomb placed beneath the floor joists under their bed exploded. His mother and a daughter were sleeping in the back of the home where they had gathered for the holidays. The force of the explosion blew the Moores and their bed to the roof. Moore died in his mother's arms on the way to the hospital; his wife passed away a week later.[94] The Moores' murderers were never found or brought to justice, but this striking image of black maternal suffering circulated widely. As Jennifer Nash has noted, black maternal grief is "one of the few spaces in which black pain is readily culturally visible," which gives it political currency.[95] In the photograph, Rosa Moore is grimacing with anguish, hand clasping her face. *The Crisis* caption under the image describes Moore's grief as paralyzing and depleting: "A grief without pang, void, dark and drear; a stifled, drowsy, unimpassioned grief, which finds no natural outlet, no relief, in work, or sigh, or tear."[96] As Rose has observed, history puts a limit on a mother's ability to mother. In this representation, disseminated on the cusp of the U.S. civil rights movement, there is no apparent way to assuage the grief of a mother whose son has been murdered because of race hatred. And yet, Moore's death—and this visual depiction of his mother's unspeakable and sacred sorrow—paved the way for Mamie Till Bradley, whose maternal grief and fury just three years later contributed to a pivotal moment in the movement for racial equality. In losing their children to racist violence both mothers lost part of themselves, but catapulted their grief into fighting for a more just future for all black Americans. They also, intentionally or not, represented the care, nurturance, and morality that pre-1920 maternalists had equated with mothering.

Some of the artistic representations of African American motherhood and grief in the early to mid-twentieth century were explicit commentaries on racism. Belying any romanticized notion of maternal bonding across race, some artists illuminated the complicity of white mothers in the lynching of black mothers' sons, which also anticipated the Emmett Till tragedy. In 1934 the NAACP sponsored an exhibition titled "Art Commentary on Lynching" at the Arthur Newton Galleries in New York City. One of the most disturbing pieces in the show was a black and white cartoon by the white painter Reginald Marsh. "This Is Her First Lynching" depicts a white mother holding a young girl, presumably her daughter, above the heads of the crowd assembled to watch the mob murder of an African American youth, in order to give her a clearer view. This mother, as interpreted by a white male artist, viewed lynching as a ritualized affair of white family life, representing part of a mother's responsibility to indoctrinate her children into the truth about race relations and white supremacy in the United States. Shouting to the woman beside her, "this is her first lynching," the mother's cartoonish face is mawkish in its hatred, obscene in its voyeuristic spectatorship. Marsh's drawing, which first appeared in the September 1934 issue of *The New Yorker*, represents lynching as communal entertainment and displays women—and mothers—initiating children in acts of race terror.[97]

Memorial Photographs, Gold Star Mothers, and Transmission of Memory as a Political Act

Memorializing lost sons and daughters in photographs was another way for black women to reclaim African American maternity during these years. In the early twentieth century, African Americans continued the tradition Euro-Americans had inaugurated but discontinued: formal portraits of the dead in final sleep.[98] Pictorially representing their departed was an avenue for early twentieth-century mothers to address and process their grief. Memorial photographs of deceased African American children in the early twentieth century also served as a way to pass on images to future generations and to keep memory, including memories of dead loved ones, alive.

Harlem, New York-based James Van Der Zee and Southerner Richard Samuel Roberts, both noted African American photographers of the 1920s and 1930s, contributed to this genre. Van Der Zee—who has been called "the custodian of memory"—described a motivation for the gentle portraiture in one of his photographs, which depicted a dead infant, peacefully lying in a crib, her teddy bear alongside her. Viewers of the photograph might believe the baby had just drifted off to sleep in the midst of play, rather than the more tragic reality of having died. "The mother was sick in the hospital and couldn't get out," Van Der Zee explained. "The child died in the meantime. If it wasn't for the picture, the mother wouldn't have seen the child for the last time."[99] In addition, for families who had migrated to Harlem, funerary portraits could be sent to relatives back home (often in the south) who were unable to attend the funerals.[100]

In another Van Der Zee photograph, a grieving mother and a father sit companionably in a wicker chair, their beautiful baby girl, wearing a christening gown, nestled in her father's arms. Asked about this artistic decision, Van Der Zee responded: "It was my suggestion to have them hold the child while the picture was being taken to make it look more natural."[101] The radio in the background and the cozy household atmosphere belie the truth, which is that the infant has died. The memorial picture suggests that these parents intended a different memory than the fact of their baby's death. Evoking domesticity and safety, this depiction portrays parental love as timeless, with the power to rewind time and erase terrible loss. Van Der Zee also sought to depict the black family in a particular way—as intact, well ordered, and home-centered—in order to visually challenge racist misconceptions about African American families.[102] At least one critic derided him for this approach: French essayist Roland Barthes sarcastically noted Van Der Zee's middle-class subjects attempting "to assume the white man's attributes."[103] Like Dorothea Lange, Van Der Zee was self-consciously trying to represent African Americans with dignity, as deserving of humanity.

Victims of pneumonia or tuberculosis in the densely populated projects of Harlem, these children died from disease rather than violence. African Americans suffered high rates of morbidity and mortality from both diseases during these decades, and tragically, children were often among the victims. During the 1920s and 1930s, the African American dead were disproportionately young.[104] In Harlem, some funeral directors described an endless procession of small caskets as black children fell victim to these infectious diseases that swept the community. In this reality—not unlike the nineteenth century—mothers could not love their children too much, because the time they would have with them was uncertain. The racial imbalance of who died in childhood supports Brittney Cooper's contention that "shortened life span according to zip code is just one example of the ways that time and space cohere in an unjust manner in the lives of black people."[105]

Like Van Der Zee, Richard Samuel Roberts depicted peaceful images of deceased children framed in familial bonds in his memorial photographs. Their shared cultural aesthetic, as Karla Holloway has noted, aimed "to construct a memorial of the dead child that contradicted the fact of the event."[106] The deliberate framing of the sensibility of home and hearth within the images stand in stark contrast to the grotesque, outdoor carnival atmosphere of many lynchings and echo the domestic settings of anti-lynching plays. One of Roberts's photographs shows a lovely female child dressed in a white flowing gown lying gently on a lace-covered bed, looking like she will open her eyes any minute. Even if an illusion, these photographs offered a way to restore dignity, order, and control to African Americans and the African American community during a time when they had little power to keep the family together, and their children alive. Like lynching plays, African American memorial photographs of the 1920s and 1930s reclaimed the familial roles, citizenship, and sheer humanity of blacks and served as a counter-narrative to the racism and antimaternalism of the times.

Memorial portraits allowed grieving mothers (and fathers) to demonstrate the importance of memory and remembrance to the healing of grief. In the black community, children's deaths made visible both the persistence of memory and the indispensable nature of memorial.[107] Memorials serve a number of personal and community functions: they insist on remembering that the past happened, that it matters. The reflective impulse of grief—which causes us to consider our own mortality and impermanence—may lead to a desire to memorialize, to remember the dead as a way to protest "the very nature of flux, transience, and loss." DeWitt Henry wrote: "with no grief, memorials, or markers, I am myself, also, passing, gone. My train itself is speeding out of sight"[108] M. Jacqui Alexander has described memory as an antidote to alienation, separation, and the amnesia that domination produces.[109] The funerary portraits of early twentieth-century African American children were a work of recovery, of anamnesis, a not-forgetting. They insisted that these children were loved, and that their lives mattered. Like Lange's photographs, these images represented maternal love, self-sacrifice, and endurance.

Another historical expression of the importance of memory and maternal grief, this one on a national scale, were the Gold Star Mother pilgrimages of 1930 to 1933. Thousands of families across the United States lost sons in World War I, and their bodies were quickly buried in shallow graves on European battlefields. At the beginning, the government was undecided whether to repatriate the bodies, which led to a movement to bring the war dead back to the United States. The federal government received scores of letters, many from mothers, saying, "My son fought for his country and died. You owe it to me to bring him back home."[110] Ultimately the government decided to give families a choice: after the war ended in 1918, the U.S. Department of War offered families the opportunity to choose between burial in their hometowns, in Virginia's Arlington National Cemetery, or in one of eight yet-to-be built cemeteries in France, Belgium, and England.

With 100,000 dead, emotional deliberations raged across America over what was best. Although most families chose burial in the United States, approximately 33,000 American casualties of the war, including those of unknown identity, were buried in U.S. cemeteries overseas.[111] Amidst uncertainty, national disagreement, and doubt over which was the correct decision and policy, mothers and widows of those buried in Europe argued persuasively over more than a decade for a government-sponsored pilgrimage to the overseas graves of their lost sons and husbands.

During the war families with members in the service displayed banners in their windows with blue stars in the center. The numbers of blue stars indicated the number of family members in the service. As soldiers were killed, the families overlaid a gold star on top of the blue star, symbolizing the supreme sacrifice made for country. Mothers' sacrifices received special attention: the idea that it was the mother's job to raise her son to be a good American citizen was still accepted by many in the culture. Therefore, as Rebecca Plant suggested, "when a son died, when a young man was lost in wartime, people's thoughts immediately went to the mother."[112] At the close of the war, the Women's Committee of the Council of National Defense suggested to President Woodrow Wilson that, instead of continuing the tradition of wearing mourning black after the loss of a family member, American women should wear black bands on their left arms imprinted with a gold star for each family member who had died in the war. The term Gold Star Mothers was applied to any mother whose son(s) died in the World War, and was meant to symbolize and honor a mother's sacrifice.[113] As the Armistice was being signed, Gold Star Mothers began lobbying on Capitol Hill.

Between 1918 and 1929, Gold Star Mothers argued to the U.S. government that their sacrifice warranted a "debt of gratitude" that could be repaid with a government-sponsored trip to the graves of their sons. New U.S. Representative and future New York City Mayor Fiorello La Guardia introduced the first pilgrimage bill in 1919. Amidst opposition from funeral directors (who wanted all bodies returned to the United States for burial), and other legal bickering, ten years passed before the mothers' petition was successful.[114] Individual mothers, some more privileged who had the funds to visit their sons' burial spots, wrote emotional letters in support of the proposed bill. Mrs. Jennie Walsh professed,

> I was so distraught over the death of my son in the war, that I lost my hearing and thought I was losing my mind. I am so thankful I had the financial means to visit my son's grave. And I feel certain if you send over the poor mothers who cannot afford to pay their own way, you will save the minds of a great many of them.

Mrs. Effie Vedder tried to express the temporal investment she had made as a mother, and the embodied connection she felt to her lost son:

Members of the Committee—I want to begin by telling you that you are all men and you have not and can not feel the way a mother feels. It is a part of her body that is lying over there. She spent 20 years, anyway, in bringing up that boy. She gave her time both day and night, and none of you can realize what a mother's loss is.[115]

Such pleas ultimately met with success. Despite an economy teetering on the brink of collapse and changing ideas about motherhood and its meaning, in 1929 President Calvin Coolidge endorsed the Gold Star pilgrimages.

From 1930 to 1933, at a cost of more than $5 million, the U.S. government sent over 6,000 women, most in their sixties, to the cemeteries of Europe. Most were first and second generation immigrants, and many could not speak English.[116] Not all mothers were to be united in these memorial pilgrimages, which one historian described as "Jim Crow Sets Sail."[117] In keeping with the segregationist policies in the United States of the 1930s, as soon as the pilgrimages were approved the War Department announced that black and white Gold Star Mothers and widows would travel in segregated groups and stay in different accommodations once they reached their destinations. Of the more than 1,500 eligible African American Gold Star Mothers and widows, only 233 received invitations due to death, remarriage (remarried widows were ineligible), illness, among other reasons. Only 55 eventually made the trip.[118] Just as their sons and husbands had largely been organized into segregated military units that were assigned to labor and support positions behind the scenes, the African American women who made the voyage were separated. There were significant differences in the perquisites provided: the white mothers voyaged on luxury liners, the black mothers on commercial steamers. The white mothers stayed in expensive hotels in the center of Paris, the African American mothers lodged in boarding houses in outlying neighborhoods of the city.[119] Historian Barbara Ransby pointed to the racism these discrepancies indicated: "[t]he government was really symbolizing in some of the most painful ways the devaluation of Black life."[120]

Yet the fact remained that African American soldiers had died in World War I, in service to the United States. Many of them faced discrimination and exclusion from their white counterparts. The experiences of Colonel Charles Young, a U.S. Army officer from Kentucky, exemplify this discrimination. The third African American graduate of West Point and the first black to achieve the rank of Colonel, after serving the United States in four wars and with the country about to enter World War I, he stood a good chance of being promoted to brigadier general. This advancement would have meant, however, that he would have outranked white officers, who would have had to report to him. In response to complaints from white officers, the War Department removed Young from active duty, claiming high blood pressure prevented him from serving.[121]

Colonel Young published a poem, "A Negro-Mother's Cradle-Song," in *The Crisis* a few years later (1921), which connects maternal grief with racial justice. In the poem, a mother rocks her son as she mourns the death of her husband—the infant's father—who "bravely fought and bled" on the battlefields of France. She prays to her dead husband, "Shade of my dead! Oh warrior one!" to "Watch from your realm upon our little son. / ... Make for him a place in the world's new March of Man." "Teach him," she asks, "that you died that all might rise and run." And to the son she cradles in her arms she sings, "Sleep, little son! Sleep, little son!/ I pray your Living Lord that victory is won;/ ... Up to the throne of God will rise in surging Throngs, / Holding high hands to Heav'n to right a Race's wrongs. —/ Mind not, my darling son, your mother's eyes that weep: /Sleep, little son! Now sleep!"[122]

Lisa Budreau has suggested that organized pilgrimages represent a coming together, or point of intersection, between individual loss and national community, and are a way to process and move on from grief. A ritual intended for unity and healing, Budreau writes that "ideally, [pilgrimages] can serve to unite groups and nation in remembrance, while offering an opportunity for participants to come to terms with grief, thus consigning the dead to memory." State-sanctioned and funded "instruments of closure," the Gold Star pilgrimages were tightly controlled by federal officials, most of them white men. The military was steadfastly determined to "play down hysteria" at the gravesites: "we see no evidence of grief, of tears at grave visits," Budreau writes, and credits this to the fact that the military were afraid of intense emotions, and were fully prepared to nip them in the bud. U.S. Army Colonel in charge Richard T. Ellis noted the need to "prevent over-emphasis of the sentimental side in order to prevent morbidness or hysteria."[123] For this reason no ceremonies were permitted at the cemeteries; the War Department stipulated that a successful visit would include "the arrangements necessary for the prompt and accurate [efficient] conduct of the pilgrim to the grave in which she was interested, the distribution of flowers or wreaths ... [and] the taking of a photograph at the grave." Budreau concludes that this automatous approach apparently dissuaded mothers from public displays of sorrow:

> Officials prepared for fits of female hysteria, but there were none. Instead, a lacuna existed where grief should have been. How could the emotive sight of thousands of white crosses cause these pilgrims no evidence of pain? Had twelve years' time really healed old wounds so well?[124]

Budreau argued that mothers who joined the state-funded pilgrimages may have supported the ideology of patriotic motherhood and that displays of grief might have struck them as unseemly, "an admission of doubt about the righteous sacrifice made on such a grand scale for questionable aims." She described the validation the pilgrimages offered Gold Star Mothers: "Death's gold star brought an opportunity for public recognition, an affirmation of a woman's patriotism, and collective reassurance that her sacrifice had been necessary."[125] Budreau also notes that expressions of mourning in general were unwelcome in American society at the time. It is also likely that the Gold Star Mothers felt indebted to the government officials who accompanied them on the voyage and cemetery visits and pressured to check public displays of sorrow. They were mothers who exemplified an earlier maternal ideal linked to sacrifice, suffering, and martyrdom. They invoked the model of Republican Motherhood, which as early as the American Revolution had claimed that women would sustain the emerging republic, not as voters but as mothers who would raise virtuous sons who would keep the new government on a safe course.[126] Gold Star Mothers must also have felt the pressure of temporal efficiency as interpreted by the United States government, and the unspoken dictate that grieving mothers are not supposed to call out social injustice.

African American Gold Star Mothers were subjected to intensified surveillance, and it is difficult to know how they registered, or checked, their grief in these public rituals. Yet what we do know about bereaved black mothers in the past and in the present is that some, as Erica Lawson has argued, take up maternal activism "to articulate their own political subjectivity for justice." Lawson writes: "subjectivity implies the *emotional* experience of a *political* subject ... caught up in a world of violence, state authority and pain."[127] She argues that black women's maternal grief is "a public feeling" in that "political identities are implicit within structures of feeling, sensibilities, [and] everyday forms of cultural expression and affiliation."[128] In this interpretation, however muted the black mothers who stood before their soldier sons' European graves in 1930–1933 might have been, they were political subjects in a racial state, one with a history of slavery that excluded black women and men from political participation and the other privileges of democracy, including freedom and the right to build and care for families. However they masked it, this truth must have informed their sensibilities and emotions during these state-sponsored, public rituals of grief and memory.

Budreau also notes that the task of commemorating conflict is inherently complicated, and there are differences of interest at stake. In the case of the Gold Star Mothers' pilgrimages, the U.S. government was invested in unifying the nation and justifying its participation in an ambiguous, ultimately unpopular war. The mothers were interested in pilgrimages of remembrance and commemoration, and possibly in serving as a symbolic antidote to misogynistic American views about the dangers of (too much) mother love. Their physical presence attested to the power and dignity of motherhood, across class and race. Ownership rights over the war dead were disputed, with families claiming their entitlement to the remains of their deceased, while the military claimed ownership of its fallen. "By default then," Budreau writes, "the dead became a widely contested commodity, an instrument of memory."[129]

We can also consider Gold Star Mothers as the keepers of memory who utilized maternal grief in an agentic way. Gold Star Mothers fought against the rapidly fading memory of the war, and the erasing of their sons' lives and sacrifices, as well as the expunging of their own losses. In his analysis of family memory and World War I in Australia, Bart Ziino describes women as the keepers of "treasured" and "cherished" letters from family soldiers, who carefully and faithfully retained the letters for their families. Women thus became known as history caretakers and family archivists: "stoic mourners, keepers of the homes and families of absent men, managers of the behavior of returned soldier husbands and the literal keepers of family history." Ziino linked this kind of preservation work with women's agency.[130] He also describes the gendering of memory, the idea that the nature of transmission of memory is connected to the roles that women play as receivers and keepers of family history. Their own experiences are embedded in the ways they share these stories with others.[131] Just as "homeplace" was a site of resistance that black women created, so transmission of family memory—whether that of a baby lost to illness or a son lost to war—can be understood as a political act, a kind of maternal reclaiming. The story of Mamie Till Bradley and her son Emmett Till, the final focus of this chapter, dramatically illustrates this.

Mamie Till Bradley and Antimaternalism

The painful story of Mamie Till Bradley and her son Emmett Till reveals the ways that the mid-twentieth century justice system used race to define worthy motherhood, and how mothers can utilize their grief to inform activism and contribute to social justice. Like the Gold Star Mothers, Bradley drew on her motherhood and her heartbreak to focus public attention on her son's death. His was a brutal lynching in a country that purported to advocate democracy and justice. Bradley employed her son's 1955 murder to shine a light on the ugliness of racial violence in America and to advocate for racial justice and equality. At the same time, Bradley illustrates the impact that antimaternalism had on African American mothers at mid-century. Not only was she blamed for not "preparing" her son for how to "behave" in the oppressive caste system of the south, but she was also denied justice and the inherent authority of her role as a mother when an all-white male jury refused to believe she could identify her own son's body.

The slaughter of Bradley's son was every black mother's worst nightmare. Although it occurred decades after the peak of lynching in the United States, the Till killing represents a country and a region—rural Mississippi— fighting against social change and a future in which racial equality might become a reality.[132] One year before Till's murder, the Supreme Court ruled in its landmark *Brown v. Board of Education of Topeka* case that segregation damaged the self-esteem of black children and that racially segregated schools were unconstitutional. Threatened and defensive, white supremacist organizations sprang up throughout the south. Some journalists and civil rights advocates directly blamed the *Brown* decision—passed on what racists called "Black Monday"—for Till's lynching.[133] The year 1955 also ended with the launch of the Montgomery bus boycott, which successfully challenged segregated public transportation in Montgomery, Alabama, and brought the young Reverend Martin Luther King Jr. into the public eye. Social and political changes, shifting feelings about racial discrimination, and mounting activism in African American communities all contributed to the civil rights movement and landmark voting rights and civil rights legislation in the mid-1960s.[134]

The murder of 14-year-old Emmett Till in late August 1955 was especially gruesome. Late Saturday night on August 28, Roy Bryant, 24 years old, and his 36-year-old half-brother J.W. Milam, kidnapped Emmett Till, a Chicago native, at gunpoint from his great uncle's cabin in Money, Mississippi. Till was on his summer vacation, visiting family. Several days later a white teenager discovered Till's body in the nearby Tallahatchie River. He had been brutally beaten, one eye was gouged out, and he was shot in the skull. His murderers had tied a 75-pound cotton gin fan to his neck with barbed wire before they dumped his body in the river. Dared by his cousins, Till allegedly had "wolf-whistled" at 21-year-old Carolyn Bryant, Roy Bryant's wife, and white mother of two young sons, in their family-owned grocery store. The two white men claimed they felt compelled to avenge what they considered a racial and sexual transgression. The murder and subsequent trial pitted the testimony of a white mother—the accuser—against the testimony of a black mother. As Ruth Feldstein highlighted, "motherhood itself was a battleground on which the meaning of Till's death was fought."[135]

Emmett Till's mother, Mamie Till Bradley, was a 33-year-old African American woman living in Chicago. Born in Mississippi, she moved to Chicago with her family when she was two. A civil servant with the Chicago Procurement Division of the U.S. Air Force, she and her only child lived in a two-family house: "We are," she stated at the trial, "what you might call the lower middle class."[136] She was a remarried widow whose husband had been a war veteran. Bradley chose to open her son's casket to the world and took a leading role in the events that followed his murder—the funeral, trial, and subsequent political mobilization. Ruth Feldstein has argued that Bradley "claimed the public role of grieving mother" and in doing so helped inject motherhood more forcefully into the political landscape, but she could not control the terms of the debate or the ways in which she herself was made a symbol.[137]

Mamie Bradley learned on Wednesday, September 1, that her son's corpse had been discovered. Till's body became a physical symbol of what the mother wanted remembered and the racist south wanted to forget. Like the fictional black mothers in African American lynching plays of the 1920s, Bradley was the witness that the upholders of the racial status quo most wanted to silence. The white sheriff of Tallahatchie County ordered that Till be buried in Mississippi, immediately. But Bradley insisted that her son's body be returned for burial in Chicago. To the sympathetic white and black Northern press chronicling Till's lynching, it was "the grieving mother of a Chicago boy" who "barely averted" this "hasty burial."

"Mother Breaks Down" announced the *Chicago Tribune*. Yet it was a clear-thinking woman who, when she saw her son's brutalized body, chose to have an open-casket funeral to "let the people see what they have done to my boy." "Lord, you gave your only son to remedy a condition, but who knows, but what the death of my only son might bring an end to lynching!" Bradley said when she first saw the body at Illinois Central Station, invoking a comparison of the martyred African American son with the martyred son of God.[138]

Bradley later described something akin to a religious conversion experience the day she learned of her son's death. The occurrence convinced her that she was the instrument of truth, the storyteller whose truth telling would change the nation. She told an interviewer that the day her son's body was found, after she insisted they bring him home to Chicago for burial, she went to her mother's home and rested in bed. "Then began one of the strangest experiences of my whole life": Bradley described a feeling as though someone, "as real to me as though we were both flesh and blood," entered the room.

> The presence said to me, "Mamie, it was ordained from the beginning of time that Emmett Louis Till would die a violent death. You should be grateful to be the mother of a boy who died blameless like Christ. Bo Till will never be forgotten. There is a job for you to do now."
>
> I sat up in bed and stretched out my hand. ... I knew that if anyone came up there and heard me talking, they would instantly think I had gone out of my mind with grief. ... "What shall I do?" I asked. The voice replied, "Have courage and faith that in the end there will be redemption for the sufferings of your people and you are the instrument of this purpose. Work unceasingly to tell the story so that the truth will arouse men's consciences and right can at last prevail."
>
> The Voice died away and the Presence left the room. I lay down and slept peacefully.[139]

Fueled by her vision and grieving her son, Bradley summoned the strength and self-possession to connect his murder to social and political change. When she received her son's body at the Illinois Central Station in early September she shouted, "Darling you have not died in vain; your life has been sacrificed for something." Till's body laid for viewing in the Chicago funeral home for three days; estimates of attendance vary widely, ranging from three thousand to six hundred thousand.[140] Although a *Daily Worker* journalist described "Strong young men ... weeping openly without shame" as they viewed Till's body, Mamie Till Bradley exhibited "a mute, speechless anger [that] stood above the wracking grief." Close to midnight Bradley pushed her way outside and spoke to the mourners in the darkness, urging them to see for themselves the horrifying evidence of the lynching, to steel themselves for the struggle to bring the killers to justice, and to "end such barbarism forever." Bradley expressed a desire to use her son's death "to make it safe for other boys," and vowed, "I want to go to the Mississippi trial; I want other people to go with me to see this thing through. I'm willing to go anywhere, to speak anywhere, to get justice."[141] Emmett Till was buried on Tuesday, September 6, the same day that a Tallahatchie County Grand Jury handed down indictments against Bryant and Milam for kidnapping and murder.

The coverage of the emotionally fraught trial that lasted from September 19th to September 23rd and has been called the first great media event of the civil rights movement, transfixed the nation.[142] Bradley testified on the fourth day of the trial, making her private grief a public and political spectacle, and connecting racial violence with a mother's horrific loss. Bradley spoke to her positive identification of the body as her son: "I was able to see that it was my boy without a shadow of a doubt," she stated. Racist whites made judgments about her mothering abilities, her warnings to her son about how to comport himself in Mississippi. In cross-examination she was asked if she had told her son how to behave in the South. Her response demonstrated that, to ensure his physical survival, she had taught Emmett to fit into systems of oppression. Bradley replied:

> I told him he was coming South and he would have to adapt himself to the customs. I told him to be careful how and to whom he spoke, to say "yes, sir" and "no, sir" at all times, humble himself if necessary by going on his knees whether he thought it was wrong or right. I told him to be careful how he walked the streets.[143]

Some blamed Bradley for her son's death: a southern white woman stated that Till had died "because his mother permit[ted] her boy to visit here ... *She* should have had better sense than to let such a child come here." Thus, Bradley had to prove her ideal motherhood not only in a universal way, but also in racialized and racist terms.[144]

The juxtaposition of the two mothers, Mamie Till Bradley and Carolyn Bryant, escalated throughout the trial. Those on the side of preserving the southern racial status quo constructed Carolyn Bryant as the messenger symbolizing that the white family was on trial and must be preserved. She took the stand in "a black dress with a white color and red sash" and "demurely told a court" that "a Negro man (the teenaged Till) had grabbed her." Although most of her testimony was deemed inadmissible, Carolyn Bryant was considered a star witness for the defense, consistently described in the press as "attractive" and "comely." A *Newsweek* journalist wrote: "It was Bryant's wife, Carolyn, an attractive, dark-haired mother of two, whom Emmett was accused of molesting." Till opponents portrayed Bryant as a "natural," "good," and "respectable" mother, in opposition to Bradley, whom segregationists characterized as a pawn of the NAACP who was exploiting her son's death for personal gain. Southern public opinion viewed Bryant as "holding the multiple attributes of respectable white motherhood."[145]

The all-white jury of Southern men, comprised mostly of cotton country farmers, rejected Bradley's identification of her son's body and precluded a definition of "natural" motherhood that encompassed black women, privileging instead the rational, "scientific" testimony of the male "experts." The jury "chose to believe" that the body was not Till's as a way to acquit the two murderers and preserve power relations in Mississippi. "What could a black mother say that would be of any value?" asked *L'Aurore*, a French daily.[146] What Mamie Till Bradley did say points to the embodiment of motherhood and the vulnerability to suffering and pain that maternity opens up for black women. Bradley's statement at the trial suggests a physical identification with the son that had emerged from her womb that was so intense it blurred identities between mother and child.

> I didn't want that body. ... That couldn't be mine. But I stared at his feet and I could identify his ankles. I said, those are my ankles. Those are my knees. I knew the knees ... And then I began to come on up ... until I got to the chin and mouth ... those were Emmett's teeth, and I was looking for his ear. You notice how mine sort of curls up ... Emmett had the same ears ... [T]he one eye that was left, that was definitely his eye, the color confirmed that, and I had to admit that that was indeed Emmett, I said that is my son. This is Bobo.[147]

Despite Bradley's clear identification of her son's body, on the final day of the trial the jury pronounced a "not guilty" verdict after deliberating just one hour and seven minutes, based on the state's failure to prove the body was Till's.[148] The defense had put on the stand a doctor, a sheriff, and two undertakers—all white, male experts—whose testimony contended that the corpse could not have been Till's, based on their allegations that the body was in the river at least ten days while Till had only been missing three. District Attorney Gerald Chatham mounted an emotional defense based on a mother's authority to identify her son's body: "All we need is someone who loved him and cared for him," he told the jury. Defining a mother as the one who knows her child best, he declared: "If there was one ear left, one hairline, one part of his nose, any part of Emmett Till's body, then I say to you that Mamie Bradley was God's given witness to identify him."[149] Highlighting the bonds between mothers and children as well as maternal power and investment, Chatham declared to the jurors: "If you found an unidentifiable body," he reminded the jurors,

> you wouldn't go to an undertaker who didn't know the child, you'd go to his mother. Here she told a forthright story and she identified the body as the body of her son. She suffered that child as a babe in her breast.[150]

"Who else could identify that child?" he queried. "Who else could say, 'That's my boy?'"[151] Journalist and social commentator Murray Kempton wrote of Chatham's summation in the *New York Post*:

> To win that fight he had to make that jury believe that the testimony of a Negro mother was worth more than the word of three white witnesses who had testified with loud assurances that the body taken from the Tallahatchie River last Aug. 31 could not be that of Emmett Till.

Pitting science against maternal knowledge and authority, the defense lawyer Sidney Carlton argued that "[t]he undisputed scientific facts" were against Mamie Till Bradley, and that sometimes mothers believe what they want to believe.[152] According to the jury foreman, the fact that Bradley did not "authentically express maternal grief" on the witness stand also affected the jury's verdict.[153] The white male jury chose to believe the white, male experts—and the white mother—over the black mother. Some of the coverage, both in the largely sympathetic Northern press and the racist Southern press, did not even mention Bradley or her testimony despite the fact that the case hinged upon believing, or not believing, a mother's ability to identify her child's body. "I wonder how the mother feels to have someone who has never seen her boy tell her she didn't know her own son," a writer queried in *The Atlanta Constitution*.[154]

Mamie Till Bradley represented a different kind of African American mother than the negative representations carried by most Americans at the time, which were deeply intensified in the south. This made her even more threatening as a symbol of motherhood and maternal power. She traveled to the trial with her pastor and two male relatives, thus challenging assumptions about black women's promiscuity and sexualized black mothers.[155] Because of her class, education, bearing, physical appearance, careful diction, and political commitment, Bradley offered white southern Americans a new model of black motherhood. As a journalist commented in *The Nation*: "When ... Mrs. Mamie Bradley took the stand it was obvious as soon as she answered a question that she didn't fit the minstrel-show stereotype that most of Mississippi's white folks cherish."[156] A *New York Post* article described Bradley as "an affront to Sumner's white population and a stranger to its black one." Bradley was aware of the scrutiny she faced, from her clothing choices to her responses on the stand: "The mother of Emmett Louis Till," wrote Murray Kempton,

> walked the long, narrow, crammed pathway from the back of the room to the witness box and sat herself down and pulled her skirt over her knee. ... She put on her glasses and looked at Special Prosecutor Robert Smith; she wore a black bolero and a printed dress with a small black hat and a piece of a veil and she was very different from the cotton

patch cropper who is the ordinary Negro witness in a Mississippi courtroom.[157]

After the verdict, progressive white journalists and the black community expressed outrage: the *Daily Worker* rebutted,

> We know our readers join with us in paying our deepest respects to the mother, Mrs. Mamie Bradley, who felt in the racist fury inflicted upon the body of her child, not only a great personal grief but an injury to the entire people.[158]

Immediately after the trial, the NAACP sponsored Bradley in public speaking venues throughout the country. In churches and before packed auditoriums she shared the story of her son's lynching and her vision of an egalitarian America. In eight weekly installments in the spring of 1956 *The Chicago Defender* ran a series of articles on Mamie Till Bradley's "untold story." She again described the experience of identifying her son's body. Although friends as well as the undertaker had advised her "it would be too horrible a shock" to view the body, she prayed for guidance and "something told me," she stated, "Your heart will be encased in glass and no arrows can pierce it."

> I looked at that horrible mangled monstrosity—the odor was terrible—what had been done to a human being created by God was a crime so foul, I don't have words to describe it. ... It looked like something from outer space, and it seemed like a weird nightmare, not a part of me. ... I looked at this and no tears came, only a deep, lonely feeling that time and space had crushed me and I was left in a vacuum.[159]

Some mothers reached across lines of race, class, and region to identify with Bradley, illustrating the subversive potential of politicizing motherhood and publicizing grief, thus challenging the split between public, masculine citizenship and private, emotional motherhood.[160] *The Crisis* included several letters in its December 1955 issue from white mothers outraged about the Till murder and trial. Mrs. E. Kirkpatrick of Toronto, Canada, wrote a scathing letter to Bryant and Milam, sarcastically sympathizing with them for having to go through the "inconvenience" of a trial. Arguing that capital punishment would be "too dignified a death" for the exonerated murderers, she suggested, "How about just tying them up in an open field and let the maggots, and the vultures and all the cravers of carion [sic] dispose of their putrid flesh."[161] On motherhood, she wrote:

> Bringing a child into the world is probably the closest we come to God on this earth. Ask your wives how they felt when they beheld their first born. And somehow I think that conversely when we wantonly take the life of a child we are as far from God as it is possible to get.[162]

The second letter is addressed to Hugh White, governor of Mississippi at the time, and expresses fury over the court's rejection of Bradley's identification of her son's body, and thus her maternal knowledge and authority. Mrs. E.H. Johnson of Fort Worth identified herself as "a white woman, a Texan, an American and the mother of a son." She queried the governor:

> Since when did the testimony of strangers, take priority over a mother's identification of a body—a mother who bore and raised the son. Do you think if someone took my boy and beat him to a pulp and threw him in the river, that I couldn't recognize him?

Tying maternal grief to the future and social change, she stated, "Think of his mother. Think of the blot on Mississippi. ... I pray that you and others to whom I am sending copies of this letter will start a great movement to see that justice is done."[163] Two months later, a grand jury refused to indict Milan and Bryant on kidnapping charges, and they were fully exonerated.

Mamie Till Bradley drew on her grief and her rage to imagine and build a more socially just future for black children, and for black mothers as well. Similar to Gold Star Mothers who pilgrimaged to their dead sons' graves, opening her brutalized son's casket was a form of maternal care, linked to the temporal progress of racial justice and a forward-looking civil rights movement. They join other activist mothers who have drawn on love, grief, anger, and fear to reclaim maternity and try and create a world that will be safer for children.[164] Patricia Hill Collins has pointed out that the black woman—"whether blood mother, othermother, or community mother," can invoke motherhood as a symbol of power.[165] She has also argued that, despite their acute awareness of their vulnerability, black mothers find motherhood an important source of self-definition above and beyond the care and nurturance it involves. Collins considers motherhood an affirming and validating site, "where Black women express and learn the power of self-definition, the importance of valuing, and respecting ourselves, the necessity of self-reliance and independence, and a belief in Black women's empowerment."[166]

Bradley asserted her dignity and maternal self-understanding for the entire world to see. Her status in the African American community stemmed from her role as a biological mother to Emmett, but also from her function as a community othermother, who chose to politicize her son's murder in service to the community. As she wrote NAACP president Roy Wilkins: "I set out to trade the blood of my child for the betterment of my race."[167] Like the Gold Star Mothers, she connected her motherhood to her citizenship as an American, but in Bradley's case she insisted that the nation admit to its complicity with death and murder, its anti-democratic impulses. Her public motherhood helped her make sense of her son's death, and contributed to social justice. Her actions also demonstrate the radical potential of motherhood in the 1950s, an era in which historians have tended to portray mothers as apolitical.[168]

Because she violated the unwritten rule of never equating maternal grief with injustice—and in appearance and decorum called into question stereotypes about black mothers and African Americans in general—Mamie Till Bradley herself became the object of social censure and criticism.[169] In addition, Bradley broke a second cardinal rule mothers have been expected to follow: mothers are asked to abolish history, "to trample over the past and lift us out of historical time." As Rose has argued, mothers are asked to nullify "the vast reach of historical, political and social anguish," "to secure a new dawn."[170] Bradley did the opposite, claiming the importance of history, of that particular vicious moment in mid-twentieth century history in Sumner, Mississippi. Called by the vision she described, Bradley became a memory keeper and a truth teller who vowed to bear witness and preserve the past, as she looked to the emergence of a new future. She insisted that the public be allowed to view her son's body because, in her words, "I wanted people to see what hatred of a human being, just because of the color of his skin, can do." She demonstrated the closest of maternal bonds with her child, declaring that her dead son's body *was* her heart. "As I stood and looked down under the glass covering of the casket," she told an interviewer in 1956, "I said to myself over and over, 'There's my heart underneath that glass.'"[171]

The image of African American women's grief and Bradley's grief in particular serves as a counter-narrative to the dehumanization that antimaternalism can reinforce. Bradley courageously utilized her care, her sorrow, and her horror to tell the truth as she saw it, and to try and build a different future for black Americans.[172] She became an icon of black maternal mourning, one that has informed our contemporary understanding of mothers' grief as a catalyst for racial justice.[173] Her life is also an important reminder of the different standards to which white and black mothers have been held in the United States. In 2007, at age 72, the white mother Carolyn Bryant—who divorced Roy Bryant and married again, twice—told a Duke University scholar that she had fabricated the most sensational part of her testimony, her claim that Till had made physical and verbal advances on her. She also described feeling "tender sorrow" for Mamie Till Bradley (who died in 2003), especially after Carolyn Bryant [later] lost one of her own sons.[174] After a long career as a teacher in the Chicago school system, after her death Bradley was buried in Chicago's Burr Oak Cemetery where her monument optimistically reads, "Her pain united a nation."[175]

Judith Butler has connected "grievability" to precariousness, which "requires not only that a life be apprehended as a life, but also that precariousness be an aspect of what is apprehended in what is living." Precariousness requires connected lives, the understanding that we depend on others for our safety, care, and well-being. Mothers are held responsible for the precariousness of life; both in the womb, and after their children are born.

> Precariousness is coextensive with birth itself (birth is, by definition, precarious), which means that it matters whether or not this infant being survives, and that its survival is dependent on what we might call a social network of hands. Precisely because a living being may die; it is necessary to care for that being so that it may live. Only under conditions in which the loss would matter does the value of the life appear. Thus, grievability is a presupposition for the life that matters.[176]

The life that is grievable is the life that would be grieved if it were lost. Grievability can be a condition of a life's emergence and sustenance, not just sorrow at the end of a life that has been lived. The anxiety or fear that something bad will happen—fearing a calamity that will cause grief—precedes and makes possible the anxiety or fear about precarious life.[177]

Butler also argued that a public expression of grief can provide a type of political community:

> Many people think that grief is privatizing, that it returns us to a solitary situation and is, in that sense, depoliticizing. But I think it furnishes a sense of political community of a complex order, and it does this by bringing to the fore the relational ties that have implications for theorizing fundamental dependency and ethical responsibility.[178]

In this interpretation, neither the African American Gold Star Mothers who stood mute before their sons' graves nor Mamie Till Bradley who felt crushed by time and space when she viewed her son's desecrated body were alone. Instead, they belonged to a broader political community that valued relational ties, including the profound bonds between mothers and their children, and believed in the ethical commitments that an alleged democracy—the United States—ought to uphold. These black mothers foregrounded maternal love and pain for Americans to contemplate, in a culture and a time that increasingly denigrated maternal–child bonds, especially those between mothers and sons, as damaging and dangerous. African American mothers rejected the antimaternalism of the early to mid-twentieth century and instead demonstrated resilience, courage, and maternal reclamation, even as they weathered tremendous loss. Theirs was a different representation of mother love.

In connecting private, maternal grief to public and political activism, Bradley challenged the post-World War II idea of motherhood as a fundamentally private experience. To the racist southerners who lynched her son, Emmett's life was not—in Judith Butler's term—"grievable," because it was not really considered a life, one sustained by regard, testimony, or social ties. Instead, as the anonymous author of the 1943 poem "Stabat Mater" wrote, the white lynch mobs who killed black sons (and daughters) left their mothers to observe, and grieve, "the tortured, half-burnt-thing/That once had been her son." The short stories and lynching plays of the 1920s and 1930s that depicted mothers who died when their children were lynched, or those who killed their babies to save them from later racist violence, illuminated figures of rebellion. These fictional mothers rejected the ideal of the Mater Dolorosa—the sorrowing Madonna who gives up "the flesh of her flesh"—to society and the world. In doing so they scorned Western notions of motherhood and seized agency to love their children intensely.

Similar to Lange's depictions of migratory mothers, the African American mothers in this chapter resisted the idea of antimaternalism. Despite a racist culture's dehumanization of them and their children, they insisted on loving, nurturing, and caring for those children and the children in their communities. Although antimaternalism and racism were tools to justify maternal disenfranchisement, black mothers fought back: by challenging or disregarding the ideal norms completely, by linking social change to maternal grief, and by embracing their maternal power and joy. They also showed the ways that mothers in extreme situations like these might utilize and experience time: by bargaining for time; by taking control of the future through drastic acts like infanticide; and by serving as eyewitnesses and agentic keepers of memory. In claiming the importance of the past and of memory and history, black mothers could chart a new future.

It is important to note that despite experiencing maternal grief, African American mothers consider motherhood to be a collective, hopeful, joyful, and dissident enterprise. Alexis Pauline Gumbs describes mothering in the face of racist hate as revolutionary, and "some of the most subversive work in the world."[179] Certainly, Mamie Till Bradley's profession of maternal love in that Sumner courtroom was revolutionary and subversive. Poet June Jordan believed that the birth and nurturance of black children was a cause for celebration, as she stated in 1977:

> Children are the ways that the world begins again and again. If you fasten upon that concept of their promise, you will have trouble finding anything more awesome, and also anything more extraordinarily exhilarating, than the opportunity or/and obligation to nurture a child into his or her own freedom.[180]

Gumbs argues in *Revolutionary Mothering* that the radical practice of mothering can be "a key to our collective liberation." Black mothers should,

Gumbs believes, "highlight the abundance of mothering, the power of mothers and the collaboration between mothers that makes the families least affirmed by the state dangerous, powerful and necessary."[181] Pro-maternal activists like Gumbs consider raising black children to be a form of resistance, an act of love that challenges patriarchal and white-focused definitions of ideal motherhood, a queer thing.

> To name oneself "mother" in a moment where representatives of the state conscripted "Black" and "mother" into vile epithets is a queer thing. To insist on Black motherhood despite Black cultural nationalist claims to own Black women's wombs and white feminist attempts to use the maternal labor of Black women as domestic servants to buy their own freedom (and to implicitly support the use of Black women as guinea pigs in their fight to perfect the privilege of sterilization) is an almost illegible thing, an outlawed practice, a queer thing.[182]

Black women have managed, Gumbs observes, to "think about the question, concept, and project of family outside of the terms set by white supremacy and patriarchy." They have challenged the demonization and pathologization of black single mothers, who pose a threat to white supremacist male-dominated culture because they "live their lives in a way that shows that they do not need patriarchy or subservience to men."[183]

In investigating present-day bereaved black mothers and maternal activism, Lawson describes maternal grief as public motherhood, rather than as a private expression of pain. She argues "the death of a beloved compels us to find new meanings in a permanently altered reality."[184] Lawson interprets Mothers of the Movement, a group of African American women whose children have been unjustifiably and violently killed, as a contemporary illustration of public motherhood.[185] Activism helps these mourning mothers make sense of the deaths of their children and advocate for legal and social change. It is a way, Lawson argues, for grieving black mothers "to articulate their own political subjectivity for justice." Activism also helps them situate the killing of their sons and daughters within professed American ideals and structures such as democracy, capitalism, and citizenship: "the murders of their children by state agents and private citizens raise questions about how mothers attempt to reclaim the value of their children's lives and express themselves as political subjects in a deeply misogynistic, racial system of governance."[186]

Multiple scholars have argued that the afterlife of slavery still plays out in the lives of black people in the U.S. racial state. Lawson and others contend that this violent past resonates in the present, and that the maternal grief of black women includes the grief of black mothers who came before them. "Black women's grief," she writes,

> is born of a suffering that is located not just in the singularity of the deaths of their children in contemporary times, but in the larger

temporality of violent racial practices that have ensnared, and continue to ensnare, black lives.[187]

Thus, she believes that "anti-Black violence transcends a fixed temporality" and invokes what Didier Fassin has called "the trace" of historical violence and its effects on black people's subjectivities and bodies.[188] LaKisha Michelle Simmons agrees, arguing that black feminist relationality is "always in conversation with the dead and with the past. Black women understand pregnancy and infant loss within a wider relational model that collapses notions of time, space, and generation."[189] The temporal line connecting enslaved mothers to Mamie Till Bradley to the Mothers of the Movement is collapsible.

In *Pedagogies of Crossing*, M. Jacqui Alexander describes the Atlantic Crossing, when captured Caribbean and Africans were forced into fetid, overcrowded ships en route to America and lives of slavery. She describes Mojuba, a slave-trading intersection in her native Trinidad, as "an expansive memory refusing to be housed in any single place, bound by the limits of time, enclosed within the outlines of a map, encased in the physicality of body, or imprisoned as exhibit in a museum." Some grief is simply too deep to contain. As Alexander writes of that Trinidadian intersection that is stained with the horrors of the Crossing that was to come, centuries later "the scent of jostled grief [is] so thick that no passage of human time could absorb it."[190] In this reading grief stands outside of time, and in grieving, time becomes meaningless. As Alexander writes, "Power is not owned by corporate time keepers or by the logic of hegemonic materialism." The grieving and agentic African American mothers portrayed in this chapter reject "dominant corporate, linear time" which has become "existentially irrelevant." In the case of these grieving mothers who experienced great loss, "[time] ceases to have any currency at all."[191]

Notes

1 Dani McClain, "What All Parents Can Learn from Black Mothers," *The Nation*, Vol. 308, No. 10 (April 15, 2019): 14–19; see also Nicole R. Fleetwood, "Raising a Black Boy not to Be Afraid," *Literary Hub*, October 3, 2018. https://lithub.com/raising-a-black-boy-not-to-be-afraid/.
2 See Isabel Wilkerson, *The Warmth of Other Suns: The Epic Story of America's Great Migration* (New York: Random House, 2010).
3 Marian S. Harris, "Best Practices in Kinship Care for African American Mothers and Their Children," in Joyce E. Everett, Sandra P. Chipungu, and Bogart R. Leashine, eds., *Child Welfare Revisited: An Afrocentric Perspective* (New Brunswick, NJ, and London: Rutgers University Press, 2004), 158–168. See 156–158.
4 Hortense Spillers, "Mama's Baby, Papa's Maybe: An American Grammar Book," *Diacritics*, Vol. 17, No. 2 (1987): 64–81; Hazel Carby, *Reconstructing Womanhood: The Emergence of the Afro-American Woman Novelist* (New York: Oxford University Press, 1987).

5 Deborah Gray White, *Ar'n't I a Woman?: Female Slaves in the Plantation South* (New York and London: W.W. Norton & Co., 1999), 1985.
6 Barbara Christian, "An Angle of Seeing: Motherhood in Buchi Emecheta's *Joys of Motherhood* and Alice Walker's *Meridian*," in Barbara Christian, ed., *Black Feminist Criticism* (New York: Pergamon, 1985), 214.
7 Toni Morrison, *Beloved* (New York: Vintage Books, 1987, 2004), 296.
8 Patricia Hill Collins, "The Meaning of Motherhood in Black Culture and Black Mother-Daughter Relationships," *Sage: A Scholarly Journal of Black Women*, Vol. 4 (1987): 2–10. See 5.
9 Carol B. Stack, *All Our Kin: Strategies for Survival in a Black Community* (New York: Harper & Row, 1974), 83. The Flats was a fictitious name for an urban area in the Midwest.
10 Stack, *All Our Kin*, 28.
11 Harris, "Best Practices in Kinship Care," 158.
12 McClain, "What All Parents Can Learn from Black Mothers," 14. See also Dani McClain, *We Live for the We: The Political Power of Black Motherhood* (New York: Bold Type Books, 2019).
13 Hill Collins, "The Meaning of Motherhood," 5.
14 Brittney Cooper, "The Racial Politics of Time," TEDWomen, 2016, https://www.ted.com/talks/brittney_cooper_the_racial_politics_of_time.
15 Cooper, "The Racial Politics of Time."
16 Jennifer C. Nash, "The Political Life of Black Motherhood," *Feminist Studies*, Vol. 44, No. 3 (2018): 699–712. See 701. See Dorothy Roberts, *Killing the Black Body: Race, Reproduction, and the Meaning of Liberty* (New York: Pantheon Books, 1997).
17 Roberts, *Killing the Black Body*, 13.
18 See the website of the organization Sister Song: https://www.sistersong.net/reproductive-justice.
19 Ruth Feldstein, *Motherhood in Black and White: Race and Sex in American Liberalism, 1930–1960* (Ithaca, NY: Cornell University Press, 2000), 29–31; 57–60.
20 Angela Y. Davis, *Women, Race, & Class* (New York: Vintage Books, 1983); Marisa J. Fuentes, *Dispossessed Lives: Enslaved Women, Violence, and the Archive* (Philadelphia, PA: University of Pennsylvania Press, 2016).
21 Erica S. Lawson, "Bereaved Black Mothers and Maternal Activism in the Racial State," *Feminist Studies*, Vol. 44, No. 3 (2018): 713–735. See 720; Fuentes, *Dispossessed Lives*.
22 Quoted in Feldstein, *Motherhood in Black and White*, 57.
23 Robert Staples, "The Myth of the Black Matriarchy," *The Black Scholar*, Vol. 1 (1970): 3–4, 8–16. See 8.
24 Koritha Mitchell, *Living with Lynching: African American Lynching Plays, Performance, and Citizenship, 1890–1930* (Urbana, Chicago, and Springfield, IL: University of Illinois Press, 2011), 148; Kimberly Wallace-Sanders, *Mammy: A Century of Race, Gender, and Southern Memory* (Ann Arbor, MI: University of Michigan Press, 2008).
25 Rebecca Jo Plant, *Mom: The Transformation of Motherhood in Modern America* (Chicago, IL: University of Chicago Press, 2010), 13–14.
26 Quoted in Plant, *Mom*, 113.
27 Plant, *Mom*, 13; 135n46.
28 Plant, *Mom*, 14.
29 John H. Owens, "To Mother," *The Crisis*, Vol. 37, No. 5 (May 1930): 163. Edited by sociologist and civil rights activist W.E.B. Du Bois from 1910–1934, *The Crisis* is the nation's oldest African-American publication.
30 Fuentes, *Dispossessed Lives*.

31 Cheryl Rodriguez, "Mothering While Black: Feminist Thought on Maternal Loss, Mourning and Agency in the African Diaspora," *Transforming Anthropology*, Vol. 24, No. 1 (2016): 61–69. See 61.
32 Lawson, "Bereaved Black Mothers"; Temma Kaplan, *Crazy for Democracy: Women in Grassroots Movements* (New York: Routledge, 1997).
33 LaKisha Michelle Simmons, "Black Feminist Theories of Motherhood and Generation: Histories of Black Infant and Child Loss in the United States," *Signs*, Vol. 46, No. 2 (Winter 2021): 311–335.
34 Mari Jo Buhle, Teresa Murphy, and Jane Gerhard, *Women and the Making of America* (Upper Saddle River, NJ: Pearson Prentice Hall, 2009), 526. See also Christopher Waldrep, ed., *Lynching in America: A History in Documents* (New York and London: New York University Press, 2006); Amy Louise Wood, *Lynching and Spectacle: Witnessing Racial Violence in America, 1890–1940* (Chapel Hill, NC: The University of North Carolina Press, 2011).
35 "Lynching Memorial Shows Women Were Victims, Too," *The Conversation*, April 24, 2018, https://theconversation.com/lynching-memorial-shows-women-were-victims-too-95029. Downloaded April 23, 2021. Christen A. Smith, "Facing the Dragon: Black Mothering, Sequelae, and Gendered Necropolitics in the Americas," *Transforming Anthropology*, Vol. 24, No. 1 (2016): 31–48. See 42.
36 Smith, "Facing the Dragon," 34–35. See also Kimberle Crenshaw, "Mapping the Margins: Intersectionality, Identity Politics, and Violence against Women of Color," *Stanford Law Review*, Vol. 43, No. 6 (July 1991): 1241–1299.
37 An example is Wells-Barnett's 1892 speech "Southern Horrors: Lynch Law in All Its Phases." See Paula J. Giddings, *Ida: A Sword among Lions: Ida B. Wells and the Campaign against Lynching* (New York: HarperCollins, 2008).
38 "Tulsa Race Massacre," History.com, https://www.history.com/topics/roaring-twenties/tulsa-race-massacre. Updated May 26, 2021. Downloaded June 16, 2021.
39 Billie Holiday, "Strange Fruit Lyrics," Genius, https://genius.com/Billie-holiday-strange-fruit-lyrics.
40 Lopez D. Matthews, "Celebrating the Faithful Colored Mammies of the South," The National Archives Rediscovering Black History, April 4, 2013 blog. http://rediscovering-black-history.blogs.archives.gov/2013/04/04/celebrating-the-faithful-mammies-of-the-south/.
41 Quoted in Matthews, "Celebrating the Faithful Colored Mammies."
42 Tony Horwitz, "The Mammy Washington Almost Had," *The Atlantic*, May 31, 2013, http://www.theatlantic.com/national/archive/2013/05/the-mammy-washington-almost-had/276431/.
43 Jodi Vandenberg-Daves, *Modern Motherhood: An American History* (New Brunswick, NJ and London: Rutgers University Press, 2014), 43.
44 Both quoted in Vandenberg-Daves, *Modern Motherhood*, 43.
45 "Opinion of W.E.B. Du Bois," *The Crisis*, Vol. 24, No. 6 (October 1922): 247–253. Quote from 247.
46 Florence Lewis Bentley, "Two Americans," *The Crisis*, Vol. 22, No. 6 (October 1921): 250–252.
47 Robert W. Bagnall, "Lex Talionis," *The Crisis*, Vol. 23, No. 6 (April 1922): 254–258. See 257. Both "Two Americans" and "Lex Talionis" are included in Tom Pomplun and Lance Tooks, eds., *African-American Classics: Graphic Classics Vol. 22* (Mount Horeb, WI: Eureka Productions, 2011).
48 Georgia Douglass Johnson, "A Sunday Morning in the South," National Humanities Center Toolbox, The Making of African American Identity, Volume 111, 1917–1968. http://nationalhumanitiescenter.org/pds/maai3/segregation/text3/sundaymorningsouth.pdf.

49 Rodriguez, "Mothering While Black," 65.
50 Simmons, "Black Feminist Theories of Motherhood and Generation," 312.
51 Smith, "Facing the Dragon," 37, 43; Rhaisa Kameela Williams analyzes her grandmother's suicide two weeks after her daughter's murder in "Toward a Theorization of Black Maternal Grief as Analytic," *Transforming Anthropology*, Vol. 24, No. 1 (2016): 17–30.
52 Mitchell, *Living with Lynching*, 147.
53 Mitchell, *Living with Lynching*, 148–149.
54 Hannah Rosen, *Terror in the Heart of Freedom: Citizenship, Sexual Violence, and the Meaning of Race in the Postemancipation South* (Chapel Hill, NC: University of North Carolina Press, 2009), 180.
55 Mitchell, *Living with Lynching*, 148.
56 Susan Fraiman, *Extreme Domesticity: A View from the Margins* (New York: Columbia University Press, 2017), 17.
57 Evelyn Higginbotham, *Righteous Discontent: The Women's Movement in the Black Baptist Church, 1880–1920* (Cambridge, MA: Harvard University Press, 1993), 202.
58 Alice Walker, "In Search of Our Mothers' Gardens," in Angelyn Mitchell, ed., *Within the Circle: An Anthology of African American Literary Criticism from the Harlem Renaissance to the Present* (Durham, NC, and London: Duke University Press, 1994), 401–409.
59 bell hooks, "Homeplace (a Site of Resistance)," in *Yearning: Race, Gender, and Cultural Politics* (Boston, MA: South End Press, 1990), 41–49. See 42.
60 hooks, "Homeplace," 47.
61 Feldstein, *Motherhood in Black and White*, 2.
62 Mitchell, *Living with Lynching*, 2. Lynching plays are considered historically relevant today as they resonate for modern audiences. See Jill Radsken, "In Anti-Lynching Plays, a Coiled Power," *The Harvard Gazette*, May 23, 2016; "Deaths of Unarmed Black Men Revive Anti-Lynching Plays," *NPR Codeswitch*, April 17, 2015.
63 Kathy A. Perkins and Judith L. Stephens, eds., *Strange Fruit: Plays on Lynching by American Women* (Bloomington, IN: Indiana University Press, 1998), 4.
64 Mitchell, *Living with Lynching*, 32.
65 Mitchell, *Living with Lynching*, 148–149.
66 Mitchell, *Living with Lynching*, 151.
67 Mitchell, *Living with Lynching*, 151.
68 *Safe* did not appear in print until 1990. In contrast, the Krigwa Players of Washington, D.C. performed another of Johnson's lynching plays, *Blue Blood*, in1927. It was published in 1928 in Frank Shay's *Fifty More Contemporary One-Act Plays*. Mitchell, *Living with Lynching*, 222–223, n10.
69 Mitchell, *Living with Lynching*, 161. See also Phillip Dray, *"At the Hands of Persons Unknown": The Lynching of Black America* (New York: Random House, 2002). Seeing the murdered Hosea's knuckles turned W.E.B. Du Bois into an anti-lynching activist.
70 Georgia Douglas Johnson, *Safe*, in Elizabeth Brown-Guillory, ed., *Wines in the Wilderness: Plays by African American Women from the Harlem Renaissance to the Present* (New York, Westport, CT and London: Greenwood Press, 1990), 26-32. See 27-28; see also Mitchell, *Living with Lynching*, 162.
71 On race as a caste system, see Isabel Wilkerson, *Caste: The Origins of Our Discontent* (New York: Random House, 2020).
72 When African American George Floyd was killed on Memorial Day 2020 in Minneapolis by a white police officer that knelt on his neck for nearly nine minutes, in his final moments he called out for his dead mother. Floyd's death, along with the deaths of other black Americans killed by police violence,

inspired Black Lives Matter, a national racial justice movement. Johnson, "Safe," in Brown-Guillory, ed., *Wines in the Wilderness*, 28-30.
73 Johnson, *Safe*, in Brown-Guillory, ed., *Wines in the Wilderness*, 30.
74 Johnson, *Safe*, and Mitchell, *Living with Lynching*, 163. Morrison, *Beloved*.
75 Johnson, *Safe*, in Brown-Guillory, ed., *Wines in the Wilderness*, 30.
76 Jacqueline Rose, *Mothers: An Essay on Love and Cruelty* (New York: Farrar, Straus and Giroux, 2018), 92.
77 Rodriguez, "Mothering While Black," 66.
78 Lisa Dawkins, "From Madonna to Medea: Maternal Infanticide in African American Women's Literature of the Harlem Renaissance," *Literature Interpretation Theory* 15 (2004): 223–240. See 223.
79 Dawkins, "From Madonna to Medea," 223, 226.
80 Dawkins, "From Madonna to Medea," 226.
81 See Dawkins, "From Madonna to Medea."
82 "The Mother," *The Crisis*, Vol. 46, No. 4 (April 1939), 120. On Richmond Barthe see Steven Orfinoski, *African Americans in the Visual Arts* (New York: Facts on File Books, 2003), 15–16.
83 Julia Kristeva and Arthur Goldhammer, "Stabat Mater," *Poetics Today*, Vol. 6, No. ½ (1985): 133–152. See 135.
84 Kristeva and Goldhammer, "Stabat Mater," 139.
85 Kristeva and Goldhammer, "Stabat Mater," 141.
86 Fanny Soderback, "Motherhood According to Kristeva: On Time and Matter in Plato and Kristeva," *philoSOPHIA: A Journal of Continental Feminism*, Vol. 1, No. 1 (2011): 65–87. See 85.
87 This is an abridged version of the Latin hymn. For the full transcription into English of the hymn, see https://www.preces-latinae.org/thesaurus/BVM/SMDolorosa.html.
88 Rose, *Mothers*, 12.
89 Gloria Clyne, "Stabat Mater," *The Crisis*, Vol. 50, No. 5 (May 1943): 153.
90 Rodriguez, "Mothering While Black," 62; Simmons, "Black Feminist Theories of Motherhood and Generation."
91 Rodriguez, "Mothering While Black," 65.
92 Jennifer C. Nash, "Black Maternal Aesthetics," *Theory & Event*, Vol. 22, No. 3 (July 2019): 551–575. See 555.
93 Dana-Ain Davis, "'The Bone Collectors' Comments for Sorrow as Artifact: Black Radical Mothering in Times of Terror," *Transforming Anthropology*, Vol. 24, No. 1 (2016): 8–16.
94 Gloster B. Current, "Martyr for a Cause," *The Crisis*, Vol. 59, No. 2 (February 1952): 73–81+. The assassination of the Moores made front-page news around the world. United Nations delegates discussed it, including U.S. representative Eleanor Roosevelt who warned: "The harm it will do us among the people of the world is untold." See "Harry T. Moore-Mims, Florida—Research," DeLaura Junior High School Multicultural Project, 12/25/95, downloaded February 10, 2016. http://www.nbbd.com/godo/moore/research/delaura9512.html.
95 Jennifer C. Nash, "The Political Life of Black Motherhood," *Feminist Studies*, Vol. 44, No. 3 (2018): 699–712. See 700.
96 *The Crisis*, Vol. 59, No. 2 (February 1952), 72.
97 Dora Apel, *Imagery of Lynching: Black Men, White Women, and the Mob* (New Brunswick, NJ, and London: Rutgers University Press), 89–90. The editors of *The Crisis* reprinted the cartoon in the January 1935 issue.
98 Karla F.C. Holloway, *Passed On: African American Mourning Stories* (Durham, NC: Duke University Press, 2002), 26.
99 Quoted in Holloway, *Passed On*, 27–28. See also James Van Der Zee, Owen Dodson, and Camille Billops, *The Harlem Book of the Dead* (New York: Morgan & Morgan, 1978).

144 *Reclaiming Maternity*

100 Mia Tramz, "Death in Harlem: James VanDerZee's Funerary Portraits," *Time*, February 25, 2014. http://time.com/3807384/death-in-harlem-james-vanderzees-funerary-portraits/ Tramz termed Van Der Zee "the custodian of memory."
101 Van Der Zee et al., *The Harlem Book of the Dead*, 83.
102 Holloway, *Passed On*, 140.
103 Quoted in Jose E. Munoz, "Photographies of Mourning: Melancholia and Ambivalence in Van Der Zee, Mapplethorpe, and *Looking for Langston*," in Harry Stecopoulos and Michael Ulebel, eds., *Race and the Subject of Masculinities* (Durham, NC, and London: Duke University Press, 1997), 337–360.
104 Holloway, *Passed On*, 139.
105 Cooper, "The Racial Politics of Time."
106 Holloway, *Passed On*, 28.
107 Holloway, *Passed On*, 139.
108 Henry Dewitt, ed., *Sorrow's Company: Writers on Loss and Grief* (Boston, MA: Beacon Press, 2001), VIII.
109 M. Jacqui Alexander, *Pedagogies of Crossing: Meditations on Feminism, Sexual Politics, Memory, and the Sacred* (Durham, NC, and London: Duke University Press, 2005).
110 Kurt Piehler, from Script, "Gold Star Mothers: Pilgrimage of Remembrance WILL-TV," PBS Documentary, 2003.
111 Lisa Budreau, "The Politics of Remembrance: The Gold Star Mothers' Pilgrimage and America's Fading Memory of the Great War," *The Journal of Military History*, Vol. 72, No. 2 (April 2008): 371–411. See 372. See also John W. Graham, "History of Gold Star Mothers' Pilgrimages," https://www.memorialdayfoundation.org/education-and-history/gold-star-mothers.html.
112 Rebecca Plant, from Script, "Gold Star Mothers."
113 Graham, "History of Gold Star Mothers' Pilgrimages," While President, Donald Trump inadvertently drew attention to contemporary Gold Star Fathers, in Trump's criticism of Khizr Khan, father of a Muslim soldier who died at war. But in the early twentieth century, it was Gold Star Mothers who were front and center in the American public eye. Maggie Haberman and Richard A. Oppel, Jr., "Donald Trump Criticizes Muslim Family of Slain U.S. Soldier, Drawing Ire," *New York Times*, July 30, 2016.
114 Graham, "History of Gold Star Mothers' Pilgrimages."
115 Both quotes from Script, "Gold Star Mothers."
116 Lisa Budreau, from Script, "Gold Star Mothers."
117 Budreau, "The Politics of Remembrance," 400.
118 Budreau, "The Politics of Remembrance," 401.
119 Holly S. Fenelon, *That Knock at the Door: The History of Gold Star Mothers in America* (Bloomington, IN: iUniverse, Inc., 2012), 90–91.
120 Barbara Ransby is quoted in Script, "Gold Star Mothers."
121 Wikipedia, "Charles Young (United States Army Officer)," downloaded August 25, 2020.
122 Colonel Charles Young, "A Negro-Mother's Cradle-Song," *The Crisis*, Vol. 26, No. 6 (October 1923), 272.
123 Budreau, "The Politics of Remembrance," 374, 404.
124 Budreau, "The Politics of Remembrance," 405.
125 Budreau, "The Politics of Remembrance," 405.
126 Vandenberg-Daves, *Modern Motherhood*, 17–18; Linda Kerber, "The Republican Mother: Women and the Enlightenment—An American Perspective," *American Quarterly*, Vol. 28, No. 2 (Summer 1976): 187–205.
127 Lawson, "Bereaved Black Mothers," 715.

128 Lawson, "Bereaved Black Mothers," 715.
129 Budreau, "The Politics of Remembrance," 409.
130 Bart Ziino, "'A Lasting Gift to His Descendants': Family Memory and the Great War in Australia," *History & Memory*, Vol. 22, No. 2 (2010): 125–145. See 139.
131 Ziino, "A Lasting Gift," 127.
132 In 2018 the Equal Justice Initiative (EJI) opened the National Memorial for Peace and Justice in Montgomery, Alabama: it is the first museum in the United States dedicated to the victims of American white supremacy. The Memorial includes descriptions and representations of the lynching of American blacks, including jars of soil from the documented lynching sites. Campbell Robertson, "A Lynching Memorial is Opening. The Country Has Never Seen Anything Like It," *The New York Times*, April 25, 2018.
133 U.S. Representative John Bell Williams, a Mississippi Democrat, coined the term "Black Monday" on the floor of Congress to denote the date of the Supreme Court decision. Wikipedia, "Black Monday," downloaded August 26, 2021. One Mississippi local told investigative journalist William Bradford Huie: "They shouldn't have killed him. They should have striped him, told him to get the hell back Up Yonder. But they shouldn't have killed him. And they wouldn't have killed him except for Black Monday. The Supreme Court of the United States is responsible for the murder of Emmett Till." William Bradford Huie, From *Wolf Whistle and Other Stories* (1959) in Christopher Metress, ed., *The Lynching of Emmett Till: A Documentary Narrative* (Charlottesville, VA, and London: University of Virginia Press, 2002), 235–247. Quote from 241.
134 Feldstein, *Motherhood in Black and White*, 87, 4.
135 Ruth Feldstein, "'I Wanted the Whole World to See': Race, Gender, and Construction of Motherhood in the Death of Emmett Till," in Rima D. Apple and Janet Golden, eds., *Mothers & Motherhood: Readings in American History* (Columbus, OH: Ohio State University Press, 1997), 131–170. See 133.
136 Murray Kempton, "The Future," *New York Post*, September 23, 1955, in Metress, ed., *The Lynching of Emmett Till*, 84–87. See 86.
137 Feldstein, "'I Wanted the Whole World to See,'" 266.
138 Mattie Smith Collin, "Mother's Tears Greet Son Who Died a Martyr," *Chicago Defender*, September 10, 1955, in Metress, ed., *The Lynching of Emmett Till*, 29–30. See 29.
139 Mamie Till Bradley, as told to Ethel Payne, "From Mamie Bradley's Untold Story," *Chicago Defender*, April–June, 1956 in Metress, ed., *The Lynching of Emmett Till*, 226–235. See 232–233.
140 Metress, ed., *The Lynching of Emmett Till*, 31; Feldstein, "I Wanted the Whole World to See," 271.
141 Carl Hirsch, "50,000 Mourn at Bier of Lynched Negro Child," *Daily Worker*, September 10, 1955. Reprinted in Metress, ed., *The Lynching of Emmett Till*, 31–34. See 32.
142 See Metress, ed., *The Lynching of Emmett Till*, 44.
143 Ralph Hutto, "Mother, 'Surprise Witness,' Gives Dramatic Testimony: Mamie Bradley Says Corpse was that of Her Slain Son," [part 1], *Jackson State Times*, September 22, 1955. Reprinted in Metress, ed., *The Lynching of Emmett Till*, 79–83. See 81.
144 Quoted in Feldstein, "I Wanted the Whole World to See," 146.
145 Feldstein, "I Wanted the Whole World to See," 148.
146 "L'affaire Till in the French Press," *The Crisis*, Vol. 62, No. 10 (December 1955), 596–602. See 600.

146   *Reclaiming Maternity*

147 Quoted in Jerry Thomas and Tribune Staff Writer, "Emmett's Legacy," *Chicago Tribune*, September 5, 1995.
148 Metress, ed., The *Lynching of Emmett Till*, 99.
149 "Called Lynch-Murder, 'Morally, Legally' Wrong," *Cleveland Call and Post*, October 1, 1955, in Metress, ed., *The Lynching of Emmett Till*, 101–104. See 103.
150 Murray Kempton, "2 Face Trial as 'Whistle' Kidnapers [sic]—Due to Post Bond and Go Home," *New York Post*, September 25, 1955, in Metress, ed., *The Lynching of Emmett Till*, 107–111. See 110.
151 John N. Pophamspecial, "Mississippi Jury Acquits 2 Accused in Youth's Killing," *New York Times*, September 24, 1955, 1.
152 Kempton, "2 Face Trial." See 109–110.
153 Feldstein, "I Wanted the Whole World to See," 148.
154 Metress, *The Lynching of Emmett Till*, 152.
155 Feldstein, "I Wanted the Whole World to See," 145.
156 Dan Wakefield, "Justice in Sumner," *The Nation*, October 1, 1955, in Metress, ed., The Lynching, 120–124. See 121.
157 Murray Kempton, "The Future," *New York Post*, September 23, 1955, in Metress, ed., *The Lynching of Emmett Till*, 84–87. See 84.
158 "The Shame of Our Nation," *Daily Worker*, September 26, 1955, in Metress, ed., *The Lynching of Emmett Till*, 118–119. See 118.
159 From "Mamie Bradley's Untold Story," Mamie Till Bradley as told to Ethel Payne, *Chicago Defender*, April–June 1956, in Metress, ed., *The Lynching of Emmett Till*, 226–235. See 227.
160 Feldstein, "I Wanted the Whole World to See," 154.
161 "Inside You and Me," *The Crisis*, Vol. 62, No. 10 (December 1955), 592–595.
162 "Inside You and Me."
163 "Inside You and Me."
164 Lawson, "Bereaved Black Mothers"; Rodriguez, "Mothering While Black."
165 Collins, "The Meaning of Motherhood," 6.
166 Quoted in Rodriguez, "Mothering While Black," 64.
167 Quoted in Feldstein, "I Wanted the Whole World to See," 153.
168 Feldstein, "'I Wanted the Whole World to See.'"
169 Feldstein, "'I Wanted the Whole World to See.'"
170 Rose, *Mothers*, 188.
171 "From Mamie Bradley's Untold Story," in Metress, ed., *The Lynching of Emmett Till*, see 227.
172 In 2005, the Emmett Till Memorial Commission, comprising a multi-racial group of citizens in Sumner, Mississippi, opened the Emmett Till Interpretive Center. Their website states that the Center exists to tell the story of the Emmett Till tragedy and to point a way toward racial healing. https://www.emmett-till.org/history. In 2018, the Emmett Till murder trial was reopened, more than 60 years after Till's death. The Department of Justice said it had reopened the case based on "new information" received. Jennie Jarvie, "The Emmett Till Case is Reopened Nearly 63 Years after the Teen's Killing Spotlighted Racial Violence," *Los Angeles Times*, July 12, 2018. In 2022, 66 years after Till's murder, the U.S. Senate finally and unanimously approved a bill that would make lynching a federal hate crime. The bill carries the name of Emmett Till. Since 1900, when North Carolina Representative George Henry White first introduced legislation to make lynching a hate crime in 1990 (the House never voted upon it), more than 200 bills like it have been filed. Emily Cochrane, "Congress Gives Final Approval to Make Lynching a Hate Crime," *The New York Times*, March 7, 2022.

173 Williams, "Toward a Theorization of Black Maternal Grief," 21.
174 Sheila Weller, "How Author Timothy Tyson Found the Woman at the Center of the Emmett Till Case," *Vanity Fair*, January 26, 2017, downloaded April 26, 2021.
175 Wikipedia, "Mamie Till," https://en.wikipedia.org/wiki/Mamie_Till, downloaded April 27, 2021.
176 Judith Butler, *Frames of War: When Is Life Grievable?* (New York and London: Verso, 2009), 14.
177 Butler, *Frames of War*, 14–15.
178 Cited in Lawson, "Bereaved Black Mothers," 713. Judith Butler, *Precarious Life: The Powers of Mourning and Violence* (London and New York: Verso, 2004).
179 Alexis Pauline Gumbs, "m/other Ourselves: A Black Queer Feminist Genealogy for Radical Mothering," in Gumbs et al., *Revolutionary Mothering*, 19–31. See 20.
180 June Jordan, "The Creative Spirit: Children's Literature," in Alexis Pauline Gumbs, China Martens, and Mai'a Williams, eds., *Revolutionary Mothering: Love on the Front Lines* (Oakland, CA: PM Press, 2016), 11–18. See 12–13.
181 Gumbs, " m/other Ourselves," 30–-31.
182 Gumbs, "m/other Ourselves," 21.
183 Gumbs, "m/other Ourselves," 29–30.
184 Lawson, "Bereaved Black Mothers," 713.
185 Lawson, "Bereaved Black Mothers," 713, 714.
186 Lawson, "Bereaved Black Mothers," 715, 718.
187 Lawson, "Bereaved Black Mothers," 716.
188 Lawson, "Bereaved Black Mothers," 717, 721; Didier Fassin, "The Trace: Violence, Truth, and the Politics of the Body," *Social Research: An International Quarterly*, Vol. 78, No. 2 (July 2011): 281–298.
189 Simmons, "Black Feminist Theories of Motherhood and Generation," 319.
190 M. Jacqui Alexander, *Pedagogies of Crossing: Meditations on Feminism, Sexual Politics, Memory, and the Sacred* (Durham, NC: Duke University Press, 2006), 288.
191 Alexander, *Pedagogies of Crossing*, 7.

Reference List

Alexander, M. Jacqui. *Pedagogies of Crossing: Meditations on Feminism, Sexual Politics, Memory, and the Sacred*. Durham, NC and London: Duke University Press, 2005.

Bagnall, Robert W. "Lex Talionis." *The Crisis*, Vol. 23, No. 6 (April 1922): 254–258.

Bentley, Florence Lewis. "Two Americans." *The Crisis*, Vol. 22, No. 6 (October 1921): 250–252.

Budreau, Lisa. "The Politics of Remembrance: The Gold Star Mothers' Pilgrimage and America's Fading Memory of the Great War." *The Journal of Military History*, Vol. 72, No. 2 (April 2008): 371–411.

Buhle, Mari Jo, Teresa Murphy, and Jane Gerhard. *Women and the Making of America*. Upper Saddle River, NJ: Pearson Prentice Hall, 2009.

Butler, Judith. *Frames of War: When is Life Grievable?* New York and London: Verso, 2009.

Carby, Hazel. *Reconstructing Womanhood: The Emergence of the Afro-American Woman Novelist*. New York: Oxford University Press, 1987.

Christian, Barbara. "An Angle of Seeing: Motherhood in Buchi Emecheta's *Joys of Motherhood* and Alice Walker's *Meridian*." In Barbara Christian, ed., *Black Feminist Criticism*. New York: Pergamon, 1985, 211–252.

Clyne, Gloria. "Stabat Mater." *The Crisis*, Vol. 50, No. 5 (May 1943): 153.

Collins, Patricia Hill. "The Meaning of Motherhood in Black Culture and Black Mother-Daughter Relationships." *Sage: A Scholarly Journal of Black Women*, Vol. 4 (1987): 2–10.

Cooper, Brittney. "The Racial Politics of Time." *TEDWomen*, 2016. https://www.ted.com/talks/brittney_cooper_the_racial_politics_of_time.

Davis, Angela Y. *Women, Race, & Class*. New York: Vintage Books, 1983.

Davis, Dana-Ain. ""The Bone Collectors" Comments for Sorrow as Artifact: Black Radical Mothering in Times of Terror." *Transforming Anthropology*, Vol. 24, No. 1 (2016): 8–16.

Dawkins, Lisa. "From Madonna to Medea: Maternal Infanticide in African American Women's Literature of the Harlem Renaissance." *Literature Interpretation Theory* 15 (2004): 223–240.

Dewitt, Henry, ed. *Sorrow's Company: Writers on Loss and Grief*. Boston, MA: Beacon Press, 2001.

Du Bois, W.E.B. "Opinion of W.E.B. DuBois." *The Crisis*, Vol. 24, No. 6 (October 1922): 247–253.

Feldstein, Ruth. ""I Wanted the Whole World to See": Race, Gender, and Construction of Motherhood in the Death of Emmett Till." In Rima D. Apple and Janet Golden, eds., *Mothers & Motherhood: Readings in American History*. Columbus, OH: Ohio State University Press, 1997, 131–170.

Feldstein, Ruth. *Motherhood in Black and White: Race and Sex in American Liberalism, 1930–1965*. Ithaca, NY: Cornell University Press, 2000.

Fraiman, Susan. *Extreme Domesticity: A View from the Margins*. New York: Columbia University Press, 2017.

Fuentes, Marisa J. *Dispossessed Lives: Enslaved Women, Violence, and the Archive*. Philadelphia, PA: University of Pennsylvania Press, 2016.

Graham, John W. "History of Gold Star Mothers' Pilgrimages." *The Memorial Day Foundation*. https://www.memorialdayfoundation.org/education-and-history/gold-star-mothers.html.

Gumbs, Alexis Pauline. "m/other ourselves: A Black queer feminist genealogy for radical mothering." In Alexis Pauline Gumbs, China Martens, and Mai'a Williams, eds., *Revolutionary Mothering*. Oakland, CA: PM Press, 2016, 19–31.

Harris, Marian S. "Best Practices in Kinship Care for African American Mothers and Their Children." In Joyce E. Everett, Sandra P. Chipungu, and Bogart R. Leashine, eds., *Child Welfare Revisited: An Afrocentric Perspective*. New Brunswick, NJ, and London: Rutgers University Press, 2004, 158–168.

Higgenbotham, Evelyn. *Righteous Discontent: The Women's Movement in the Black Baptist Church, 1880–1920*. Cambridge, MA: Harvard University Press, 1993.

Holloway, Karla F.C. *Passed On: African American Mourning Stories*. Durham, NC: Duke University Press, 2002.

hooks, bell. "Homeplace (a Site of Resistance)." In *Yearning: Race, Gender, and Cultural Politics*. Boston, MA: South End Press, 1990, 41–49.

Horwitz, Tony. "The Mammy Washington Almost Had," *The Atlantic*, May 31, 2013.

"Inside You and Me," *The Crisis*, December 1955, 592–595.

Johnson, Georgia Douglass. "Safe." In Elizabeth Brown-Guillory, ed., *Wines in the Wilderness: Plays by African American Women from the Harlem Renaissance to the Present*. New York, Westport, CT and London: Greenwood Press, 1990, 26–32.

Jordan, June. "The Creative Spirit: Children's Literature." In Alexis Pauline Gumbs, China Martens, and Mai'a Williams, eds., *Revolutionary Mothering: Love on the Front Lines*. Oakland, CA: PM Press, 2016, 11–18.

Kristeva, Julia and Arthur Goldhammer. "Stabat Mater." *Poetics Today*, Vol. 6, No. ½, The Female Body in Western Culture: Semiotic Perspectives (1985): 133–152.

Lawson, Erica S. "Bereaved Black Mothers and Maternal Activism in the Racial State." *Feminist Studies*, Vol. 44, No. 3 (2018): 713–735.

"Lynching Memorial Shows Women Were Victims, Too." *The Conversation*, April 24, 2018. https://theconversation.com/lynching-memorial-shows-women-were-victims-too-95029.

Matthews, Lopez D. "Celebrating the Faithful Colored Mammies of the South." The National Archives Rediscovering Black History, April 4, 2013 blog. http://rediscovering-black-history.blogs.archives.gov/2013/04/04/celebrating-the-faithful-mammies-of-the-south/.

McClain, Dani. "What All Parents Can Learn from Black Mothers." *The Nation*, Vol. 308, No. 10 (April 15, 2019): 14–19.

Metress, Christopher, ed. *The Lynching of Emmett Till: A Documentary Narrative*. Charlottesville, VA and London: University of Virginia Press, 2002.

Mitchell, Koritha. *Living with Lynching: African American Lynching Plays, Performance, and Citizenship, 1890–1930*. Urbana, Chicago and Springfield, IL: University of Illinois Press, 2011.

Morrison, Toni. *Beloved*. New York: Vintage Books, 1987, 2004.

Munoz, Jose E. "Photographies of Mourning: Melancholia and Ambivalence in Van Der Zee, Mapplethorpe, and *Looking for Langston*." In Harry Stecopoulos and Michael Ulebel, eds., *Race and the Subject of Masculinities*. Durham, NC and London: Duke University Press, 1997, 337–360.

Nash, Jennifer C. "The Political Life of Black Motherhood." *Feminist Studies*, Vol. 44, No. 3 (2018): 699–712.

Nash, Jennifer C. "Black Maternal Aesthetics." *Theory & Event*, Vol. 22, No. 3 (July 2019): 551–575.

Owens, John H. "To Mother." *The Crisis, The Crisis*, Vol. 37, No. 5 (May 1930): 163.

Perkins, Kathy A. and Judith L. Stephens, eds. *Strange Fruit: Plays on Lynching by American Women*. Bloomington, IN: Indiana University Press, 1998.

Piehler, Kurt. From Script, "Gold Star Mothers: Pilgrimage of Remembrance WILL-TV." PSB Documentary, 2003.

Plant, Rebecca Jo. *Mom: The Transformation of Motherhood in Modern America*. Chicago, IL: The University of Chicago Press, 2010.

Rodriguez, Cheryl. "Mothering While Black: Feminist Thought on Maternal Loss, Mourning and Agency in the African Diaspora." *Transforming Anthropology*, Vol. 24, No. 1 (2016): 61–69.

Roberts, Dorothy. *Killing the Black Body: Race, Reproduction, and the Meaning of Liberty*. New York: Vintage Books, 1997, 2016.

Rose, Jacqueline. *Mothers: An Essay on Love and Cruelty*. New York: Farrar, Straus and Giroux, 2018.

Simmons, LaKisha Michelle. "Black Feminist Theories of Motherhood and Generation: Histories of Black Infant and Child Loss in the United States." *Signs*, Vol. 46, No. 2 (Winter 2021): 311–335.

Smith, Christen A. "Facing the Dragon: Black Mothering, Sequelae, and Gendered Necropolitics in the Americas." *Transforming Anthropology*, Vol. 24, No. 1 (2016): 31–48.

Soderback, Fanny. "Motherhood According to Kristeva: On Time and Matter in Plato and Kristeva." *philoSOPHIA: A Journal of Continental Feminism*, Vol. 1, No. 1 (2011): 65–87.

Spillers, Hortense. "Mama's Baby, Papa's Maybe: An American Grammar Book." *Diacritics*, Vol. 17, No. 2 (1987): 64–81.

Stack, Carol B. *All Our Kin: Strategies for Survival in a Black Community*. New York: Harper & Row, 1974.

Staples, Robert Staples. "The Myth of the Black Matriarchy." *The Black Scholar*, Vol. 1 (1970): 3–4, 8–16.

The National Association for the Advancement of Colored People (NAACP). *The Crisis*, The Crisis Publishing Co., Inc., 1920–1960 Archives.

Tramz, Mia. "Death in Harlem: James VanDerZee's Funerary Portraits." *Time*, February 25, 2014.

Vandenberg-Daves, Jodi. *Modern Motherhood: An American History*. New Brunswick, NJ and London: Rutgers University Press, 2014.

Walker, Alice. "In Search of Our Mothers' Gardens." In Angelyn Mitchell, ed., *Within the Circle: An Anthology of African American Literary Criticism from the Harlem Renaissance to the Present*. Durham, NC, and London: Duke University Press, 1994, 401–409.

Weller, Sheila. "How Author Timothy Tyson Found the Woman at the Center of the Emmett Till Case." *Vanity Fair*, January 26, 2017.

White, Deborah Gray. *Ar'n't I a Woman?: Female Slaves in the Plantation South*. New York and London: W. W. Norton & Co., 1999, 1985.

Williams, Rhaisa Kameela. "Toward a Theorization of Black Maternal Grief as Analytic." *Transforming Anthropology*, Vol. 24, No. 1 (2016): 17–30.

Young, Colonel Charles. "A Negro-Mother's Cradle-Song." *The Crisis*, Vol. 26, No. 6 (October 1923): 272.

Ziino, Bart. ""A Lasting Gift to His Descendants": Family Memory and the Great War in Australia." *History & Memory*, Vol. 22, No. 2 (2010): 125–145.

4 Herself
Irish American Catholic Mothers, Maternal Power, and Antimaternalism

Jacqueline Rose has argued that motherhood is the place in Western culture where we lodge, or bury, the reality of our own conflicts, of what it means to be truly human. "It is the ultimate scapegoat for our personal and political failings," she writes, "for everything that is wrong with the world, which it becomes the task—unrealisable, of course—of mothers to repair." She asks her readers to consider what the consequence of this might be for us, but more importantly for mothers, of whom we ask the impossible:

> [w]hy are mothers so often held accountable for the ills of the world, the breakdown in the social fabric, the threat to welfare, to the health of the nation…Why are mothers seen as the cause of everything that doesn't work in who we are?

she asks. Mother blaming could, Rose suggests, deflect from our awareness of human responsibility for the world. Like Adrienne Rich, she argues that it is the very *dependence* of human life on the mother that makes the mother figure so threatening; furthermore, motherhood is disconcerting because of its proximity to death, not only because of the physical dangers of childbirth but because it reminds us of our mortality: "the fact of being born can act as an uncanny reminder that once upon a time you were not here, and one day you will be no more."[1] We make mothers responsible not only for the tribulations of the world but also for the rage that the inevitable disappointments of an individual life incite.

The way this blame plays out, and the degree of maternal criticism and attack, depends upon the race, class, religion, sexuality, location, and ethnicity of the mother, as well as the historical moment. White, patriarchal, native-born Americans have scapegoated and otherized immigrant mothers, ethnic mothers, and working-class mothers in the past, and continue to do so today. As we have seen, dominant American culture has dehumanized and sidelined certain groups, and mothers in those groups, to justify the undemocratic treatment they receive(d). In this chapter I turn to consider the ways that White Anglo-Saxon Protestant (WASP) culture, along with

DOI: 10.4324/9781003334712-5

strands of Irish American culture, deployed antimaternalism as a weapon against Irish American Catholic mothers.

White Protestant Americans viewed both white Irish immigrants and African Americans as threats to American ideals, as "foreigners" whom they stereotyped as poor, undisciplined, animal-like, and disordered. The Nursery and Child's Hospital, in operation in New York City from 1854 to 1910, considered Irish women, like black women, to be strong, "lustful," naturally fertile, impervious to pain, and oblivious to privacy.[2] When the Protestant white elite hired Irish wet-nurses to breastfeed their babies, their belief in the racial inferiority of the Irish made them associate Irish wet-nurses with the animal, making them fit producers of human milk, and differentiating them from their more civilized employers, who claimed the status of moral mothers.[3] Irish Americans harbored fears about the emasculation of Irish American Catholic men (parallel to black men, de-masculinized because of slavery), which put pressure on both groups of women to hold men up and mask their own struggles and strengths. Like African Americans, Irish Americans too had a legacy of loss that included a tragic history in Ireland of brutal colonization and starvation, the trauma of leaving home, and social exclusion in the new country. Native-born whites condemned both groups of mothers in the 1920–1960 decades as unfit, and as matriarchs who damaged husbands and were responsible for a host of social ills. Although Irish American Catholic mothers did not face the same threat of violence and maternal loss that black mothers did, they too struggled to support their families in a hostile social climate, and were judged and subjected to increasing demands and expectations. Like African American women, Irish American Catholic women played a critical role in the financial survival and upward mobility of their families. Like the rural and African American mothers of previous chapters, Irish American Catholic mothers did not have access to time as a commodity because of antimaternalism. Ultimately their whiteness and changing economic circumstances made their assimilation into middle-class American society more possible than the other two groups.

In this chapter I consider the ways that xenophobia and ethnic and religious bias constructed the Irish American Catholic mother as "other" to the motherhood ideal, as well as Irish American dissemination of antimaternalism. I trace this by first considering white Protestant bias toward the Irish in general, then examining the lives and challenges of Irish American Catholic mothers in these years. I analyze how Catholicism constructed the "good mother" and conclude by interpreting antimaternalist writings by Irish American Catholic male writers James Farrell and Andrew Greeley. I begin by briefly outlining the history of the racialization of the Irish in the United States.

Irish Catholic immigrants were, from the start, racialized in America. Their tragic history in Ireland informed their racialization in their new country. The greatest of Irish tragedies occurred in the 1840s, when the subsistence crop, the potato, failed. The devastation began in the fall of 1845 when a fungus decimated the crop over one-third of Ireland. The following summer, the crop was destroyed throughout the country. In 1847, famine and disease were endemic, and 1848 marked the nadir: blight destroyed the entire potato crop. From that year on, emigration became a feasible, often inevitable alternative to life on the land at home in Ireland. To compound the tragedy, the British government responded tepidly, continuing to export grain and livestock from Anglo-Irish estates to England. One million Irish died of starvation and related diseases, and over 1.6 million emigrated to the United States in the first ten years after what came to be known simply as "the Famine." Between 1840 and 1900 the population of Ireland plunged from nine to six and a half million. The pattern of emigration continued throughout the century, with half a million people leaving Ireland every ten years up to World War I.[4] As David Eng and Shinhee Han have eloquently described, the experience of immigration is constructed on a structure of mourning: "[w]hen one leaves one country of origin—voluntarily or involuntarily—one must mourn a host of losses both concrete and abstract," Eng writes. "These include homeland, family, language, identity, property, status in community—the list goes on." Assimilation into the new country poses another kind of loss or mourning: "[t]he process of assimilation," Eng and Han note, "is a negotiation between mourning and melancholia." In psychoanalytic terms that negotiation includes conflict and trauma and sadness, connected to the loss of "home" but also driven by the history of social exclusions connected to immigration, assimilation, and racialization.[5]

Some suggest that the racialization of the Irish began in the eighteenth and nineteenth centuries and was driven by the idea of a "missing link" between ape and Anglo-Saxon. This representation increased with the rise of the Fenian movement in Ireland and the United States, which supported independence from British rule. Historians have also drawn parallels with the arrival in 1860 of the first chimpanzees and gorillas in London.[6] These portrayals were linked to racist depictions of black Americans; native-born whites characterized "Celts" and blacks with "wild look and childish manner, barbarity and violence, rampant sexuality, lack of control and intelligence, superstition, tribal organization, and immoral character."[7] A quote from British historian Edward A. Freeman in an 1881 letter reveals a paired hatred of the Irish and African Americans: "This [the United States] would be a grand land," he wrote, "if only every Irishman would kill a Negro, and be hanged for it."[8]

Beginning with the first wave of famine emigrants, the dominant Anglo-Saxon culture referred to Irish Catholics as a "race," with some historians even suggesting that the Celts had originated in Africa. Xenophobes described the Irish as "low-browed and savage, growling and bestial, lazy and wild, simian and sensual."[9] Most historians argue that the defamation of the Irish arose after the Famine, when British colonizers sought to justify their failure to save millions of starving Irish, which some have linked to genocide.

> So, [the British] depicted the Irish as drunken, violent, lazy animals. Surely, no one would want to give money or food to that kind of people. Cartoonists of the day depicted the Irish as apes with turned-up noses and animal-like pointed ears. ... a symptom of untreated syphilis (it denotes to the view that clearly the Irish were immoral). Most often they had a bottle of whiskey sticking out of their pocket and a gun in their hand. The association of the Irish with apes in caricature was carried across the Atlantic and American cartoonists such as Thomas Nast drew the Irish as ... out of control violent guerillas.[10]

Some scholars have connected the question of whiteness, or not-whiteness, to the Irish, arguing that historically the Irish in America have occupied an ambivalent position between white and black. In *How the Irish Became White*, Noel Ignatiev noted how in the early years of Irish immigration the white, Protestant, native-born elite blurred the racial identities of Irish immigrants and blacks: "Irish were frequently referred to as 'niggers turned inside out'; the Negroes, for their part, were sometimes called 'smoked Irish.'"[11] Sarah Heinz has described Irish American identities as "Not White, Not Quite," and characterized perceptions of the Irish as oscillating between whiteness and otherness. Native-born white Protestant Americans considered Irish Catholics to be from the lower, uneducated classes and influenced by a foreign religion that kept them subject, childlike, and primitive. Individuals who compared Irish and African Americans were not only those who emphasized the undesirable characteristics of each group; opponents of Irish colonization or African slavery also made the association, in order to highlight the similar injustices both groups suffered.[12] Andrew Greeley has argued that every accusation made against African Americans was also made against the Irish:

> Their family life was inferior, they had no ambition, they did not keep up their homes, they drank too much, they were not responsible, they had no morals, it was not safe to walk through their neighborhoods at night, they voted the way crooked politicians told them to vote, they were not willing to pull themselves up by their bootstraps, they were not capable of education, they could not think for themselves, and they would always remain social problems for the rest of the country.[13]

In his now-classic text *White*, Richard Dyer argued that cultural critics and scholars, assuming whiteness as the norm, had failed to examine it. "As long as race is something only applied to non-white people, as long as white people are not racially seen and named," Dyer wrote, "they/we function as a human norm. Other people are raced, we are just people."[14] This idea of whiteness as the human norm then conceptualizes non-white skin as dirty, or as "a deviation, degeneration, or genetic aberration."[15] Non-white skin, as we have seen, is also connected to temporal chaos, or temporal disobedience: "The black skin of the other is linked to savagery, barbarism, backwardness, and emotionality. It is therefore linked to an irrevocable inferiority. In contrast, the white skin of the self signalizes rationality and intelligence, and therefore superiority and supremacy."[16] White, Protestant Americans considered the Irish, like Americans of color, to be temporally disobedient or impaired, which affected the social exclusions and ethnic stereotyping the Irish faced in their new country. All of these negative characterizations affected the ways that WASPS viewed, and stereotyped, Irish Catholic women and mothers.

White, Anglo-Saxon Protestant Bias toward the Irish

Once in the United States, the Irish had to contend with nativism and anti-Catholic bias. America is a historically Protestant country, and initially Irish Catholic immigrants—including women and mothers—faced difficulties trying to assimilate. Nativists in the United States internalized British ideas that the Irish were "feminine, emotional, lazy, improvident, and dependent [in contrast to the British who were] masculine, rational, industrious, thrifty with resources and committed to individual freedom."[17]

White Protestant Americans viewed the Irish as uncivilized, undomesticated, frivolous with time, and undisciplined. Even the transcendentalist writers of the mid-nineteenth century were prejudiced against the Irish in America. Although he optimistically believed the newcomers could "construct a new race, a new religion, a new state, a new literature" to match Europe, Ralph Waldo Emerson also wrote, in his essay "Fate":

> The German and the Irish millions, like the Negro, have a great deal of guano in their destiny. They are ferried over the Atlantic and carried over America, to ditch and to drudge, to make corn cheap, and then to lie down prematurely to make a spot of green on the prairie.[18]

Thoreau was less charitable: "The culture of an Irishman is an enterprise to be undertaken with a sort of moral bog hoe," he wrote in *Walden*. He described one John Field, "an honest, hard-working but shiftless man," and continued,

> poor John Field! … thinking to live by some derivative old country mode in this new country … with his horizon all his own, yet he is a poor man, born to be poor, with his inherited Irish poverty or poor life, his Adam's grandmother and boggy ways, not to rise in this world, he nor his posterity, till their wading webbed bog-trotting feet get *talerin* [wings] to their heels.

Like stereotyped views about black Americans and time, Thoreau's interpretation of the Irish in the United States linked them to the past, to the unchanging bog—which famously preserves things in their current state indefinitely—not to the future, or to the kind of innovation or prosperity that he believed America represented. The colonized Irish were "born to be poor," and even though the Irish in America had left the colonizer behind, Thoreau believed they still "lived by some derivative old country mode in this new country." *The Atlantic* editor William Dean Howells described the Irish as inherently disordered and intemperate with money, expressing surprise that an Irish wife could keep a tidy home: "If Mrs. Clannahan, lady of an Irish cabin, can show a kitchen so capably appointed and so neatly kept," he wrote, "the Country may yet be an inch or two from the brink of ruin, and the race which we trust as little as we love may turn out no more spendthrift than most heirs."[19] Here thrift, cleanliness, and domesticity are considered positive traits that might redeem these immigrants whom native-born white Protestants "trust"[ed] as little as [they] loved."

Leaders in the woman suffrage movement were anti-immigrant, and anti-Irish. Lucy Stone protested in 1850: "The meanest foreigner who comes to our shores, who can not speak his mother-tongue correctly, has secured for him the right of suffrage."[20] Elizabeth Cady Stanton notoriously condemned the granting of suffrage to immigrant men she considered ignorant—"Patrick and Sambo and Hans and Ung Tung"—while native-born, refined white women were denied the vote.[21]

American politicians, policy makers, and cultural commentators have long rendered immigrants as less than human, dirty, and criminal. Martin Manalansan has explained the genealogy of this disdain:

> In various times in history, immigrants have been portrayed as animals, unruly subhumans, or diseased, sex-crazed criminals. While people might see the overt, flagrant demonizing of immigrants today as something new, people on the move and other itinerant strangers have always been met with suspicion or derision.[22]

This suspicion includes assumptions about immigrants' understanding and use of time. Much as white nativist critics had constructed Irish American men in negative ways, xenophobes condemned Irish women for breaking American cultural codes about time's essential connection to productivity, and the importance of measuring, tracking, and quantifying time. Nativists typecast Irish women in America—lumped together as Bridgets—as slovenly and vulgar, and cast them as symbols of disorder, inefficiency, and a careless use of time.[23] Despite WASP culture's efforts to portray Irish immigrant women and mothers as animal-like and disordered, their labor, sacrifices, and leadership in the family helped Irish Americans survive, and build a future for themselves in the United States.

Irish Women in the United States

The story of Irish women's immigration to America is a unique one in the history of immigration. Seven hundred thousand young, mostly unmarried women, traveling alone, emigrated from Ireland between 1885 and 1920, many headed for the United States. This large, continuous migration of unmarried women is an anomaly in the history of European emigration.[24] European emigrant men, including Jewish, Italian, Scandinavian, and those hailing from the other British Isles, customarily outnumbered women, and if women emigrated, they were part of a family migration. In contrast, Irish emigrant women left Ireland because demographic and economic changes in Irish life in the half-century before 1880 made their chances of becoming wives—and consequently adults with economic and social status—slim. To avoid becoming celibate dependents on family farms, more and more Irish women emigrated. Historian James Connolly noted women's lack of legal or familial protection in Ireland, describing laws written by men that "shut them out of all hope of inheritance in their native land" while at the same time their male relatives exploited Irish women's labor and "returned them never a penny as reward."[25] As late as 1921, females aged 15 to 24 made up 41.8 percent of the total Irish emigration in that year.[26] Historians have interpreted their emigration as a feminist act: "In view of Irish women's increasingly restricted lives," Janet Nolan concluded, "their decision to emigrate becomes a remarkable example of female self-determination." Emigration might prove a welcome route out of dependency into independence: Irish women immigrants viewed themselves as entrants rather than exiles, seeking opportunity as independent "sisters" rather than dependent "daughters."[27] Thus, a dispossessed generation of women sought control over their own destinies by seeking new lives abroad.

Despite how emigrant Irish women saw themselves, once in the United States, Irish Americans conceived of women's roles in strict terms of duty. Single women were expected to work, to be "young women out in the world," and the married woman's role was to be a mother.[28] As Maureen Waters described the message she received from the nuns in her New York City Catholic elementary school in the 1940s:

> There was no talk of professional careers beyond teaching or nursing. They didn't press us to enter the convent—that was a matter of grace, a rare thing. Most of us were expected to become wives and the mothers of large families; there was perhaps more emphasis on the latter vocation.[29]

The Irish and Catholic establishment attached great importance to women's sexual morality and to ensuring that Irish women would continue to be "suitable" mothers for the next generation of Irish Catholic children.[30] Irish opposed to the massive emigration of women grew concerned that those who would have made the best mothers and wives were departing, leaving at home in Ireland "the timid, the stupid, and the dull to help in the deterioration of the race and to breed sons as sluggish as themselves."[31] Catherine Nash has argued that concern over Irish women's emigration was (and is) constructed in terms of the reproduction and continuance of the Irish "race": thus projecting both ideas of racial pride and racial fears onto the female body.[32]

Twentieth-century Protestant Americans, including white reformers and childhood advocates, conflated immigrant and African American mothers, viewing both as a threat to American ideals. For example, white social worker Margaret Quilliard teamed up with African American pediatrician Alonzo deGrate Smith to create the Inter-Community Child Study Committee in 1929. Quilliard linked African American race and culture with "foreignness" and believed that educating (proselytizing to) the next generation was the best way to ensure their successful assimilation. She wrote in a 1930 letter:

> I feel the foreign born groups and the Negroes both present situations which hold many potential difficulties for the American people if they are not handled wisely. I know of no better way to establish relationships between the ideals which we are trying to work out in America today and the foreign born and Negro groups than through the medium of child study activities.[33]

As noted in Chapter 2, adherence to clock time in child rearing became a gauge for determining the assimilation of immigrant (and black) mothers in the early twentieth century. Educating immigrant and mothers of color in "American" child-rearing norms was one way to address the social problems they represented.

Yet, scholarship suggests that Irish American wives and mothers took control of their own lives and children, often working outside of the home, cleverly managing their money, and frequently serving as the sole financial support of their families.[34] Along with African American women, Irish women dominated domestic service in the United States from the early nineteenth century to the 1920s, which sharply affected their lives and the ways that native-born whites depicted them. In these years, Irish immigrant women held nearly 15 percent of domestic service jobs nationally and up to 50 percent of such positions in urban centers with large Irish populations.[35] The cultural representations of the Irish "Bridget" and her comparison to the Black Mammy both shaped and reflected white, Anglo Protestant views on race. Historians have written about the circulation of similar representations of the two groups of women: in April Schultz's words, "cultural arbiters characterized [the Irish Bridgets] with a physiognomy that put them in much closer proximity to those Americans of African descent."[36] These traveling representations resonated forward and influenced American stereotypes about Irish American women, and mothers, in the twentieth century.

Middle-class white Protestants depicted Irish domestics in insulting and classist ways. In their 1869 *American Woman's Home*, the Beecher sisters, Catharine and Harriet Beecher Stowe, portrayed Irish domestics as brawny, dim-witted, and physically slow, thoroughly unfit to keep an orderly, well-run American home. While the Beechers admired "the Old New-England motto, 'get your work done in the forenoon,'" in their estimation Irish servants toiled from dawn to dusk to complete the amount of work a native-born Protestant could efficiently finish in a morning.[37] The Beechers shared the story of a New England "lady" in dire need of a servant. Desperate, she sent away to a distant city, receiving

> a raw Irish maid-of-all-work, a creature of immense bone and muscle, but of heavy, unawakened brain. In one fortnight she established such a reign of chaos and Old Night[38] in the kitchen and through the house that she made more work each day than she performed, and [the lady] dismissed her. "At her wit's end," the "lady" found a "tall, well-dressed, un-obtrusive, self-respecting" neighboring farmer's daughter and hired her: "In a single day the slatternly and littered kitchen assumed that neat, orderly appearance that so often strikes one in New England farmhouses."[39]

This classist and ethnocentric description sets up a contrast between Irish Catholic immigrant women (raw, immense, heavy, chaotic) and native-born white Protestant daughters (neat, orderly, efficient, light). In this interpretation, Irish Catholic immigrant women were careless and disordered, impaired in their understanding and use of time. The Beechers expressed surprise that given the preponderance of Irish women in domestic service, who represented "the raw, untrained Irish peasantry, all the unreasoning heats and prejudices of the Celtic blood, [and] all the necessary ignorance and rawness, there should be the measure of comfort and success there is in our domestic arrangements."[40] The overuse of the adjective "raw" to describe the working-class Irish immigrant is striking. Raw can mean inexperienced or new, coarse or crude, unpolished, passionate, and evokes images of not-whiteness, or ambivalence between white and black, or dirtiness.[41] If the self always needs an other to define itself, Native Anglo Protestants represented Irish Catholic domestics as their inferiors and temporal opposites.

Because domestic service was a racially stigmatized occupation rooted in slavery, the women who worked as domestics were marked as racially inferior, underserving of adequate wages and labor protections. Danielle Phillips-Cunningham has traced the parallels in the labor histories of Irish women and black domestics in the United States. She has shown the ways that Irish domestics, like black domestics, were considered inferior beings.[42] Phillips-Cunningham has argued that both Irish immigrant and Southern black migrant women used slavery as a metaphor to confront labor exploitation of women from the Irish immigrant and black communities, in order to oppose and redefine gendered class and racial hierarchies. She believes that Irish immigrant and southern black migrant women were organic and strategic thinkers on the subject of race, migration, and labor, an intellectual labor often attributed to men.[43]

According to April Schultz, depictions of Irish American domestic servants grew particularly nasty by the end of the nineteenth century. Portrayed in cartoons and fiction in publications like *Puck* and *Godey's Ladies Book*, Anglo-American artists and writers ridiculed the Irish urban poor through references to dirt, ignorance, child abuse, drunkenness, and violence. Irish American female domestics were depicted as apelike, stealing from their employers and aiding Irish revolutionaries. They were blamed for their poverty, marked as "ethnic," and categorized as working class. Schultz has argued that the highest point of these nativist images coincided with the peak of Irish women's domination of domestic service, and was the historical moment when second-generation Irish Americans were beginning to enter the middle class.[44] Still, as late as 1920, Irish-born women made up 43 percent of white, female, foreign-born domestics in the United States.[45]

In addition to the social exclusions they faced as immigrants hoping to assimilate, the young Irish women who made the journey alone and worked for American families as live-in servants were often lonely, and longed for home. Transatlantic letters between Irish servants and their families in Ireland illustrate close ties, and lives that were still partially rooted in Ireland. Irish servant Sarah Brady, who immigrated in 1912, said that "she used to write continually" to her family in Ireland. Helen Flatley, who immigrated in 1928 said, "I wrote, I wrote a lot," and recalled that from Ireland in return came "such lovely, lovely letters from my mother and she wrote to me all the time. And then when my other sister came out, Peggy, she wrote to both of us." Photographs were exchanged, newspaper clippings sent, shamrocks tucked into letters sent from Ireland to daughters and sisters in America, especially around Saint Patrick's Day. Irish American young women who were domestic servants confessed their homesickness in their letters. From Elmira, New York, domestic Hannah Collins wrote to Nora McCarthy, who was in service in Massachusetts, "I had an awful dream about you the other night … [I]t was in this country but after a little while we were back again to dear Ballinlough … I could not get that sweet place off my mind."[46] Immigrant Irish women sent remittances home to Ireland to help the families they had left behind. Irish American immigrants, the majority of them female, sent approximately $260 million back to Ireland in the years between 1850 and 1900, which funded emigration and preserved many families from starvation.[47]

Irish American women assuaged their loneliness by establishing social lives in the United States, which gave them opportunities to meet other young people, including prospective husbands. Some scholars have argued that many farmers' daughters emigrated from Ireland in hope of finding husbands, especially in the immediate post-Famine decades, when in many parts of Ireland, females far outnumbered males.[48] Thursday nights were the domestics' nights out, and Irish dances—often sponsored by ladies' county organizations—were an important part of the social lives of Irish young women who worked in domestic service. The Irish dance hall scene was especially animated in New York City in the 1920s and 1930s. Ann Kelly described immigrating to New York in 1925 and enjoying "our country dance, you know you go and you meet all the people from home with you and have like a reunion." Mary Feely remembered, after arriving in the United States in 1927, going to a dance hall in New York, which "was fun" and "was packed for years with all the Irish girls who came there." Helen Flatley, who left Ireland in 1928, also recalled the dances: "In New York at that time, there would be ... maybe ten or twelve dances in different parts of the city ... [T]hat's another place that you would [meet] people you knew in Ireland." Flatley remembered these social gatherings fondly: "The dances were wonderful," she continued. "Our greatest joy because when you're young ... you love to dance."[49]

Despite their efforts to recreate Irish community in the United States, the structure of mourning that immigration entails, the sadness of losing "home" and nation, and the traumatic losses that Catholics had experienced in Ireland left their mark on their psyches as American immigrants. Irish-born parents passed on to their children the pain of colonialism that they had experienced. Labor activist Elizabeth Gurley Flynn wrote of her childhood in New Hampshire and the South Bronx at the end of the nineteenth century: "The awareness of being Irish came to us as small children, through plaintive song and heroic story. ... As children, we drew in a burning hatred of British rule with our mother's milk."[50] Novelist James Farrell described in 1962 the ways that tragic Irish history had resonated for him:

> I am a second-generation Irish-American. The effects and scars of immigration are upon my life. The past was dragging through my boyhood and adolescence. Horatio Alger, Jr., died only seven years before I was born. The "climate of opinion" ... was one of hope. But for an Irish boy born in Chicago in 1904, the past was a tragedy of his people, locked behind *The Silence of History*.[51]

Similarly, in her memoir about growing up in the 1940s and 1950s in an Irish-Catholic household in the Bronx, Maureen Waters recalled that the sorrowful stories her parents told her and her sister "made a deep impression on us as children, linked us firmly to the old country."

> We were made aware of the perilousness of that old life. Gaiety would shift suddenly into sadness. Ireland was never simply the land of Shamrocks or leprechauns or a memory celebrated on St. Patrick's Day. Too many had died, too many were disappointed. The hard fight for

independence, the bitter aftermath of civil war, did not bring prosperity. Emigration went on. The old family home ... collapsed in ruin.[52]

Thus, like the black community, the Irish American community also experienced intergenerational trauma that affected their emotions as well as their understanding of their own placement in their culture, and in history.

Catholicism and the Motherhood Ideal

Because of this tragic history the Catholic Church, along with Irish American culture, sought to bolster men's masculinity and temper the authority of women, especially mothers. In the years before Ireland's Great Famine, Irish women had had considerable family authority as wage earners and influential decision makers.[53] Some pre-1920 depictions of Irish mothers suggested they wielded a great deal of power over their children, as well as social importance. In 1910, Irish writer and nationalist G.W. Russell stated,

> The mother moulds the character of the generations as they pass. She gives the child its heart ... [I]n these great matters of character moulding and education in its true sense women have much more to do with in life than men have, and the whole realm of society or social intercourse is theirs to rule and govern.

In 1913, novelist Nora Tynan O'Mahony compared the honor and reverence Ireland bestowed upon mothers with that reserved for church leaders: "A mother's influence, a mother's dignity, is very sacred and holy; hardly less so, ... than that of the priesthood itself."[54]

Yet, at the same time the Church believed that mothers had undue influence over children and the family, and that fathers should assume a greater role in child-rearing. In this vein Catholic culture not only urged men to marry, but to be active participants and leaders in home life, as well as hands-on fathers. Catholic journalist Maurice Egan described in 1889 a "wretched and utterly vile tradition" found more commonly "among people of Irish birth and descent than among others," which stipulated that "children should be brought up principally by their mothers." This practice, Egan concluded, "works well with animals but not among men." The manly father was not only to help his wife, but also to exert "kind and strong rule [to] keep his children in the path of duty." The true man did not relinquish the power of child-rearing to the mother: church representatives urged the Irish American male to "not leave to the mother of your children the great and holy work of the preservation of purity in their souls."[55]

The motherhood ideal—often conceptualized and disseminated by men—was very much alive for Irish American Catholic mothers in the 1920–1960 years, but was impossible to realize. Abigail Palko observes the ways that maternal ideals and reality diverged:

In the decades following [Irish] independence, the literary depictions of good mothering were written by men and bore little resemblance to the realities under which women undertook actual mothering; the result was that often the ideal that was promulgated as the only acceptable way to mother was in fact an unattainable ideal.[56]

Catholicism exerted significant influence in maintaining this motherhood ideal, ensuring that maternity was viewed as the essence of womanhood.[57] In post-independence Ireland, both the church and the state idealized married, desexualized, at-home motherhood. The 1937 Constitution—which drew on Papal Encyclicals[58]— enshrined this philosophy by formally recognizing a woman's "life within the home," but also by using the terms "woman" and "mother" interchangeably.[59] Article 41.2.2 of the new Constitution directed: "The State shall ... endeavor to ensure that mothers shall not be obliged by economic necessity to engage in labour to the neglect of their duties in the home."[60]

Married women and mothers, then, were expected to concentrate on a restricted, married domesticity. Yet in the year the new Constitution was written, census figures show that over 54 percent of the female working population in Ireland were engaged in agriculture or domestic service.[61] Thus the Church and State ideal, which also traveled to America, was only available to a particular class of mothers.

Nonetheless the Catholic Church considered religious life and married motherhood as two ideal expressions of femaleness. As Yvonne McKenna observed, "Dominant discourses of Irish womanhood tended to idealize traits such as demureness, piety, self-sacrifice, and devotion to others ... qualities intrinsic both to the archetypal Irish mother and the nun."[62] Catholics associated motherhood with purity, asexuality, and self-denying devotion to others—similar to nineteenth century conceptions of motherhood and white, middle-class womanhood in the United States.[63] The Catholic Church, both in Ireland and the United States, celebrated motherhood by endorsing large families and highlighting women's loyalty and faith. The Irish Catholic community used the term "Irish twins" to connote closely spaced pregnancies and the prevalence of children being born in near proximity to one another.[64]

The Church modeled good Catholic mothers on the Virgin Mary who was "pious, pure, self-sacrificing, patient, and submissive to authority."[65] Irish Catholics have been strongly devoted to Mary, who symbolizes an impossible ideal: a virgin birth, uncomplaining maternal grief, along with patient understanding, and forgiveness.[66] The Church has equated Mary's sorrow with the suffering of all mothers, and seized upon her as a model of married motherhood, the ideal state for women.[67] In the Church's interpretation, children—particularly sons—especially sinned when they disobeyed Irish customs and hurt a deeply caring mother. Irish priests linked the strong maternal figure of Mary to confession, thus mingling Irish penitential guilt with the mother:

A sinner should avoid temptation not only because of Christ's agony on the cross, but also because of Mary's sorrows by her son's side. And so, part of one's penance after confession was usually the recital of several prayers known as "Hail Mary's."[68]

The Virgin Mary figure has overlapped with the Mother Ireland motifs, diminishing women from being individuals with their own identities to being representations of the homeland and the Church.[69]

What did it mean to be Catholic in the early to mid-twentieth century United States? Just as in Ireland, the Catholic Church served as a principal cultural force and national unifier of the Irish in the United States.[70] According to sociologist Andrew Greeley, Catholicism meant going to church, receiving the sacraments, and passing the faith on to one's children. The parish priest was an important figure in the Catholic neighborhood, and defining oneself as Catholic was a way of distinguishing oneself from the English (and American) Protestants. Catholics often said the rosary, fasted at Lent, and went to confession to atone for their sins. Friendship patterns in Irish American communities were largely with people in the parish.[71] Parochial schools provided social and cultural Catholic training to children. Anglo-Americans critiqued the Catholic Church as foreign, hierarchical, and thus not easily adapted for American democracy.[72] Catholics in the United States faced anti-Catholicism, potent in the 1920s and slowly declining in the decades after, with World War II bringing more religious tolerance. The 1960 election of Irish American Catholic John F. Kennedy symbolized a degree of Catholic social acceptance.[73]

Irish American Catholics were also marked by their home country's tumultuous history of colonization and rebellion, which affected the ways native-born Protestants viewed them. By 1916 many Irish were disenchanted with England and Ireland's involvement in World War I. On Easter Monday 1916 a force of 1,500 Irish Volunteers and Citizen Army members—led by Patrick Pearse, James Connolly, and Thomas Clarke—seized the center of Dublin and declared the creation of an Irish republic. The six-day rebellion ended in British executions of Pearse, Connolly, and other participants (as traitors in times of war), and the government sent over 2,000 nationalists to English prisons. When the militants were released in 1917, they returned as martyrs, and the nationalist party Sinn Fein in 1918 elections captured nearly all of Southern Ireland.[74]

The victorious Sinn Fein candidates refused to go to Westminster and gathered in Dublin, where they formed a parliament and began to rule Ireland in the name of the republic announced by Pearse on Easter Monday. Michael Collins, who emerged as a leading figure in the republic, melded the Irish Republican Brotherhood (IRB), a secret fraternal organization dedicated to Irish independence, and the Irish Volunteers into a new fighting force, the Irish Republican Army (IRA). Although efforts were made to win Irish independence at the Versailles peace conference after World War I, they were unsuccessful. From 1919 until 1921 the IRA waged guerilla warfare with the British army. By 1921, both sides were ready for peace talks, and in December representatives signed a treaty which established the Irish Free State, making Southern Ireland no longer a colony of England, but self-governing. Only 26 of Ireland's counties were included; the other predominantly Protestant six counties, all in Ulster, remained part of the United Kingdom, but with their own parliament to legislate local matters. Unhappy about the partition of the country, the IRA split between pro-and anti-treaty forces, and from June 1922 to May 1923 Ireland was convulsed by civil war.[75] As Irish feminist writers have noted, the quest for independence involved the invoking of idealized images of Mother Ireland as motivation for the political battle.[76]

Both the Easter Rising and the Irish civil war affected Americans' views about the Irish, and Irish Americans' freedom to voice Irish nationalism and pride. In addition, native-born Americans were increasingly concerned about immigrants whose loyalties allegedly remained with their countries of birth. President Woodrow Wilson's notorious "hyphenated Americans" speech, which he gave at the 1914 unveiling of a memorial to Irish-born hero of the American Revolution Commodore John Barry, praised Barry as "an Irishman whose heart crossed the Atlantic with him." In contrast, some Americans "need hyphens in their names because only part of them has come over." Wilson questioned the loyalty and patriotism of immigrants, suspecting that Irish Americans, German Americans, Italian Americans, Chinese Americans, "any man who carries a hyphen about with him ... carries a dagger that he is ready to plunge into the vitals of the republic."[77]

Anti-immigration legislation like the 1924 Johnson-Reed Act, which established small and decreasing permanent quotas for immigrant entry into the United States, fostered an anti-immigrant climate.[78] As nativism and anti-Catholicism rose during the post-World War I years, leaders of Irish ethnic-based organizations like the Ancient Order of Hibernians (AOH) found themselves, along with American blacks, targets for racist organizations like the Ku Klux Klan (KKK). In Columbus, Ohio, in 1920 the AOH placed an article in *The Catholic Columbian* protesting the nomination of Georgia's Tom Watson—described as a force for white supremacy and anti-Catholic rhetoric—for U.S. Senate. "The indications are," the author wrote, "that another wave of anti-Catholic feeling is about due." At the 1924 St. Patrick's Day celebration in Youngstown, Ohio, the Klan lit crosses and around midnight a near riot broke out downtown between the Irish and Klan members.[79] The previous year, at the fifty-third AOH national convention, the organization had resolved to fight the KKK. By 1930, three times as many Irish were emigrating to England as to America; on average, only 1,200 Irish emigrated to the United States yearly in the 1930s, a striking decline.

The Power of Irish American Catholic Mothers

Despite their country's tumultuous history and the xenophobia they faced, Irish American mothers focused on ensuring their children's and family's survival and success in the United States. Sources on the actual lives and experiences of Irish American Catholic mothers are quite limited. Joe Lee describes the absence of mothers in the historiography of Irish emigration: "The study of parenthood in general, and of motherhood in particular, the most consuming role in the life of the majority of women in the diaspora during the century, remains astoundingly neglected."[80] One way in to the lives of Irish Catholic immigrant mothers in the United States is through geographically specific studies of Irish Americans that historians have conducted. For example, Irish American women in the copper smelting town of Anaconda, Montana, which had a sizable Irish population, offer insights into the actual lives of Irishwomen in the United States in the late nineteenth through mid-twentieth centuries. Most young, single Irish women in Anaconda worked as domestic servants, and older women, especially widows, frequently rented rooms in their homes or ran boardinghouses. Irish Catholics discouraged intermarriage; as one local second-generation woman recalled, marrying a non-Irish Catholic American "was a real taboo."[81] Not until World War II and the 1940s did the Irish-Catholic community in this area accept marrying outside of ethnicity and religion.

Irish American mothers in Anaconda were hardworking, trying to contribute to the family economy while raising large broods of children. Like the itinerant rural mothers of Chapter 2, these working-class women found ways to help families survive. Their enterprises ranged from renting rooms, taking in laundry, raising chickens, and gardening, to managing their children's labor both inside and outside the home. Irish married women often handled family finances, thus gaining some economic and decision-making power. Irish women tended to become widows at younger ages than women in other ethnic groups. Anaconda smelter workers, mostly male, often died young from consumption, caused by breathing arsenic, sulfur, and other industrial poisons in the copper mining plants.[82]

Often left alone with children to support, widows had to take any work they could find to make ends meet. One Anaconda Irish American widow, Mary McNelis, lost two husbands during the 1920s. A midwife, she was not always able to care for her two sons and periodically placed them in St. Joseph's Orphanage in Helena. In an interview, her son recalled that his mother's work kept her away from home a week at a time or more:

> [She'd] cook and wash and take care of the woman who had the baby ... and no matter how big the family was, that was it. Sometimes she'd walk in when there'd be seven or eight kids, and she'd take care of them all and see some off to school and change the [diapers] on the babies.[83]

An early twentieth-century parallel to the twenty-first century practice of immigrant mothers from the developing world leaving their own children to care for the children of more affluent First World women, this hardworking mother knew little rest.[84] Another Anaconda Irish American mother widowed in the 1920s cleaned houses until she received her husband's $2,000 life insurance policy, which allowed her to open a store. Her daughter recalled this industrious mother:

> she started up and she never looked back. ... and you know she was a young woman ... and opened that store when the shift [street] car went down at 6:00 in the morning and closed it when the last one came up at 11:20 at night, that's the kind of hours [she worked].[85]

Like other women in the United States in the 1930s, Irish American women in Montana faced labor discrimination, especially if they were married. Beginning in the 1920s, Anaconda employers refused to hire married women as salesclerks or stenographers. Not until the 1940s, when married women took advantage (and were needed) in war-related employment, did Anaconda Irish American women leave behind domestic and service work for white-collar jobs as saleswomen, secretaries, or even in professional positions.[86]

Historians have found a similar pattern in other locations: hardworking Irish American immigrant mothers who displayed tenacity and personal competence in keeping their families together, and caring for their children.[87] Patricia Kelleher's study of Irish female-headed households in Gilded Age Chicago uncovered maternal strategies that mixed self-reliance with assistance from kin and institutions. Kelleher has made a convincing case that historians have overemphasized deserting and dying Irishmen, and that the reasons for marital dissolution among Irish immigrants were complex. Whatever the reasons, she has concluded that Irishwomen have been disproportionately likely to raise their own families, and that late nineteenth-century Irish mothers in Chicago often had to make "torturous choices" in response to marital disruption.[88] These painful choices at times required mothers to separate, either temporarily or permanently, from their children. Institutionalization and "placing out" of children of single Irish mothers was a real threat in late nineteenth-century Chicago. Most cases like these required the surrendering of parental custody rights. Poor single mothers thus went to great lengths to avoid destitution and to keep their children with them.[89]

Other documents including oral histories point to the reverse emigration of young Irish Catholic children—children removed from one family and inserted into another—if, for example, their mothers died in the United States and their fathers sent them home to family in Ireland to care for them.[90] Some of these separations were temporary, but children still paid a price for such arrangements, as parents undoubtedly did as well. Irish

Catholic immigrant Joan Dolan recalled that in 1939 her mother moved her from New York City, where Joan was born, back to Ireland to live with her grandparents and her uncle. "For some reason, when I was two," she stated in a 2006 oral history, "my mom brought me back to Ireland to visit her mother and to leave me for a while. It was not an uncommon thing. I've spoken with many people who were in this position." While she was living with her grandparents in Ireland, the United States joined World War II, and, she reflected, "it became very dangerous to bring people back. You just couldn't do it. So I was there, I was left there."

Joan grew up on a small farm in Killarue, Ireland, until 1948, when her parents returned to Ireland hoping to resettle but could not find work. Ireland was expensive after the war so they decided to return to the United States. This Irish American mother retrieved her daughter when the war was over, and she believed the family had enough money to relocate to Ireland. When that proved impossible, she and her husband brought their young daughter back to the United States with them.[91] Joan Dolan recalled a difficult reunion: "So now I'm coming back with a mother and father that I don't even know. It was quite an adjustment." Although her father had kept his job at Brooklyn's Jack Frost Sugar Company, the family had given up their apartment and for the first year shared an apartment on 56th Street with another family—a mother, daughter, and granddaughter. The Dolans made do in one bedroom in the apartment for a year. Eventually Joan Dolan's mother found the family their own apartment on Third Avenue and 76th Street—the elevated train stopped at their door, at their window. It was a world apart from the rural Ireland Joan Dolan had left behind. She had a hard time fitting in at the Catholic high school she eventually attended on New York's Upper East Side. But her life improved immensely when her mother introduced her to the world of Irish music and Irish step dancing in New York City in the 1940s and 1950s.[92]

In some situations where mothers died, Irish immigrant fathers were forced to bring up children themselves, or turn to unmarried sisters or second wives for help. In a 2008 oral history, Sergeant Edward Burns described his mother Molly's life growing up in the South Bronx in the 1940s, as the first American-born child of an Irish immigrant family.[93] Molly's mother died after giving birth to Molly's younger brother; her father was a "sandhog," a laborer who worked digging the Lincoln and Holland tunnels.[94] After years of excessive drinking, her father returned to Ireland without the children to bring home a new wife to raise them.

As these family histories reveal, the real lives of working-class Irish Americans often contradicted the Church's narrow vision of gender roles.[95] Irish American Catholic women were proficient and independent as mothers, wives, and widows, which proved threatening to those concerned with bolstering Irish men's masculinity, and maintaining patriarchy. Margaret Lynch-Brennan has argued that Irish women acquired authority through motherhood, were considered to be the heart of the family, and exhibited power in their roles as mothers: "[i]t was often Irish mothers, rather than fathers," she wrote, "who controlled the family purse, commanded the children, and made decisions regarding the children's education."[96] With fathers often absent, Irish mothers were responsible for childcare, fiscal oversight, decision making, and emotional support. Historian Laurie Mercier described Irish mothers as agentic figures who took their family obligations seriously: thus "they often asserted leadership, authority, and autonomy, hardly the passive figures church imagery projected."[97] Irish American Catholic writer Mary Gordon recalled her Irish grandmother, mother to nine, as "a tall, strong tree, an oak, imposing, something to be leaned on, taking nourishment from deep, deep roots." She elaborated:

> An immigrant, sent over by herself from Ireland at seventeen, and then never a moment's rest, never a moment free of the anxiety of feeding, clothing, sheltering all those children, who were born, with regularity, every two years, then nursed until the next one came, and the husband, "an artist," not even Irish but Sicilian, a scandal to marry, but she had courage for that: oh, she had courage, she could face anything.[98]

Angela Sheehan McCourt, the indomitable Mam in Frank McCourt's acclaimed memoir of growing up wrenchingly poor in an Irish family in Brooklyn and Limerick, Ireland, in the 1930s and 1940s, gave birth to seven children, lost three as infants, and survived her husband's alcoholism and desertion (along with poverty, squalor, and hunger) to raise her four surviving sons.[99]

Not surprisingly, scholars have judged the Irish American female-headed household as "disorganized." Classic 1940s texts like Oscar Handlin's *Boston's Immigrants, 1790–1880: A Study in Acculturation* (1941) and Robert Ernst's *Immigrant Life in New York City, 1825–1863* (1949) described disturbing Irish family dynamics not so far removed from mid-nineteenth century Anglo Protestant nativist images of the Irish. These pointed to heavy drinking, high mortality rates, overcrowded households, and reliance on public assistance in Irish families.[100] By the late 1970s, scholars emphasized the prevalence of Irish female-headed households, and blamed "the fragility of Irish family life" on men. Like Daniel Patrick Moynihan's *The Negro Family: The Case for National Action* (1965) and its focus on absent African American fathers, these academics' searches for "missing Irish fathers" zeroed in on early death, work-related absences, drunkenness, and desertion. Therapists writing in 1981 about the Irish American family described male alcoholism as the source of much family disruption, as well as Irish men's fears of women's power:

> Traditionally fathers in Irish families have been shadowy or often absent figures, and men dealt with women primarily by avoidance. Studies of psychiatric patients have indicated that Irish males tend to view women as the main source of anxiety, power, and fear.[101]

Although sociologists blamed Irishmen's unreliability for the disorganized Irish American family, they also blamed overly dominant Irish American Catholic wives and mothers, as they had blamed matriarchal black mothers, for the disordered family.[102] There were in fact similarities between Irish Catholic immigrant communities and African American communities in the mid-twentieth century. Irish Americans described living in communitarian neighborhoods very much in the African American tradition and at odds with the image of white, nuclear families tucked inside suburban homes. Irish American matrons noted "what time or with whom we [young people] arrived," and looked out for the safety of the block's children and teens. Maureen Waters wrote of her childhood in the 1940s Bronx:

> Growing up, my sister Agnes, and I felt surrounded by curious ears and eyes, by people who asserted their kinship and hence the right to know everything about us. We might as well have been living in an Irish village.[103]

Many Irish American mothers, like African American and rural mothers, sacrificed for their children. Thus the "modern" American view that motherhood no longer meant sacrifice or self-denial could not have rung true for them. They worked to see that their children got an education, and would have better lives than their own. Many working-class Irish women sought to send their children to parochial schools to receive a Catholic education. These mothers sometimes worked 15-hour days to earn money for children's clothes and school expenses; as one Irish American daughter recalled of her widowed mother and others like her, they "went without a lot of things to see that their kids got an education." Another daughter of an Irish immigrant mother in the 1980s recalled her mother saying, "The poor Irish would go without if they thought their son or daughter could amount to something."[104] Irish American mothers' emphasis on Catholic education for their children paid off, especially for their daughters. Nuns and teaching sisters fostered Irish American women's upward mobility.[105] In addition to an extensive national network of parochial schools built and run by parishes and staffed by teaching nuns, many of them Irish, by 1918, 14 parishes had collaborated to open Catholic women's colleges. By 1926, 25 Catholic women's colleges were open, and a greater proportion of female Irish Americans attended college than did their WASP counterparts.[106]

Marriage often, but not always, provided the route out of domestic service for Irish American women. It was easier to marry in the United States—which did not support the cultural expectation of a dowry—than in Ireland. Irish domestics tended to marry Irish men, who shared their cultural and religious backgrounds.[107] According to Margaret Lynch-Brennan, Irish domestics did not view themselves as comprising a servant class and considered service a temporary experience or life stage. Marriage did not, however, always provide a respite for mothers from waged labor. In her 1914 book,

Mothers Who Must Earn, Katharine Anthony focused on women whose husbands—due to injury or death on the job, incapacitation by diseases like tuberculosis, or improvidence or desertion—could not financially support their families. In her study of 370 married mothers living on New York City's West Side, 95 were Irish-born, making the Irish the largest ethnic group represented in her sample.[108] Anthony described an Irish mother's regrets, noting an "almost universal" statement by the Irish women she surveyed: "If I had to do it over again, I'd never marry."[109]

When they did marry and become mothers, because they had learned the manners and traditions of the middle class during their time in service, Irish American women were able to speed the assimilation of their American-born children. According to Janet Nolan, it was the economic and social choices that young Irish Catholic women immigrants to the United States made that "eased their transition from one world to another and reduced the psychological dislocation of an otherwise abrupt entrance into an alien environment." She contends that Irish women immigrant's successful adaptation to American life—measured by their presence in the female work force, their children's social and economic mobility, and their participation in public life—was largely responsible for Irish upward mobility in America. "In fact, if Irish social mobility in the United States is measured by the accomplishments of women," she concluded, "Irish Americans enjoyed a rapid climb from a gloomy world of rural poverty into a new world of urban prosperity."[110] Nolan portrayed Irish American women not as passive followers of men, but as sculptors of their own social and economic destinies which helped spearhead the mobility of all Irish Americans.[111] Margaret Lynch-Brennan agrees that Irish women helped move the Irish into the middle-class in the United States. She argued that their physical proximity to white Protestant Americans in their homes is what led to their eventual acceptance by the dominant culture.

> If native-born idle- and upper-class Americans ... had any direct experience with the Irish, it was probably through proximity to the Irish Bridget who lived and worked in the intimate spheres of the private American home. ... native-born Americans came to see the Irish less as "others," and more as fellow humans. Credit is due to the Irish Bridget for pioneering the way for the Irish to become accepted by native-born Americans and for helping the Irish, as a group, move into the American middle class.[112]

Their whiteness, of course, smoothed the way for their assimilation and acculturation. Whatever similarities in experiences of poverty, political oppression, and economic exploitation Irish Americans had shared with American blacks, their white skin ultimately allowed them the opportunity to find a place in American society that blacks were denied. April Shultz has argued that a strictly racial definition of servitude could not sustain

Irish servants within that racialization: "As perceptions of Irish Americans became more compatible with their status as 'white'," she wrote, "domestic service became increasingly dominated by women of color."[113] Phillips-Cunningham has shown that despite the similar exploitation they faced as domestic servants, Irish immigrant women eventually drew on coded racial metaphors like "ladyhood," "respectable," "refined," and "hardworking" to distance themselves from African American employees. They did this in an effort to expand the boundaries of whiteness to include them.[114] By 1944, African American women constituted more than 60 percent of domestic workers.[115] Irish American domestics also were advantaged over non-English speaking or limited-English speaking immigrant domestics. Mary Feely, who came to the United States from Ireland in 1927 and worked as a domestic, recognized her language skills as an asset when she stated that the girls who did housework who

> come from Sweden and Norway and Germany ... didn't speak a word of English when they come here. But they learned. Some of them took care of the kids for a couple of months until they learned enough that they could get by on.[116]

Second-generation Irish American women were much less likely to enter domestic service but instead moved into other occupations such as teaching and nursing.[117]

A number of scholars have argued that Irish Americans of both genders capitalized on their whiteness to gain a foothold in the American middle class. David Roediger asserted that although the Irish arrived in the United States without a sense of themselves as white and WASP culture viewed them as racial subordinates, over time they took advantage of their whiteness by entering the low-wage working class and supporting racist policies against blacks.[118] Noel Ignatiev has argued that both blacks and Irish Americans felt labor competition for the types of low-skilled labor to which they were consigned. Part of the Irish becoming "white," Ignatiev contends, was their displacement of African Americans from their jobs, followed by their refusal to work with blacks.[119] "This whitening of the Irish," Sarah Heinz asserted, also extended to the immigrants' sense of self, affiliations with church and class, and their aspirations for upward mobility. This was all part of a quest to be seen as "true Americans" by distancing and differentiating themselves from blacks: "For Catholic Irish immigrants, becoming American meant becoming white: and proximity to African Americans, whether spatial, cultural, or political, was inimical to such a process."[120] By the twentieth century, some Irish, especially in the 1920s and 1930s, were known for being racist and discriminatory toward African Americans, Jews, and Italians. Studies have demonstrated a clear pattern of outmigration by the Irish in direct response to black population movements.[121]

In addition to taking advantage of skin privilege, through the 1920s, 1930s, and 1940s, the Irish began to make inroads into professions and to build political power and economic resources. As Irish populations began to flourish in cities, the Irish flexed their influence by building political machines capable of getting out the vote and getting Irish Americans elected to office. Irish Americans' growing dominance in unions, politics, police, and fire companies fueled their economic mobility and helped them improve their economic security. World War II proved a watershed in Irish Americans' great leap forward in to the American middle class.[122] Described by one scholar as "a white ethnic group bent on assimilation with a vengeance," by World War II Irish Americans were the least segregated and most suburbanized of any ethnic group.[123] Second-and-third generation Irish Americans were increasingly prone to mixed marriages, further demonstrating the Irish impulse toward assimilation. The loss of traditional Irish communities did not come without a cost, but symbolized "the inconstancy of American society generally, and the social and economic precariousness of the American Irish specifically." Irish writers of the time embraced a literary trope of loss, and tied it to the demise of the Irish neighborhood.[124] In 1920, the Irish-born population in the United States numbered a little over a million. This dwindled to 500,000 by 1930 and about 400,000 in 1960. Yet, in 2015, about 33 million Americans claimed Irish ancestry, making Irish Americans 10.5 percent of the United States population. In comparison black Americans—who did not have the same access to political or economic resources in the 1920–1960 years—made up 13.4 percent of the United States population in 2019.[125]

Antimaternalism and the Dominant Irish Mother

In the face of perceived loss of homeland and community, and women's and mothers' increasing autonomy and power in the family, Irish American Catholic male writers and cultural authorities turned to antimaternalism. They blamed mothers for pushing their children to achieve and for acquisitiveness and social climbing. These mid-twentieth century, largely male writers and historians portrayed Irish American Catholic mothers as matriarchs who damaged men and children.[126] Irish American author James T. Farrell painted a darkly negative portrayal of Irish American Catholic mothers in his Studs Lonigan trilogy.[127] Seven years before Philip Wylie published *Generation of Vipers*, his damning critique of American middle-class "momism," in *Judgment Day* (1935), the final novel in his Studs Lonigan trilogy, Farrell appraises Irish American middle-class culture and its consequences. One of the culture's most significant symbols that he savages is the character of the matriarch as a moral example. In Farrell's fictional handling, "the saintly mother becomes a monster of bourgeois respectability."[128] The class-striving mother in the Lonigan trilogy represents the social climbing "lace curtain Irish," while Studs Lonigan and his father identify with the "shanty Irish" who were poor.[129] Two decades later, in *The Black Bourgeoisie*, African American sociologist E. Franklin Frazier described an effeminate and frolicsome black middle class, and portrayed black women as "selfish social climbers, dominating emasculators, and sexually frustrated self-haters."[130] In both interpretations, women, and mothers, are viewed as class-striving traitors to their own cultures. Because Irish immigrants criticized Protestant American culture and questioned the Protestant work ethic and the meaning of success (despite their desire to assimilate), it is not surprising that one strand of Irish American antimaternalism focused on mothers' financial practicality and pursuit of respectability.[131] On the other hand, therapists have described Irish Americans of both genders, because of the British colonization of Ireland, as carrying a longing for respectability: "Propriety has been the curse of the Irish since they came to America building respectability layer on layer."[132]

The fictional Lonigans live in Chicago's South Side Irish community, eventually moving to the suburbs to keep ahead of the large-scale migration of African Americans from the rural south to Chicago after World War I, thus depicting the ways in which, as Fanning writes, "the Irish immigrant's quest for safe shelter becomes racist flight."[133] The mother, Mary Lonigan, is strong willed, tenaciously links motherhood with respectability, and symbolizes "the powerful, distorting grip of the mother on her child," even when that child is an adult and soon to be a married man. The series charts Studs Lonigan's bleak descent into delinquency, poolroom society, alcohol, illness, and finally death at 29. As Studs is dying, he feverishly envisions a montage of personalities that have affected his life, including his parents. Stud's Ireland-born mother Mary Lonigan dominates the dream, a "thin, distorted figure" with a "witch's face" who warns him, "you'll never have another mother." "I'm damn glad of that," Studs replies. She returns two more times in the death fantasy, the second time knocking over a nun to remind him, "No one loves you like your mother," and stepping in front of President Woodrow Wilson to tearfully state that "the home is the most sacred thing on earth." Studs awakens screaming "Save me! Save me!" but his death is inevitable and imminent.[134]

Farrell shortened the death fantasy sequence substantially as he edited the manuscript for publication. The earlier version of *Judgment Day* included even uglier depictions of Mary Lonigan's crippling maternal dominance. In a dream in which Studs reviews his sexual sins, Studs' mother appears, shouting, "Honor thy God and thy Mother!" and Studs feels "that her long, talon-like finger would be dug into his eye." Farrell satirizes the romanticization of domesticity and motherhood as well as Catholic and Christian imagery that connected the mother with the Virgin Mary, as Mary Lonigan pronounces that "the home is next to heaven, your father is next to God, and your mother is next to the Blessed Virgin Mary." The fantasy sequence ends with a sardonic rhyme that, had it not been cut from the text, would have to stand as one of the more antimaternal statements in American literature.

Herself 175

S ing 'em, sing 'em, sing them blues, said Studs,
M is for the million things she did for you.
O means only that she's growing older.
T is for the tears she shed to save you.
H is for her heart of purest gold.
E is for her eyes with lovelight shining.
R is right and right she'll always be.
Put them all together, they spell Mother
A word that means the world to me.[135]

Another theme of maternal destruction that runs through Farrell's Studs Lonigan trilogy echoes larger, post-Freudian criticisms of the sexual innuendos between mothers and sons. In his characterization of the encounter between Studs' pregnant fiancée, who comes to visit her child's father as he lies dying, and Studs' mother, Farrell distilled an American, psychology-driven suspicion circulating in the 1920s and beyond that mothers sexually desired their sons, thus fueling competition with their sons' lovers or wives. When Catherine, Studs' fiancée, admits to Mary Lonigan that she is pregnant, Mary hisses,

> I won't say that you killed my son. But I will say that by making a chippy of yourself, you have helped to ruin his chances. If you hadn't thrown yourself on him like a street-walker, he might not be on his deathbed this very minute.

In shock at this verbiage coming from "that thin, hard, wrinkling face, calculating, intense, insane, yes, insane," Catherine faints.[136] Mary Lonigan feels "envy, that this girl was young, and she had known her own flesh, her own son in a way that she herself never could have known him." She also feels humiliation at her son's impending death, as it will lower her own respectability and prestige in the community; Fanning writes,

> All that remain [for Mary Lonigan] are the acquisitive drives to possess her children permanently and to achieve social prominence in the community. ... To Mary Lonigan, Catholicism has become a set of forms whose main relevance is its contribution to her dream of herself as a respectable mother."[137]

The antimaternalism that Lonigan's trilogy exemplifies continued to grow in the 1940s and 1950s. Mothers were blamed for producing prejudiced children, children with sexual dysfunction, sons with damaged masculinity. In his 1940s study of alcoholism in Irish American families, psychologist Robert Freed Bales blamed dominant mothers (and weak fathers) as well as mother–son dependence for the Irish male's greater tendency to alcoholism than other ethnic groups: "The father in many cases seems to have dropped into a role of impotence and insignificance, and the mother became the dominant member of the family," he wrote. He described mothers who "tended to bond her sons to her in the way which was usual and natural in Ireland." In the United States however, Bales believed that a strong attachment between a son and his mother made it difficult or impossible for the son to successfully transition to adult status. In his view, overbearing mothers resulted in alcoholic and impaired sons: "In a survey of some 80 cases of alcoholic patients of Irish descent," Bales concluded, "I found this mother-son dependence and conflict in some 60 percent."[138] Some expert claims went beyond blaming Irish American mothers to blaming all American mothers for their sons' failures. In *The Authoritarian Personality* (1952), a group of social psychologists and theorists tried to understand how and why American men developed unhealthy personalities. They drew a connection between individuals who would be willing to succumb to an authoritarian leader (they used the "F-scale," with F representing "fascist") and mothers who were either excessively "sacrificing, kind, submissive," or "domineering, dictatorial, and self-centered."[139] Thus, mothers could damage sons with too much kindness or not enough kindness.

Literary scholar Charles Fanning blamed the de-masculinization of Irish men on their historical sorrows under British colonialism, and the Irish wife and mother's emergence as a stronger figure in the family than the husband.

> [T]he greatest humiliations came in areas of traditional male dominance. For the most part, Irish women had not led the unsuccessful revolutions, nor sung the poems in outlawed Gaelic, nor lost and then had to work the stolen fields. And when the Great Hunger of the late 1840s came, it brought the worst horror of all; for now the men were even powerless to keep their families alive. The men of Ireland bore the brunt of guilt and remorse for all these failures.[140]

Ignoring the humiliations immigrant Irish women faced as domestic workers and laborers struggling to support their families, Fanning argued that the fact they were able to get jobs in the United States more easily than men was also "potentially damaging to the male self-image." Then, in his interpretation, women gained influential roles in the home as full-time wives and mothers, while their Irish immigrant husbands had to risk "insult, humiliation, and mockery" as they tried to make their way as working-class Irish Catholic men in the dominant culture. Fanning contended that the role of full-time mothering not only reinforced Irish women's sense of self-worth but also the role of homemaker allowed them "to replenish their self-images constantly." The result, he concluded, was "a subtle transfer of power and family control—from the insecure, struggling male provider to the less threatened, securely located 'woman of the house.'"[141] Like African American women, Irish American women have been expected to help heal masculine pride that has been damaged by racial and ethnic oppression.

They are expected to suppress their own self-worth and mask their considerable strengths in order to encourage and support the diminished male.

Popular mid-century Catholic priest and sociologist Andrew Greeley offered a contemptuous indictment of the emasculating Irish and Irish American mother and matriarch in *That Most Distressful Nation: The Taming of the American Irish* (1972). Like Fanning, he tied women's and wives' employment and breadwinning to their increasing power and destructive influence in the Irish and Irish American family. He recounted Irish social scientists telling him that in Ireland, "herself" (the term they used for the Irish matriarch) was more prevalent in urban than rural areas which, Greeley concluded, "suggest[s] that when the man is no longer able to work on the land he loses the fundamental basis of his dignity and authority."[142] Greeley described the Irish mother as grim and calculating, asserting

> there is a tendency for Irish women to have far more power in the family life than do women in some other ethnic cultures and in some instances this produces a situation in which a strong and domineering mother rules either by sheer force of will or by the much more subtle manipulation of constantly appealing to the sympathies and the guilts of her husband and children.

Greeley categorized several types of Irish matriarchs: the ruthless "Woman of Property" who buys, sells, and rents property while her "shadowy" husband sits "in the background saying practically nothing"; "The Pious Woman" whose religious devoutness and habitual ill health requires the family's full devotion; and "The Respectable Woman" who insists her family achieve, and "whose whole life is governed by the categorical imperative, 'what will people say?'" The adjectives he used to describe these incarnations of the Irish matriarch included: loud, compulsive, acquisitive, ambitious ("she has more than enough of that quality for five men"), complaining, manipulative, focused on appearances, consumerist, and vindictive.[143]

One antimaternalist image of the conventional Irish mother was a woman who threatens, or actually does, withhold emotional support, thus starving her children's emotions and making them overly dependent upon her. William Shannon notes that Irish mothers were known for "their willingness to sacrifice on behalf of the children," but expected compensatory sacrifices in return.[144] Fanning points to a recurring theme in both Irish and Irish American fiction: "the dutiful self-immolation of children on behalf of their parents." Greeley blamed the "coldness" of the Irish family on the mother, and summarized the withholding approach of the Irish mother this way: "There is not enough chicken soup to go around; and if you don't love Mother enough, you'll go to bed hungry." The mother's coldness cast a chill on the entire family: "The harshness, inflexibility, and oppression reported in previous studies," Greeley concluded, "might be more characteristic of women. ... [I]t is the woman who is more responsible than her husband for the 'coldness' of Irish family life."[145] It is clear from reading the sources that these male writers drew upon one another's conclusions as well as Farrell's misogynistic description of the fictional mother Mary Lonigan. Therefore, the stereotype of the dominant Irish mother kept moving forward in time. It is still alive in contemporary fictional representations. In Colm Toibin's coming-of-age immigrant story, *Brooklyn*, the Irish mother is depicted as the one who uses guilt to try and lure her daughter Eilis back to Ireland after she has begun a new and happy life in America.[146]

Antimaternalist representations largely focused on the unhealthy relationships between Irish and Irish American mothers and their children. Greeley argued that mothers discouraged their sons from marrying, and controlled and manipulated adult sons, daughters, and daughters-in-law—many of whom "breathe a sign of relief when she [the mother] goes forth for whatever reward the Almighty has in store for her."[147] In his 1960s study of rural Irish immigrants to Dublin, Alexander Humphrys described mothers who spoiled sons by waiting on them hand and foot, displacing their affections from husband to son, and expressing dread about their sons marrying.[148] Historian Kerby Miller portrayed post-Famine Irish wives trapped in loveless May-December arranged marriages who, when they became middle-aged widows, displaced their unfulfilled emotions on their children: "[Widowed mothers] projected frustrated affections on sons and bitter jealousy on daughters and prospective daughters-in-law."[149] The 1922 film *The Man with Two Mothers* highlights a supposedly helpless Irish widow who immigrated to the United States with her son and lives so near him she demands his attention whenever she likes, "in effect, manipulating his life." One scholar blamed this controlling behavior and sons' vulnerability to it on Irish Catholicism: "In real life, the Irish son's dependency stemmed partly from Irish devotion to the Virgin Mary: In a twisted version of Marion devotion, the son feels responsible for his long-suffering mother."[150]

Greeley's antimaternalism led him to blame what he considered the taming of the Irish in America—their reluctance to believe in possibility, to take risks, to express passion, and to keep their history and culture alive—on the Irish mother. In his view this represented a colossal cultural loss: "[T]he American Irish forgot their past, and successfully imitated the achievement and style of 'big-city Protestants,'" he wrote: "much of the poetry, the laughter, the mysticism, and the style of the Irish past was lost." It was the all-powerful mother's fault.

> The Irish mother encourages underachievement, in order that she may continue to dominate [her children]. One knows all too many Irish families made up of old maids and bachelors (some of them priests and nuns) who are completely dominated by a tiny, frigid, ailing old woman whose virtue everyone proclaims and praises (and she drove her husband to kill himself with drink thirty years before). No matter how old

her children are, she is still the center of their lives, and any outside interest, be it career or potential spouse, that is seen as a threat to her control, that must be demolished.[151]

Greeley describes a "powerful self-defeating neuroses" in Irish American youth symbolized by his students, whom he portrays as lacking in self-assurance in comparison to self-confident Jewish students who have praising mothers. In his view, through her coldness, caution, acquisitiveness, and social climbing, the Irish American Catholic matriarch not only held back her own children, but the entire group of Irish immigrants to the United States.

> The primary agent of this seduction by respectability is the Irish mother … The Irish mother manipulates her children by starving them for affection. …
>
> There is no need for women's liberation in Ireland. The mothers have been running the country for centuries—together with the clergy, who, in their turn, are dominated by their mothers and housekeepers. When a real chance for respectability arrived, the Irish matriarch wasted no time in setting her male off in hot pursuit. If his enthusiasm seems to flag, she set him in motion once again with her most powerful weapon, "What will people say?"

"And so the WASPS won," he concluded. "Seduced by the bright glitter of respectability and egged on by their mothers, the Irish have become just like everyone else."[152]

My own Irish American Catholic mother read Andrew Greeley's novels and nonfiction books voraciously in the 1960s and 1970s. Mother to five daughters, what must she have taken away, and how did Greeley's ideas impact her own sense of maternal self-worth? I will never know.

Why did these Irish American male Catholic writers of the mid-twentieth century express such antimother misogyny and hatred? Perceptions of masculinity-in-crisis and fear of loss in uncertain times are often "magnified, gendered and signified as a form of emasculation." Antimaternalist narratives are resentment-fueled and hate-filled discourse about mothers, particularly for their perceived roles in feminizing their sons.[153] As Irish American Catholic women gained more choices, freedoms, and power, Irish American Catholic men responded by attacking mothers, whom Rose and Rich (and Freud) have theorized to be deeply threatening to men because of their power in giving birth and in being the primary caregivers to children. Some scholars have argued that it is easy to blame mothers for the social and personal problems of the Irish—which include high rates of alcoholism and mental illness—but the more likely culprit is colonialism, which tolerated famine, starvation, emigration, and poverty, all of which took a painful toll on the Irish, including Irish men.[154] The mourning and melancholia that assimilation entails, the Irish trope of loss, found its way into Irish men's constructions of the dominating, matriarchal mother.[155]

Roots of Irish antimaternalism can also be traced to traditional Irish Catholic views about motherhood that have been tied both to nationalism and to ideologies about the Virgin Mary. Concepts of nation are closely entwined with notions of gender, typically some incarnation of a "militarized masculinity and an eternal, essentialized, culture-keeping femininity."[156] Gerardine Meaney has observed that fusing religious and national identity connects women's roles as reproducers to the process of nation-building: "Women are obviously crucial to national expansion and consolidation in their role as biological reproducers of the members of national collectivities." Thus, women's capacity to procreate gives them enormous power in a nation urgently wanting to expand its population.[157] Siobhan Mullally has contended that this postcolonial Irish mission stripped away women's multidimensionality: "[w]oman's reproductive autonomy [in Ireland] was sacrificed to the greater good of a postcolonial political project, and women were defined not by their capacity for moral agency, but by their reproductive and sexual functions."[158] When Irish and Irish American women and mothers refused to perform as passive reproductive vessels for the state—or as idealized virgin mothers who willingly give up their sons to redeem all people—men responded with antimaternalism.

Ron Ebest has argued that the "demon matriarch" so often associated with Irish American families is a literary icon rather than a cultural (i.e., real) one.[159] Considering the history of Irish and Irish American mothering, Polly Radosh has concluded that the antimaternalist myth is far from the truth:

> Irish mothers, who are often blamed for preserving and promoting intergenerational sexual inhibitions, emotional repression, perennial personal guilt, extraordinarily high rates of celibacy, and population decline until the late twentieth century, practiced mothering with goals of preservation, nurturance, and training as transcendent and diffused mechanisms of survival.[160]

Abigail Palko has asked: how have women negotiated "the parameters imposed upon their mothering by the social, political, cultural, historical, and biological realities that mark the situations in which they mother?"[161] This is one of the central questions driving this book. Like so many mothers, Irish American Catholic mothers had less access to time than men (and fathers) did, and would have been hard pressed to achieve the synchronized family lives and idealized domesticity that middle-class culture admired. With little time for leisure or rest, often as single mothers working to help their families survive, they had little power in their negotiations over how their time would be used. Many Irish American working-class mothers did not have the luxury of caring for their own children or tending to their own homes, but instead performed these services for other women and their families. Thus, for them, domesticity—the domestic labor they gave to other women's homes—sustained their own families' lives and led to family survival in the most basic sense. It is difficult to know whether they yearned for homes like those they cleaned. Their overwhelming and gendered care obligations limited their access to time as a commodity and resource. Because of their need to earn wages, many Irish American Catholic mothers were unable to fulfill the Church's ideal of full-time, stay-at-home motherhood. Especially for the immigrant generation, they moved—in memory, and in body—between the past (Ireland) and the present (America). They were colonized in their home country, and in their new country faced ethnic, religious, and gender discrimination. Yet, their labor and sacrifices ensured the survival of both extended family in Ireland and nuclear family in the United States, and built toward a better future for themselves and their children.

The contested image of the strong Irish American mother, building a future for her children and family in the United States, illuminates once again American (and Irish) anxieties and fears about maternal power. Despite cultural messaging about the dangers of intense mother-love and self-sacrifice, Irish American Catholic mothers in these years described and experienced motherhood in ways that departed markedly from mainstream American culture. They embraced an earlier interpretation of motherhood that included self-sacrifice, emotional ties with children, and self-identity informed by mothering. As I have argued about diverse, working-class mothers in the post-1920 years, Irish American Catholic mothers both persevered and experienced agency and deep meaning in their experiences of motherhood. Otherized as immigrants and Catholics by WASP culture and as matriarchs by their own, they exercised their power as mothers while they kept their eyes persistently on the future. As Adrienne Rich wisely concluded, although powerless in many ways, these and other culturally marginalized women "used mothering as a channel—narrow but deep—for their own will to power."[162]

Notes

1 Jacqueline Rose, *Mothers: An Essay on Love and Cruelty* (New York: Farrar, Straus and Giroux, 2018), 1, 6, 25.
2 Deirdre Cooper Owens, *Medical Bondage: Race, Gender, and the Origins of American Gynecology* (Athens, GA: University of Georgia Press, 2017), 5, 96–97, 103, 107.
3 Andrew Urban, *Brokering Servitude: Migration and the Politics of Domestic Labor in the Long Nineteenth Century* (New York: New York University Press, 2018), 19–20, 53, 96–97, 223.
4 Charles Fanning, *The Irish Voice in America: 250 Years of Irish-American Fiction* (Lexington, KY: The University Press of Kentucky, 2nd ed. 2000), 73–74; Wesley Johnston, "Prelude to the Irish Famine 4, Demographics,"

https://www.wesleyjohnston.com/users/ireland/past/famine/demographics_pre.html, downloaded October 15, 2021.
5 David L. Eng and Shinhee Han, *Racial Melancholia, Racial Dissociation: On the Social and Psychic Lives of Asian Americans* (Durham, NC: Duke University Press, 2019), 48, 60. See all of Chapter 1.
6 Sarah Heinz, "'Not White, Not Quite': Irish American Identities in the U.S. Census and in Ann Patchett's Novel *Run*," *Amerikastudien/American Studies*, Vol. 58, No. 1 (2013): 79–100. See 85; See also Curtis L. Perry, Jr., *Apes and Angels: The Irishman in Victorian Caricature* (Newton Abbot, Devon: David & Charles, 1971); Richard Dyer, *White* (London: Routledge, 1997).
7 Heinz, "'Not White, Not Quite,'" 85.
8 Quoted in Nicole M. Creech, "The History of the Ancient Order of Hibernians and Ladies Ancient Order of Hibernians in Ohio: A Comparative Analysis," Master's thesis in history, the University of Toledo, 2005, 66, https://etd.ohiolink.edu/apexprod/rws_olink/r/1501/10?clear=10&p10_accession_num=toledo1115246819.
9 Quoted in April Schultz, "The Black Mammy and the Irish Bridget: Domestic Service and the Representation of Race, 1830–1930," *Eire-Ireland*, Vol. 48, Nos. 3 & 4 (Fall/Winter 2013): 176–212. See 181; see also David Roediger, *The Wages of Whiteness: Race and the Making of the American Working Class*, rev. ed. (London: Verso, 2000).
10 Creech, "The History of the Ancient Order of Hibernians," 78.
11 Noel Ignatiev, *How the Irish Became White* (New York and London: Routledge, 1995), 41.
12 Heinz, "'Not White, Not Quite,'" 85, 85n8.
13 Andrew M. Greeley, *That Most Distressful Nation: The Taming of the American Irish* (Chicago, IL: Quadrangle Books, 1972), 119–120.
14 Dyer, *White*, 1.
15 Heintz, "'Not White, Not Quite,'" 84. Here Heinz is drawing on Claudia Benthien, *Skin: On the Cultural Border between Self and the World* (New York: Columbia University Press, 2002).
16 Heinz, "Not White, Not Quite," 84.
17 Creech, "The History of the Ancient Order of Hibernians," 65.
18 Quoted in Shaun O'Connell, "Boggy Ways: Notes on Irish-American Culture," *The Massachusetts Review*, Vol. 26, No. 213 (Summer-Autumn 1985): 379–400. See 382.
19 Quotes from O'Connell, "Boggy Ways," 382, 383.
20 Elizabeth Cady Stanton, Susan B. Anthony, and Matilda Joslyn Gage, eds., *History of Woman Suffrage*, vol. I: 1848–1861 (Rochester, NY: Charles Mann, 1881), 804.
21 Elizabeth Cady Stanton, Susan B. Anthony, and Matilda Joslyn Gage, *History of Woman Suffrage*, vol. II: 1861–1876 (Rochester, NY: Charles Mann, 1887), 353.
22 Martin F. Manalansan, "Messy Mismeasures: Exploring the Wilderness of Queer Migrant Lives," *South Atlantic Quarterly*, Vol. 117, No. 3 (July 2018): 491–506. Quote from 493–494.
23 Schultz, "The Black Mammy and the Irish Bridget," 181.
24 Janet Nolan, *Ourselves Alone: Women's Emigration from Ireland, 1885–1920* (Lexington, KY: The University Press of Kentucky, 1989), 2.
25 Cited in Kerby Miller, *Emigrants and Exiles: Ireland and the Irish Exodus to North America* (New York: Oxford University Press, 1985), 407.
26 Miller, *Emigrants and Exiles*, 581.
27 Nolan, *Ourselves Alone*, 3, 93.

28 Timothy J. Meagher, "'Sweet Good Mothers and Young Women Out in the World': The Roles of Irish American Women in Late-Nineteenth and Early-Twentieth Century Worcester, Massachusetts," in Rima D. Apple and Janet Golden, eds., *Mothers & Motherhood: Readings in American History* (Columbus, OH: Ohio University Press, 1997): 319–333. See 329.
29 Maureen Waters, *Crossing Highbridge: A Memoir of Irish America* (Syracuse, NY: Syracuse University Press, 2001), 44.
30 Mary E. Daly, *The Slow Failure: Population Decline and Independent Ireland, 1920–1973* (Madison, WI: The University of Wisconsin Press, 2005). See 265.
31 Quote is from George Russell, *Co-operation and Nationality* (Baltimore, MD: Norman, Remington & Company, 1913). Cited in Catherine Nash, "'Remapping and Renaming': New Cartographies of Identity, Gender and Landscape in Ireland," *Feminist Review*, Vol. 44 (1993): 39–57. See 49.
32 Nash, "'Remapping and Renaming,'" 49.
33 Quoted in Julia Grant, *Raising Baby by the Book: The Education of American Mothers* (New Haven, CT: Yale University Press, 1998), 98.
34 Colleen McDannell, "'True Men as We Need Them': Catholicism and the Irish-American Male," *American Studies*, Vol. 27, No. 2 (Fall 1986): 19–36. See 33.
35 Schultz, "The Black Mammy and the Irish Bridget," 180.
36 Schultz, "The Black Mammy and the Irish Bridget," 179. See also Danielle T. Phillips-Cunningham, *Putting Their Hands on Race: Irish Immigrant and Southern Black Domestic Workers* (New Brunswick, NJ, and London: Rutgers University Press, 2019).
37 See Schultz, "The Black Mammy and the Irish Bridget," 189–190; Catharine Beecher and Harriet Beecher Stowe, *The American Woman's Home: or, Principles of Domestic Science* (New York: J.B. Ford and Co., 1869), 318–319.
38 Here the Beechers are referring to Milton's *Paradise Lost*, when Satan struggles through the turmoil of Chaos, which with its consort Night, sits between heaven and hell. In this reading Chaos—which the Beechers associate with the anti-domestic Irish Bridget—represents darkness, disorder, and the potential of destruction.
39 Quoted in Schultz, "The Black Mammy and the Irish Bridget," 190.
40 Quoted in Schultz, "The Black Mammy and the Irish Bridget," 191.
41 See Merriam-Webster online Dictionary. https://www.merriam-webster.com/.
42 Danielle Phillips-Cunningham, "Slaving Irish 'Ladies' and 'Black Towers of Strength in the Labor World': Race and Women's Resistance in Domestic Service," *Women's History Review* (2020): 1–18, online publication, ahead of print, Routledge.
43 Phillips-Cunningham, "Slaving Irish 'Ladies.'"
44 Schultz, "The Black Mammy and the Irish Bridget," 196, 206.
45 Margaret Lynch-Brennan, *The Irish Bridget: Irish Immigrant Women in Domestic Service in America, 1840–1930* (Syracuse, NY: Syracuse University Press, 2009), 421.
46 Quoted in Lynch-Brennan, *The Irish Bridget*, 121, 125. These quotes are drawn from interviews that Lynch-Brennan conducted in 1996.
47 Polly F. Radosh, "Sara Ruddick's Theory of Maternal Thinking Applied to Traditional Irish Mothering," *Journal of Family History*, Vol. 33, No. 3 (July 2008): 304–315. See 307.
48 Miller, *Emigrants and Exiles*, 408.
49 All quoted in Lynch-Brennan, *The Irish Bridget*, 133–134.
50 Elizabeth Gurley Flynn, *The Rebel Girl* (New York: International Publishers, 1955), 23.
51 Quoted in Fanning, *The Irish Voice in America*, 257.

52 Waters, *Crossing Highbridge*, 26.
53 Radosh, "Sara Ruddick's Theory of Maternal Thinking," 306. Women in pre-Famine Ireland produced lace, dairy products, woolen goods, and other saleable items. Thus, the separation of spheres was less pronounced in Irish families than it was in families in other Western countries at the time.
54 Both quoted in Lynch-Brennan, *The Irish Bridget*, 34–35.
55 McDannell, "'True Men as We Need Them,'" 28.
56 Abigail L. Palko, *Imagining Motherhood in Contemporary Irish and Caribbean Literature* (New York: Palgrave Macmillan, 2016), 223.
57 Meagher, "'Sweet Good Mothers and Young Women Out in the World,'" 328.
58 Papal encyclicals are letters written by the Pope to Catholic bishops throughout the world. They are used as a kind of papal teaching to apply Catholic beliefs to contemporary religious, social, economic, or political spheres. Sharon Tighe-Mooney, "Exploring the Irish Catholic Mother in Kate O'Brien's *Pray for the Wanderer*," available on-line: http://mural.maynoothuniversity.ie/2745/1/STM _ExploringTheIrishCatholicMother.pdf.
59 Yvonne McKenna, "Embodied Ideals and Realities: Irish Nuns and Irish Womanhood, 1930s-1960s," *Eire-Ireland*, Vol. 41, Nos. 1 & 2 (Spring/Summer 2006): 40–63. See 44.
60 Quoted in Tighe-Mooney, "Exploring the Irish Catholic Mother," 74.
61 Tighe-Mooney, "Exploring the Irish Catholic Mother," 78. She cites Caitriona Clear, *Women of the House: Women's Household Work in Ireland 1922–1961* (Dublin: Irish Academic Press, 2000), 14.
62 McKenna, "Irish Nuns and Irish Womanhood," 45.
63 See Barbara Welter, "The Cult of True Womanhood: 1820–1860," *American Quarterly*, Vol. 18, No. 2, Part 1 (Summer 1966): 151–174.
64 In his oral history Edward Burns Sr. called his two sons "Irish twins because they were born so close to one another in the tradition of many Catholic Irish families." Edward Burns Sr. Oral History, Ireland House Oral History Collection, Tamiment Library and Robert F. Wagner Labor Archive, NYU, Irish American Archives.
65 Patricia A. Lamoureux, "Irish Catholic Women and the Labor Movement," *U.S. Catholic Historian*, Vol. 16, No. 3 (Summer 1998): 22–44. See 29.
66 Lee Lourdeaux, *Italian and Irish Filmmakers in America: Ford, Capra, Coppola, and Scorsese* (Philadelphia, PA: Temple University Press, 1990), 91.
67 McKenna, "Embodied Ideals and Realities," 43.
68 Lourdeaux, *Italian and Irish Filmmakers in America*, 48.
69 Palko, *Imagining Motherhood*, 52.
70 Monica McGoldrick and John K. Pearce, "Family Therapy with Irish Americans," *Family Process*, Vol. 20, No. 2 (June 1981): 223–241. I used an online version of this article which was renumbered, so journal page numbers are not available.
71 Greeley, *That Most Distressful Nation*, 82.
72 Lourdeaux, *Italian and Irish Filmmakers in America*, 55, 99.
73 Wikipedia, "Anti-Catholicism in the United States," https://en.wikipedia.org/wiki/Anti-Catholicism_in_the_United_States, downloaded May 5, 2021.
74 This history is informed by Miller, *Emigrants and Exiles*, 451–453.
75 Fanning, *The Irish Voice in America*, 239.
76 Palko, *Imagining Motherhood*, 52.
77 Quoted in Fanning, *The Irish Voice in America*, 239.
78 Fanning, *The Irish Voice in America*, 239.
79 Creech, "The History of the Ancient Order of Hibernians," 74.
80 Quoted in Marion R. Casey, "Family, History, and Irish America," *Journal of American Ethnic History*, Vol. 28, No. 4 (Summer, 2009): 110–117. See 112.

81 Quoted in Laura K. Mercier, "'We Are Women Irish': Gender, Class, Religious, and Ethnic Identity in Anaconda, Montana," *Montana: The Magazine of Western History*, Vol. 44, No. 1 (Winter 1994): 28–41. See 30.
82 Mercier, "'We Are Women Irish,'" 31.
83 Quoted in Mercier, "'We Are Women Irish,'" 32.
84 See Arlie Russell Hochschild, "Love and Gold," in Barbara Ehrenreich and Arlie Russell Hochschild, eds., *Global Woman: Nannies, Maids, and Sex Workers in the New Economy* (New York: Henry Holt, 2003), 15–29.
85 Quoted in Mercier, "'We Are Women Irish,'" 32.
86 Mercier, "'We Are Women Irish,'" 32.
87 Catherine Ahern, "Women and the Economy: Analyzing the Roles of Women in Irish-American Communities during the Late Nineteenth and Early Twentieth Centuries" looks at women in three western communities, including San Francisco, http://blogs.nd.edu/irishstories/files/2012/08/Ahern-Women-and-Economy.pdf.
88 Patricia Kelleher, "Maternal Strategies: Irish Women's Headship of Families in Gilded Age Chicago," *Journal of Women's History*, Vol. 13, No. 2 (Summer 2001): 80–106. See 81.
89 Kelleher, "Maternal Strategies," 91.
90 See Casey, "Family, History, and Irish America," 112.
91 Joan Dolan Oral History, Ireland House Oral History Collection, Archives of Irish America, New York University, Tamiment Library and Wagner Labor Archives, Box 1, Folder 45.
92 Joan Dolan oral history.
93 Sergeant Edward Burns Oral History, November 14, 2008. See n2. Ireland House Oral History Collection, Tamiment Library and Robert F. Wagner Labor Archive, NYU, Irish American Archives.
94 In New York City "sandhogs" were traditionally drawn from the Irish and West Indian communities. Irish and West Indian immigrants built the Lincoln and Holland tunnels as well as the tunnels that carry water from the Croton Reservoir on the Hudson into New York City. Sergeant Edward Burns Oral History. See n2.
95 Mercier, "'We Are Women Irish,'" 38.
96 Lynch-Brennan, *The Irish Bridget*, 35.
97 Mercier, "'We Are Women Irish,'" 38.
98 Mary Gordon, *Circling My Mother: A Memoir* (New York: Anchor Books, 2007), 93–94.
99 Frank McCourt, *Angela's Ashes: A Memoir* (New York: Scribners, 1996).
100 Kelleher, "Maternal Strategies," 82. See Oscar Handlin, *Boston's Immigrants, 1790–1880: A Study in Acculturation* (Cambridge, MA: Harvard University Press, 1941); Robert Ernst, *Immigrant Life in New York City, 1825–1863* (New York: King Crown's Press, 1949).
101 McGoldrick and Pearce, "Family Therapy with Irish Americans."
102 Kelleher, "Maternal Strategies," 82.
103 Waters, *Crossing Highbridge*, 14. Irish American writer James Farrell painted a similar portrait of his early twentieth century Chicago South Side neighborhood in James T. Farrell, "My Beginning as a Writer," in *Reflections at Fifty and Other Essays* (New York: Vanguard Press, 1954), 157–163.
104 Quotes from Mercier, "'We Are Women Irish,'" 38–39.
105 Sally Barr Ebest, "Irish American Women: Forgotten First-Wave Feminists," *Journal of Feminist Scholarship* 3 (Fall 2012): 56–69. See 62.
106 Ebest, "Irish American Women," 62. See Maureen Dezell, *Irish America: Coming Into Clover* (New York: Doubleday, 2000), 83.
107 Lynch-Brennan, *The Irish Bridget*, 142–146.

108 Cited in Lynch-Brennan, *The Irish Bridget*, 157. See Katherine Anthony, *Mothers Who Must Earn* (New York: Survey Associates, 1914).
109 Anthony, *Mothers Who Must Earn*, 20.
110 Nolan, *Ourselves Alone*, 94–95.
111 Janet Nolan, "Silent Generations: New Voices of Irish America," *American Literary History*, Vol. 17, No. 3 (Autumn, 2005): 595–603. See 601. See also Hasia R. Diner, *Erin's Daughters in America: Irish Immigrant Women in the Nineteenth Century* (Baltimore, MD: Johns Hopkins University Press, 1983).
112 Lynch-Brennan, *The Irish Bridget*, xxi–xxii.
113 Schultz, "The Black Mammy and the Irish Bridget," 210.
114 Phillips-Cunningham, "Slaving Irish 'Ladies.'"
115 Lynch-Brennan, *The Irish Bridget*, 161.
116 Quoted in Lynch-Brennan, *The Irish Bridget*, 172.
117 Schultz, "The Black Mammy and the Irish Bridget," 206.
118 David R. Roediger, *The Wages of Whiteness: Race and the Making of the American Working Class* (London: Verso, 1991).
119 See Ignatiev, *How the Irish Became White*, 98–121.
120 Heinz, "Not White, Not Quite," 85.
121 Irish American support for the anti-Semitic Irish American priest Father Coughlin in the 1930s was one demonstration of this. Ron Ebest, "The Writing of the Irish-Americans, 1900–1935," PhD diss. (Southern Illinois University, 2002), 230.
122 Lawrence J. McCaffrey, "Irish America," *The Wilson Quarterly*, Vol. 9, No. 2 (Spring 1985): 78–93; Library of Congress, "Immigration and Relocation in American Society, Irish: Joining the Workforce," https://www.loc.gov/classroom-materials/immigration/irish/joining-the-workforce/, downloaded October 8, 2021.
123 Ebest, "The Writing of the Irish-Americans," 284; 207–208.
124 Ebest, "The Writing of the Irish-Americans," 222.
125 Sara Goek, "From Ireland to the U.S.: A Brief Migration History," *The Irish Times*, October 8, 2021, https://www.irishtimes.com/life-and-style/abroad/generation, downloaded October 8, 2021; Drew Desilver, "The Fading of the Green: Fewer Americans Identify as Irish," Pew Research Center, March 17, 2017, https://www.pewresearch.org/fact-tank/2017/03/17/the-fading-of-the-green/, downloaded October 8, 2021; From U.S. Department of Commerce, "We, the Americans: Blacks," September 1993, https://www.census.gov/prod/cen1990/wepeople/we-1.pdf, Downloaded October 8, 2021.
126 Some women writers portrayed this maternal stereotype as well. In *The Last of Summer* (1943), Irish novelist Kate O'Brien sketched a mother character who systematically destroys the relationship between her son and his fiancé, in order to retain her own primary emotional and psychic grip on her son. See Tighe-Mooney, "Exploring the Irish Catholic Mother," 81–82.
127 Charles Fanning, "James T. Farrell's Fiction and American Catholicism," *U.S. Catholic Historian*, Vol. 23, No. 3 (Summer 2005): 41–56. See 45.
128 Fanning, *The Irish Voice in America*, 271, 267.
129 These derogatory categorizations of Irish Americans by social class were common in the nineteenth and twentieth century United States. Wikipedia, "Lace Curtain and Shanty Irish," https://en.wikipedia.org/wiki/Lace_curtain_and_shanty_Irish, downloaded October 28, 2020. "Shanty Irish" were presumed to live in shanties, or roughly built cabins. The Irish translation of "shanty" equates to an adjective meaning "of the house," or "the matriarch of the house."
130 E. Franklin Frazier, *Black Bourgeoisie* (New York: Free Press, 1966; originally published 1957).
131 Lourdeaux, *Italian and Irish Filmmakers in America*, 98, 57.

132 Goldrick and Pearce, "Family Therapy with Irish-Americans."
133 Fanning, *The Irish Voice in America*, 267.
134 Farrell apparently cut this from the final version of *Studs Lonigan*. Quote is from Charles Fanning, *The Irish Voice in America*, 273.
135 Quoted in Fanning, *The Irish Voice in America*, 274.
136 James T. Farrell, *Studs Lonigan: A Trilogy* (New York: The Library of America, 2004 ed.), 919.
137 Quoted in Fanning, *The Irish Voice in America*, 274–275.
138 Robert Freed Bales, "Cultural Difference in Rates of Alcoholism," *Quarterly Journal of Studies in Alcohol*, Vol. 6 (1945–1946): 484.
139 Quoted in Ruth Feldstein, *Motherhood in Black and White: Race and Sex in American Liberalism, 1930–1965* (Ithaca, NY, and London: Cornell University Press, 2000), 48. See 48–49.
140 Charles Fanning, "Elizabeth Cullinan's House of Gold: Culmination of an Irish-American Dream," *MELUS*, Vol. 7, No. 4 (Winter, 1980): 31–48. Quote from 31–32.
141 Fanning, "Elizabeth Cullinan's House of Gold," 32–33.
142 Greeley, *That Most Distressful Nation*, 110.
143 Greeley, *That Most Distressful Nation*, 110–113.
144 Quoted in Margaret Hallissy, *Reading Irish-American Fiction: The Hyphenated Self* (New York: Palgrave Macmillan, 2006), 22.
145 Greeley, *That Most Distressful Nation*, 57, 269, 166–167.
146 Colm Toibin, *Brooklyn* (New York and London: Scriber, 2009).
147 Greeley, *That Most Distressful Nation*, 112.
148 Described in Greeley, *That Most Distressful Nation*, 98–99. See Alexander Humphreys, *The New Dubliners* (New York: Fordham University Press, 1966).
149 Miller, *Emigrants and Exiles*, 406–407.
150 Lourdeaux, *Italian and Irish Filmmakers in America*, 58.
151 Greeley, *That Most Distressful Nation*, 126, 251.
152 Greeley, *That Most Distressful Nation*, 268–269.
153 Julie Stephens, "Mother Hate: The Anti-Maternal Fantasies of the alt-Right," *Arena Magazine*, No. 160 (June–July 2019): 36–39. See 36.
154 Radosh, "Sara Ruddick's Theory of Maternal Thinking," 314.
155 Eng and Han Lee, *Racial Melancholia*, 60.
156 Matthew Frye Jacobson, *Special Sorrows: The Diasporic Imagination of Irish, Polish, and Jewish Immigrants in the United States* (Cambridge, MA, and London: Harvard University Press, 1995), 6.
157 Quoted in Palko, *Imagining Motherhood*, 52.
158 Quoted in Palko, *Imagining Motherhood*, 52.
159 Ebest, "The Writing of the Irish-Americans," 287.
160 Radosh, "Sara Ruddick's Theory of Maternal Thinking," 305.
161 Palko, *Imagining Motherhood*, 22.
162 Rich, *Of Woman Born*, 38.

Reference List

Ahern, Catherine. "Women and the Economy: Analyzing the Roles of Women in Irish-American Communities during the Late Nineteenth and Early Twentieth Centuries." http://blogs.nd.edu/irishstories/files/2012/08/Ahern-Women-and-Economy.pdf.

Bales, Robert Freed. "Cultural Difference in Rates of Alcoholism." *Quarterly Journal of Studies in Alcohol*, Vol. 6 (1945–1946): 480–499.

Beecher, Catharine and Harriet Beecher Stowe. *The American Woman's Home; or, Principles of Domestic Science*. New York: J.B. Ford and Co., 1869.

Burns, Edward Sr. and Jr. *Oral Histories*. Ireland House Oral History Collection, Tamiment Library and Robert F. Wagner Labor Archive, NYU, Irish American Archives.

Casey, Marion R. "Family, History, and Irish America." *Journal of American Ethnic History*, Vol. 28, No. 4 (Summer, 2009): 110–117. Quote from 112.

Cooper-Owens, Deirdre. *Medical Bondage: Race, Gender and the Origins of American Gynecology*. Athens, OH: University of Georgia Press, 2017.

Creech, Nicole M. "The History of the Ancient Order of Hibernians and Ladies Ancient Order of Hibernians in Ohio: A Comparative Analysis." Master's thesis in history, the University of Toledo, 2005.

Daly, Mary E. *The Slow Failure: Population Decline and Independent Ireland, 1920–1973*. Madison, WI: The University of Wisconsin Press, 2005.

Diner, Hasia R. "The World of Whiteness." *Historically Speaking*, Vol. 9, No. 1 (September/October 2007): 20–22.

Dolan, Joan. Oral History. Ireland House Oral History Collection, Archives of Irish America, New York University, Tamiment Library and Wagner Labor Archives, Box 1, Folder 45.

Dyer, Richard. *White*. New York and London: Routledge, 1997.

Ebest, Ron. "The Writing of the Irish-Americans, 1900–1935." PhD diss. Southern Illinois University, 2002.

Ebest, Sally Barr. "Irish American Women: Forgotten First-Wave Feminists." *Journal of Feminist Scholarship*, Vol. 3 (Fall 2012): 56–69.

Eng, David L. and Shinhee Han. *Racial Melancholia, Racial Dissociation: On the Social and Psychic Lives of Asian Americans*. Durham, NC: Duke University Press, 2019.

Fanning, Charles. "Elizabeth Cullinan's House of Gold: Culmination of an Irish-American Dream." *MELUS*, Vol. 7, No. 4 (Winter, 1980), Ethnic Women Writers II "Of Dwelling Places": 31–48.

Fanning, Charles. *The Irish Voice in America: 250 Years of Irish-American Fiction*. Lexington, KY: The University Press of Kentucky, 2nd ed. 2000.

Fanning, Charles. "James T. Farrell's Fiction and American Catholicism." *U.S. Catholic Historian*, Vol. 23, No. 3 (Summer 2005): 41–56.

Farrell, James T. *Studs Lonigan: A Trilogy*. New York: The Library of America, 2004.

Gordon, Mary. *Circling My Mother: A Memoir*. New York: Anchor Books, 2007.

Grant, Julia. *Raising Baby by the Book: The Education of American Mothers*. New Haven, CT: Yale University Press, 1998.

Greeley, Andrew M. *That Most Distressful Nation: The Taming of the American Irish*. Chicago, IL: Quadrangle Books, 1972.

Gurley Flynn, Elizabeth. *The Rebel Girl*. New York: International Publishers, 1955.

Hallissy, Margaret Hallissy. *Reading Irish-American Fiction: The Hyphenated Self*. New York: Palgrave Macmillan, 2006.

Heinz, Sarah. "'Not White, Not Quite': Irish American Identities in the U.S. Census and in Ann Patchett's Novel *Run*." *Amerikastudien/American Studies*, Vol. 58, No. 1 (2013): 79–100.

Ignatiev, Noel. *How the Irish Became White*. New York and London: Routledge, 1995.
Jacobson, Matthew Frye. *Special Sorrows: The Diasporic Imagination of Irish, Polish, and Jewish Immigrants in the United States*. Cambridge, MA and London: Harvard University Press, 1995.
Kelleher, Patricia. "Maternal Strategies: Irish Women's Headship of Families in Gilded Age Chicago." *Journal of Women's History*, Vol. 13, No. 2 (Summer 2001): 80–106.
Lamoureux, Patricia A. "Irish Catholic Women and the Labor Movement." *U.S. Catholic Historian*, Vol. 16, No. 3 (Summer 1998): 22–44.
Lourdeaux, Lee. *Italian and Irish Filmmakers in America: Ford, Capra, Coppola, and Scorsese*. Philadelphia, PA: Temple University Press, 1990.
Lynch-Brennan, Margaret. *The Irish Bridget: Irish Immigrant Women in Domestic Service in America, 1840–1930*. Syracuse, NY: Syracuse University Press, 2009.
Manalansan, Martin F. "Messy Mismeasures: Exploring the Wilderness of Queer Migrant Lives." *South Atlantic Quarterly*, Vol. 117, No. 3 (July 2018): 491–506.
McCaffrey, Lawrence J. "Irish America." *The Wilson Quarterly*, Vol. 9, No. 2 (Spring 1985): 78–93.
McCourt, Frank. *Angela's Ashes: A Memoir*. New York: Scribners, 1996.
McDannell, Colleen. ""True Men as We Need Them": Catholicism and the Irish-American Male."*American Studies*, Vol. 27, No. 2 (Fall 1986): 19–36.
McGoldrick, Monica and John K. Pearce. "Family Therapy with Irish Americans." *Family Process*, Vol. 20, No. 2 (June 1981): 223–241.
McKenna, Yvonne. "Embodied Ideals and Realities: Irish Nuns and Irish Womanhood, 1930s-1960s." *Eire-Ireland*, Vol. 41, Nos. 1 & 2 (Spring/Summer 2006): 40–63.
Meagher, Timothy J. ""Sweet Good Mothers and Young Women Out in the World": The Roles of Irish American Women in Late-Nineteenth and Early-Twentieth Century Worcester, Massachusetts." In Rima D. Apple and Janet Golden, eds., *Mothers & Motherhood: Readings in American History*. Columbus, OH: Ohio University Press, 1997, 319–333.
Mercier, Laura K. ""We Are Women Irish": Gender, Class, Religious, and Ethnic Identity in Anaconda, Montana." *Montana: The Magazine of Western History*, Vol. 44, No. 1 (Winter 1994): 28–41.
Miller, Kerby A. *Emigrants and Exiles: Ireland and the Irish Exodus to North America*. New York: Oxford University Press, 1985.
Nolan, Janet. *Ourselves Alone: Women's Emigration from Ireland, 1885–1920*. Lexington, KY: The University Press of Kentucky, 1989.
Nolan, Janet. "Silent Generations: New Voices of Irish America." *American Literary History*, Vol. 17, No. 3 (Autumn, 2005): 595–603.
O'Connell, Shaun. "Boggy Ways: Notes on Irish-American Culture." *The Massachusetts Review*, Vol. 26, No. 213 (Summer–Autumn 1985): 379–400.
Palko, Abigail L. *Imagining Motherhood in Contemporary Irish and Caribbean Literature*. New York: Palgrave Macmillan, 2016.
Perry, Curtis L. Jr. *Apes and Angels: The Irishman in Victorian Caricature*. Newton Abbot: David & Charles, 1971.
Phillips-Cunningham, Danielle. "Slaving Irish 'Ladies' and Black 'Towers of Strength in the Labor World": Race and Women's Resistance in Domestic

Service." *Women's History Review*, 2020, 1–18, on-line publication, ahead of print, Routledge.

Radosh, Polly F. "Sara Ruddick's Theory of Maternal Thinking Applied to Traditional Irish Mothering." *Journal of Family History*, Vol. 33, No. 3 (July 2008): 304–315.

Rich, Adrienne Rich. *Of Woman Born: Motherhood as Experience and Institution.* New York and London: W.W. Norton & Company, 1986 edition.

Roediger, David R. *The Wages of Whiteness: Race and the Making of the American Working Class.* London: Verso, 1990.

Rose, Jacqueline. *Mothers: An Essay on Love and Cruelty.* New York: Farrar, Straus and Giroux, 2018.

Schultz, April. "The Black Mammy and the Irish Bridget: Domestic Service and the Representation of Race, 1830–1930." *Eire-Ireland*, Vol. 48, No. 3 + 4 (Fall/Winter 2013): 176–212.

Stanton, Elizabeth Cady Stanton, Susan B. Anthony, and Matilda Joslyn Gage, eds. *History of Woman Suffrage*, Vol. I: 1848–1861. Rochester, NY: Charles Mann, 1881, and Vol. II: 1861–1876 (1887).

Stephens, Julie. "Mother Hate: The Anti-Maternal Fantasies of the Alt-Right." *Arena Magazine*, Vol. 160 (June/July 2019): 36–39.

Tighe-Mooney, Sharon. "Exploring the Irish Catholic Mother in Kate O'Brien's *Pray for the Wanderer*." https://mural.maynoothuniversity.ie/2745/1/STM_ExploringTheIrishCatholicMother.pdf.

Toibin, Colm. *Brooklyn.* New York and London: Scribner, 2009.

Urban, Andrew. *Brokering Servitude: Migration and the Politics of Domestic Labor during the Long Nineteenth Century.* New York: New York University Press, 2018.

Waters, Maureen. *Crossing Highbridge: A Memoir of Irish America.* Syracuse, NY: Syracuse University Press, 2001.

5 Antimaternalism and the Work of Care
How Is This Showing Up Today?

Not all mothers have accepted uncritically the experts' pronouncements on the best ways to utilize time in the household and in child rearing, or the opinions of antimaternalists. Some—including working-class mothers—resisted linear concepts of time that valorized time discipline, productivity, and scientific motherhood. Many mothers simply did not have access to the kinds of resources that would enable time discipline in the home, or were unwilling to let go of cultural traditions that encouraged a different temporality and mothering tempo. Some mothers did not have homes. American mothers throughout history have fought against renouncing the authority, power, and pleasure they gain from motherhood, and some have always resisted—in the 1920–1960 era to authorities like psychologist John Watson, mother baiters like Philip Wylie, or feminists like Simone de Beauvoir and Betty Friedan. As historian Julia Grant has noted, motherhood "is one of the few opportunities for the powerless and culturally marginalized to exert power; therefore, mothers may show substantial resistance to efforts to thwart that power."[1]

In this book, I have examined the ways that antimaternalism affected mothers, specifically rural itinerant, African American, and Irish American Catholic mothers in the years between 1920 and 1960. I have paid particular attention to the ways that proponents of scientific motherhood used time efficiency, one important component of antimaternalism, as a tool of oppression and social control. Although middle-class and patriarchal white culture has always told American mothers how to use time, I have tried to illustrate the ways that some mothers' experiences and time utilization have been at odds with cultural instructions, as have their understandings of motherhood. Rebecca Jo Plant, along with other historians, suggests that poor and working-class mothers, immigrant and ethnic mothers, and African American mothers have often described and experienced motherhood in ways that departed markedly from mainstream American culture.[2] I agree, arguing that the women whose emotions and experiences I try to render here rejected the antimaternalism of the post-1920 years and instead held tight to an earlier construction of motherhood that included self-sacrifice, a changing understanding of self based on motherhood, and

DOI: 10.4324/9781003334712-6

deep emotional ties with their children. Disadvantaged mothers of diverse backgrounds and life experiences have survived, have nurtured and held families together against the odds, and for the most part have valued their mothering. Although some tried to meet scientific motherhood's dictates about time efficiency and discipline, others concluded that it was impossible, or ill advised. In considering motherhood under duress, I conclude that diverse, working-class mothers in the United States in these years both persevered and experienced agency and profound meaning in their experiences of motherhood. As one Michigan mother wrote to the Children's Bureau in 1924:

> We, the laboring class, are as a general rule doing our share and raising up the race and also our *share* of the work. Babies mean work, but it is the kind we like to do, so it don't matter.[3]

I conclude this book with a great deal of admiration for their strength, courage, and self-possession, and with hope that the country may yet value mothers and give them the resources and support that they need, and deserve.

American ideas about motherhood changed dramatically in the 40 years examined here, repudiating the pre-1920 maternalist ideas about motherhood: that it was a full-time job incompatible with wage earning; that it was a service to the state; that mother love was powerful and good; and that mothering required selflessness or self-sacrifice.[4] The spread of Freudianism and psychology along with other factors solidified the cultural shift away from a romanticized view of mother love to an outright blaming of "moms" for a host of social troubles, including homosexuality, communism, and alcoholism.[5] But scholarly evidence points to the fact that the largely working-class, rural, Irish American, and African American mothers who are the subjects of this book simply carried on, raising their children and working for their sustenance, and for their thriving.

Historian Jodi Vandenberg-Daves has described modern motherhood in the United States as best characterized by mothers' resilience and adaptation.[6] In her view, the forces of modernization—industrialization, scientific expertise, and an expanding government—complicated motherhood ideals "without ever fully dislodging the notion of an irreplaceable maternal effect on children."[7] Instead of viewing mothers as passive victims of modernization, Vandenberg-Daves believes mothers proved adept at developing familial strategies to help them gain new resources. They preserved cultures, maintained family and community ties, socialized their children, and sacrificed for them so that their children would have better lives than their own: "The strength and flexibility of maternal-child relationships is truly a striking thread in the sources we have," Vandenberg-Daves writes. She also concludes that mothers were able to resist the prescriptions of the institution of motherhood that Adrienne Rich described: "Equally striking is mothers' general adaptability and resourcefulness when it came to mothering," Vandenberg-Daves wrote. "They often enjoyed self-confidence in their maternal roles, in spite of all the cultural messages pushing in the opposite direction. Mothering practices and motherhood as Institution often diverged."[8]

Feminism, Antimaternalism, and the Future

In its emphasis on change over continuity, smashing of tradition, and rewriting of laws, feminism as both a social movement and an idea (or set of ideas) leans toward the future.[9] Some feminists in the 1920–1960 period disseminated antimaternalist ideas, making mothers and full-time homemakers feel belittled, devalued, and distanced from the movement. Feminists prized the future and connected traditional motherhood, maternal devotion, and women's domestic labor with the past. Rita Felski describes feminism's flirtation with the future when she writes: "feminism constantly gestures toward the future. It crafts plans and projects, offers prescription and policy. It cannot help but imagine how what comes next may be different from what came before."[10] Their forward-looking focus is partly what made feminists like de Beauvoir and Friedan reject maternalism and the traditional role of mothers as somehow less than, and associated with a dated past.

Yet to erase, or ignore, the past comes with attendant dangers. One temptation of forgetting, as Tronto has pointed out, is that we then allow the future to become more important than the past as a guide for our activism and reflection.[11] Such a stance disregards past injustices, and the ways that relationships of oppression continue to affect the present. The idea of restitution for past wrongs—whether slavery in the United States, apartheid in South Africa, the Holocaust in Europe, or genocide in Bosnia and Rwanda—has fueled reparation movements in each of those locations. It is much more comfortable for perpetrators of injustice to move forward (from the past to the future) than it is for victims of injustice: "[T]here is a much greater incentive for a group of people to forget the harms that they have done to others," Tronto remarks, "than for the others to forget the harms done to them, or for the effects of those harms to disappear."[12] As I discussed in Chapter 3, African American mothers of lynched sons and daughters—Mamie Till Bradley is one famous example—had an emotional and political stake in not forgetting, and not allowing the American public to forget, what had been done to their children. African American mothers in Mothers of the Movement, a contemporary group sharing their grief to rally communities against police brutality and gun violence, have an investment in remembering their children's deaths.[13] Historians of United States feminism write with the hope that Americans will never forget the struggles that women endured for each new victory, and the same is true of historians of other social movements: "Only if we are willing to give the past its due," Tronto concludes, "will we have any firm ground to stand upon and pursue hope for the future."[14]

Remembrance is another way of not forgetting, and for mothers, it has served as a powerful antidote to the devaluing of motherhood embedded in antimaternalism. Whether Gold Star Mothers who made pilgrimages to their sons' World War I European graves, Depression-era photographers who captured the images of impoverished American families on the road, or Irish Americans who passed on to their children the horrors of famine and colonialism, remembering what is/has been lost is a powerful need in personal experiences and public expressions of grief. Pilgrimages of remembrance and rituals of commemoration play an important role in our nation's history, whether in the journeys of Gold Star Mothers or in national memorials like Veteran's Day, Labor Day, 9/11 ceremonies, and recognition of those who have died in the COVID-19 pandemic. Dana Luciano has cautioned that the need for historical memory, which she terms "monumental pedagogy," can be symptomatic of the search for a distinctively American cultural identity, which often supports the work of nation-building and in its selectivity "depends as much upon forgetting as it does upon remembering."[15] With this important caveat in mind it is still important to note that to not remember cuts us off from our own placement in, and contextual grounding in, linear time.[16] The work of historians is critical to keeping the past alive and reminding us of the past's relevance to the present, and the future. One reason the historian Mary Ritter Beard, widely considered the mother of the discipline of women's history, was so incensed by de Beauvoir's *The Second Sex* was that she found it profoundly ahistorical, and thus dangerous. (As we have seen, Beard was also a maternalist who believed in the social and historical importance of motherhood and women's capacity to care, and objected to de Beauvoir's light dismissal of motherhood.)[17] In their emphasis on the future and their repetition of antimaternalist ideas, both de Beauvoir and Friedan made full-time housewives and mothers feel diminished, planting the seeds for what we in the twenty-first century have come to know as the "mommy wars," the debate over stay-at-home mothers versus career women.[18]

As I have maintained, mothers—especially working-class mothers and mothers of color—have been silenced in history, and motherhood deserves a major salvaging and reclaiming. Academic feminism that has been institutionalized through women's, gender, and sexuality studies departments and programs have a lacuna, an absence through exclusion, where motherhood studies and maternal theory might be.[19] This is a contemporary form of antimaternalism. Given that a large percentage of the world's women are mothers, my Rutgers students are amazed that my course is the only one in the large and esteemed Department of Women's, Gender, and Sexuality Studies to focus solely on motherhood. Samira Kawash, a former department member, pointed to the absence of the maternal in feminist theory since the 1990s, noting that "feminism cannot possibly hope to remain relevant without acknowledging motherhood in all its contradictions and complexities."[20] Tatjana Takseva has argued more recently that still, both in the field of women's and gender studies and in much of feminist theory, the concepts of empowerment, self-direction, and gender equality are constructed on Western, neoliberal ideas about individualism, self, and agency. The idea of care that is core to maternalism is viewed as less than and inferior: "The maternal—as based on the work of care and rooted in a subjectivity that is structurally relational and characterized by vulnerability, exposure, and interdependence—" Takseva observes, "stands as an undeniable 'other' to the neoliberal model of preferred selfhood."[21] Some scholars have even placed motherhood in opposition to history, as Elizabeth Freeman has noted: "History ... emerges as textual, humanmade, and linear only in contradistinction to a mute female body laboring 'naturally' and recurrently in childbirth."[22]

Philosopher Fanny Soderback concludes that twenty-first century feminism must represent the past as well as the future and not allow patriarchy to bury our history and stories, including our maternal history.

> Feminism is the vision that things can be otherwise, that the future holds unprecedented opportunities and the potential for change—that we can break with a past that has excluded women and other minorities to protect white male privileges. Yet feminism must also be an antidote to the forgetfulness that characterizes our culture: the covering over of our maternal origins and our place in nature as well as our tendencies to conceal nonwhite or nonheterosexual aspects of human experience. In this sense, it is patriarchy instead that marks a break with certain aspects of history, and our task would be a work of recovery, of anamnesis, of unearthing a forgotten history and silenced stories.[23]

In *The Second Sex*, de Beauvoir connected women's maternity and domesticity to repetition and to being trapped in the unchanging present:

> Woman is shut up in a kitchen or in a boudoir, and astonishment is expressed that her horizon is limited. Her wings are clipped, and it is found deplorable that she cannot fly. Let but the future be opened to her, and she will no longer be compelled to linger in the present.[24]

As I have argued, women and mothers have often "lingered in the present" with their eyes steadfastly on the future, on building a better life for their children. In this way they did not passively wait for the future to be opened to them; they opened it themselves.

Mothering, Antimaternalism, and Time

Economist and sociologist Juliet Schor, who published the influential book *The Overworked American* in 1991, said that it was her husband who piqued her interest in the subject of time and leisure. A native of India, he had an attitude toward time that was alien to Schor when they met: "The idea of spending time doing nothing was completely abhorrent to me, whereas he was much less concerned about wasting time," she said. But after a visit to India, she changed her mind: "I began to see that Americans have a kind of insane relationship with time, in which we are in a sense being used by time and trapped by it."[25]

The sense of being used and trapped by time is greatly accentuated for mothers. In *Contemporary Motherhood: The Impact of Children on Adult Time*, Australian scholar Lyn Craig found that time constraint is a major consequence of having children: that the time impacts of children are highly gendered, in that fathers and mothers parent differently, both in how much time they spend with children, and in how they spend that time.[26] Drawing on data from the Australian Time Use Survey and the Multinational Time Use Study (the United States is one of 30 countries included), she concluded that motherhood limits women's market work opportunities, and that working mothers place high value on giving care. Single mothers compensate in parenting time for the absence of a partner. Social and personal consequences of the act of caring that Craig points to include delayed child bearing, lowered fertility, stress, detrimental effects on children, lifetime financial losses for mothers, and loss of female contributions to the workforce. Her policy suggestions are to reduce care penalties through well-paid part-time work; affordable, accessible, and high-quality child care; parental leave; and reasonable working hours for all (40 hours per week maximum). As a more radical solution, she proposes the redistribution of care, including a universal basic income; time banking in the labor market over the life course; and understanding care as a social obligation. Similar powerful critiques of the impact that motherhood has on women's access to time and all that flows from that access include sociologist Arlie Russell Hochschild's work, legal scholar Joan Williams's work, journalist Ann Crittenden's *The Price of Motherhood: Why the Most Important Job in the World is Still the Least Valued*, among others.[27]

The COVID-19 pandemic laid bare the continuing gender inequities in access to time when it comes to work, and care.[28] Many mothers in the United States found themselves in untenable positions; without childcare or schools open, they left their jobs or scaled back to part-time work. Because men out earn women, it is often the assumed best short-term economic solution for women to be the ones to leave their jobs, but they pay a large price in terms of lifetime earnings, professional achievement, and financial security.[29] If men in heterosexual families with children take all the time to themselves and their work and leisure and leave women to carry the weight of child care primarily themselves, women will not be freed to achieve creatively, professionally, or as leaders in the same ways that men will. The challenges of the pandemic-induced recession have fallen most heavily on low-income and minority women and single mothers, who have the most unpredictable work schedules, the fewest benefits, and the least resources to pay for childcare.[30] The pandemic has precipitated a drop in female labor force participation that may have long-term ramifications for women.[31] Described in *The*

Antimaternalism and the Work of Care 197

New York Times as a "rare and ruinous one-two-three punch" for women, the kinds of industries that the coronavirus epidemic decimated—restaurants, retail businesses, health care, local and state government jobs—are ones where women workers predominate. The knockout blow was the closing of childcare centers and the shift to remote schooling; the increased time and care commitments fell largely on "the usual backup plan: mothers."[32] As *The New York Times* concluded, "In the United States, mothers remain the fallback plan."[33] In some cases, the remote work arrangements the pandemic precipitated have intensified mothers' guilt, in that they highlight a potential way—burdening and impossible as it is—for mothers to both hold down full-time jobs and care for their young children full-time at home.

One young professional mother told me:

> COVID changed my perspective about work and motherhood, because before COVID, I never questioned that if I worked a full-time job, I'd have to have full-time childcare. The pandemic kind of turned this idea on its head because suddenly, all of us were forced to fit full-time childcare into our already full work lives. It was extremely difficult (and I'd argue not worth the benefits), but it was *possible*, which was not something I was expecting. Of course, it meant working less hours, working after bed-time, having kids with you on Zoom calls, and feeling pulled in a million directions all the time, but that's what everyone was doing. This added another layer of complication onto things for me, because now it doesn't feel so cut and dried that a full-time job = needing full-time childcare. I still believe that's the right choice for me and my family, but seeing that some people with similarly tough jobs haven't gone back to traditional childcare does leave me with some guilt.[34]

Long-term ramifications that the pandemic has had on women's earnings and their job security include rising unemployment, a surging global gender poverty gap, increased domestic and childcare burdens, and loss in potential lifetime earnings.

Globally, the pandemic-induced poverty surge will widen the gender poverty gap, meaning more women—particularly those of child-bearing age—will be pushed into extreme poverty than men. U.N. Women's Antra Bhatt notes: "Women typically earn less and hold less secure jobs than men. With plummeting economic activity, women are particularly vulnerable to layoffs and loss of livelihoods." The burden of unpaid domestic work and childcare has exploded: even before COVID-19, women around the world spent an average of 4.1 hours per day performing unpaid work, while men spent 1.7 hours. That means women did three times more unpaid work than men.[35] According to Oxfam International, in 2020 alone, women globally lost more than 64 million jobs, which equals five percent of the total jobs held by women. This loss of jobs due to the COVID-19 crisis cost women around the world at least $800 billion in earnings, a number greater than the combined GDP of 98 countries.[36] American women are leaving the workplace at an alarming rate. Between February 2020 and February 2021, more than 2.3 million women left the labor force, compared to 1.8 million men. The mass exodus was largely linked to the closing of day care centers and schools, causing millions of women to be burdened by both work and childcare responsibilities. During the pandemic, mothers have been twice as likely as fathers to worry that their job performance is being judged negatively because of their caregiving obligations.[37] The U.S. Supreme Court's overturning of the constitutional right to abortion in June 2022 will only exacerbate these trends in America.

Beliefs that mothers are ultimately responsible for homemaking and child rearing persist in the twenty-first century, and the United States still lacks the kinds of policies that would help American parents carry loads that are often impossibly heavy. Even in lesbian and gay couples, who tend to divide chores more equally, after children, couples often begin to allocate domestic labor as heterosexual couples do, with the lower earner assuming a greater amount of childcare and household responsibilities.[38] The "time squeeze"—that is, the enormous pressure that is experienced by two-earner families with children and by single parents to balance work and family life—has tightened in the pandemic, and women are bearing the brunt of this tightening temporal squeeze.[39] In some cases, it has led to overwhelm, exhaustion, and physical and mental health repercussions.[40] This was true, of course, before the pandemic. As Mona Harrington wrote in 2009, "a whole generation of mothers have appeared in workplaces designed for workers who did not hold primary responsibility for family care." She suggested that "a mothers' movement" that addresses time for workers' families across class would be "a clear response to a real and urgent need—but better yet would be a mothers' and fathers' movement backing time for family care as a norm in workplaces of all kinds and seeking governmental supports for it."[41]

There are very real repercussions from the "time squeeze" that twenty-first-century wage-earning parents face. One is a declining birth rate, correlated to the lack of support that children and families receive in this country. Over the past decade, delayed child bearing has become a far-reaching pattern across classes of American women. The result has been the slowest growth of the American population since the 1930s. The demands of intensive parenting and "mom shaming" have grown, making some women in their twenties and thirties reluctant to sacrifice educational or work opportunities to begin a family.[42] The financial costs of raising a child also affect decisions about child bearing. A professional who had just turned 40 told me:

> with my six figures of debt from doctoral school, if I were to choose to be a single parent, I would also be choosing to be a dependent myself—on another person, or on the state. The only people I know who have

chosen to be single mothers are people who have money, or significant family support.[43]

Some researchers suggest that it has become more difficult to work and have children, motivating some mothers even pre-pandemic to leave the workforce. According to one study, women underestimate the costs of motherhood, which in the United States became more intensive in the 1990s: "Parents now spend more time and money on child care. They feel more pressure to breast-feed, to do enriching activities with their children and to provide close supervision."[44] All over the world, countries are facing population stagnation and a fertility bust, inciting alarm in affluent countries like Italy, Germany, South Korea, and Japan.[45] How the reversal of *Roe v. Wade* will affect the birth rate, and the quality of women's lives in the United States, has yet to be seen.

The impacts of time shortage and gendered labor in the home that we feel today can be traced back to the antimaternalist messages that experts gave mothers about time efficiency and time management in the 1920–1960 period. Mothers continue to be overwhelmed by the impossible burdens of fulfilling the domestic and motherhood ideals as they care for children, earn wages, and tend to the home, but now in a 24/7-work culture with an internet that constantly delivers new work, along with impossible-to-meet images of perfect mothering. As one contemporary mother of a one and a three-year-old described her life:

> There's never enough time for everything, and I am doing all of it sub-par for sure: being under prepared at work and then coming home and feeling like I'm not carrying my fair share with everything my husband has been doing, which feels terrible. Free time is not a thing. I end up staying up really late and not getting enough sleep so I am tired—30 minutes to chill before going to bed. My evening is filled with laundry, cleaning the house—which is a disaster—planning for the next day.

This young woman described her reactions to perfect mothering projected on social media: "How are their kids so clean? How does the house look so beautiful? Everything is sparkling; it all looks so idyllic."[46]

In addition, cultural messages about over-invested and clutching mothers and mothers of adult children who can't release them to live independent lives are still present. As *The New York Times* journalist Margaret Renkl commented in 2018:

> The notorious "helicopter parent," the meddling mother, the critical mother-in-law — these are all tropes at least as pervasive and unchallenged as any Madonna and Child image of manifest womanhood. A mother who can't "let go" is a grasping, desperate creature, entirely to be pitied if not openly reviled.[47]

Julie Stephens concurs, arguing that contemporary antimaternal stereotypes hold mothers "responsible for having enfeebled boys and thus somehow to have made the nation vulnerable to external threats and internal decay."[48] These could easily have been two mid-twentieth century mothers' responses to the ideas of a Philip Wylie, Edward Strecker, or Andrew Greeley.

Antimaternalism continues to show up in our present-day rejection of earlier, positive ideas about motherhood: that it was a service to the state, that it was powerful and good, and that mothering involved selflessness. Today motherhood is perceived as a much more individual pursuit, one that should be hidden or easily balanced with work demands or one's social life. A young white mother shared with me her feelings of being judged in the workplace, and social pressure she felt to not discuss the challenges (and joys) of parenting: "a lot of people during COVID critique parents: why are they complaining? Don't they know what they signed up for?" She expressed an emotion I remember feeling as a young mother with friends who were single and did not have children, a certain expectation—which I worked hard to meet—to not talk about my children, and to continue to be available in the same way as a friend. "It is tough to talk to my friends on the phone," this young mother said. "I don't want to use my rare moments of alone time to talk on the phone. My single friends don't get this." Another young mother told me, "generally it is better not to talk about your kids [in the workplace]." If she does, the presumption is that she is less available, is "not as good as a worker."[49]

We have largely renounced the pre-1920 idea that motherhood was a full-time job incompatible with wage earning (although some still believe this), yet our policies and expectations have not made it any easier for women to combine the two. "The message," one professional mother of young children told me, "is that you can and should be both having a job and being a good and present mother." These cultural pressures come from her friends as well as her colleagues. Yet, this mother feels guilty to enjoy her work, and she and her husband have concluded that they both cannot pursue ambitious work at this life stage. She reflects:

> It is hard to see other people my age making big career moves and knowing I can't do that now, or the cost would be too high—both for me not seeing my children and for the added burden it would put on my husband.

A mother of a three-year-old, pregnant with a second, described to me a recent Twitter thread about "phased work" that went viral. Lettering artist Jessica Hische wrote:

> This will be my new answer for the "how has having kids changed your work?" question. When I see other artists doing huge ambitious projects or pushing themselves a lot artistically I shrink a little, because it has been a while/will be a while until I'm capable of that.
>
> The key as a parent is just making sure your creative pilot light never goes out. The system is running on "energy save" for a while. There will

be a time when you can crank it again and it's easier to turn it up if it's not entirely extinguished.[50]

And I reflect upon Dorothea Lange and her conclusion that in order to be a great documentary photographer one has to go in over one's head, not just up to one's neck. And the ways that she suffered in not meeting that standard, but trying to. And yet, I remember, her work has endured. I also consider the fact that I did not earn tenure, or begin publishing books, until my late fifties.

Contemporary mothers' writings show that mothering involves intense emotions and bonding with children, along with a bittersweet recognition of the finite nature of childhood. In describing her experiences of pregnancy and childbirth, Julia Kristeva summons the word "FLASH"—"an instant of time or a timeless dream; atoms swollen beyond measure, atoms of a bond, a vision, a shiver, a still shapeless embryo, unnameable."[51] Trying to use language to capture the emotions a nursing mother might feel in the night, she pronounces,

> Childhood regained, recreated, dreamed-of peace, in sparks, flash of the cells, moments of laughter, a smile in the black of a dream, night, an opaque joy that holds me fast in my mother's bed and propels him, a son, a butterfly, drinking dew from his hand, there, beside me in the night.[52]

In their recognition of the finiteness of their time with their children, some mothers resist temporal regulation, and the use of time to organize people toward maximum productivity. In describing her first year with her newborn son, contemporary writer Anne Lamott noted: "Sam is growing so fast that it almost makes me light-headed. It's time-lapse photography speeded up."[53] A mother of a newborn son described the first month after his birth as "the shortest and the longest month of my life."[54] Others have written of their acute awareness of the threat of the passage of time in early motherhood. In her poem "Lapse," Jorie Graham describes pushing her 22-pound daughter, "so recently inside me," on a swing. The movement of the swing back and forth symbolizes the passage of time, the seasons, the years. The title of the poem—"Lapse"—literally means an interval or passage of time. To Graham, the child's "flashing" as she goes by on the swing captures the rapid movement of time. "This is our time," the new mother insists.

> let no one dare pick this fruit I think
> as I cast the roundness of you up again now so high
> into a mouth of sky agape yet without wonder
> as if it eats everything and anything and does not know what day is
> or time—this is our time—or that this next-on meal is being fed it,

> as just under you the oval puddle from the recent rain lies
> in the worn declivity where each one before you
> has dug in her feet to push off or to stop—
> and in it you flash as you go by[55]

Other mothers express sorrow and loss as their children's babyhood or childhood ends. One writes: "It is February 9, 2010. 9:06 PM. Time has passed as it does. Weaning is a catch in my throat, a hand grabbing and squeezing my exposed heart."[56] Writer and musician Patti Smith also voiced sorrow at the passage of time, and the fleeting nature of her son's and daughter's childhoods.

> I have relived moments that were perfect in their certainty ... Our daughter, Jesse, standing before me stretching out her arms.
> Oh, Mama, sometimes I feel like a new tree.
> We want things we cannot have. We seek to reclaim a certain moment, sound, sensation. I want to hear my mother's voice. I want to see my children as children, Hands small, feet swift. Everything changes. Boy grown, father dead, daughter taller than me, weeping from a bad dream. Please stay forever, I say to the things I know. Don't go. Don't grow.[57]

And I realize that the dreams I have of my adult daughters as children, in their girl bodies, is a gift.

Antimaternalism and Policy

The antimaternalism that I have described in this book has affected public policies that impact the lives of contemporary mothers in the United States. Although a topic that deserves its own volume, I would be remiss if I did not at a minimum pull some of these ideological threads forward from the 1920–1960 years to today. The offensive label "Welfare Queen," which emerged in the early 1970s, can be traced back to the early twentieth century debates about mothers' pensions and ideas about public assistance and deserving versus undeserving (poor) mothers. Although public concerns about "cheaters" and "relief frauds" came much earlier, historian and writer Rickie Solinger has argued that only after 1950 did women become the particular target of accusations of scamming and vilification over misusing public funds, which makes perfect sense as this was the ascendant period of antimaternalism.[58] As the civil rights movement garnered some successes, negative representations of the poor increasingly highlighted African Americans and connected them to the most negative aspects of poverty. White Americans began to accuse black women of child bearing for government handouts: "[O]ne of the least sympathetic subgroups," Solinger wrote, "was the iconic poor woman of color, a 'person' many Americans associated with the figure of the prostitute: she had sex for money—the money she got from the government for having children."[59] This association, as we have seen, was made about African American mothers as early as the 1920s and 1930s.

New Deal relief policies of the 1930s virtually excluded blacks by barring agriculture and domestic workers from eligibility.[60] Thus the itinerant, rural mothers—and their partners—whom I focused upon in Chapter 2 were ineligible for financial assistance from the government, as were the Irish American and black domestics I discussed in Chapter 4. The historical assumption about African American women from the days of slavery onward has been, as political scientist Gwendolyn Mink noted, that black women "were ... a distinct class of womanhood to which the ideal of domesticity did not apply." Thus, New Deal welfare policies incorporated a presumption of employability applied selectively to black women, assuming they would be wage earners.[61] Thus the "no win" paradox in which mothers have found themselves has taken a particular contour for black mothers, who were assumed to be unwomanly if they worked (since this emasculated their male partners), while convention and public policy pressured them to earn wages. Policy makers viewed stay-at-home black mothers as an aberration: "A Black mother who didn't work was violating her natural status as a worker," Solinger observed, "pretending to fulfill a mothering role she had no feel for, and staying home to look after children whose tending would do society no good."[62]

Solinger has maintained that after 1960, when the birth control pill became widely available, and 1973, with the legalization of abortion, Americans began to think of pregnancy and child bearing in terms of choice, which influenced their ideas about federal funding for poor mothers. In the 1940s, a poor white widow who headed a family was expected to make her own decisions about her role as a mother. In 1942, the federal Bureau of Public Assistance defended a mother's "right to choose aid" over employment and called for higher assistance payments so mothers could stay home and care for their children. The 1946 federal *Handbook of Public Assistance* described the value of ADC (Aid to Dependent Children, inaugurated in 1934), explaining that the funds should "make it possible for a mother to choose between staying at home to care for her children and taking a job away from home."[63] Yet, by the early 1970s, Mamie Blankley, a black Detroit welfare rights activist and mother, felt pressed to defend the physical and emotional labor that motherhood entailed, and the valuable social role that all mothers played. In her 1972 testimony before the United States Congress on "Problems in Administration of Public Welfare Programs," she declared:

> Let us talk a minute about a one-parent family. That woman has to be ... mother and father ... Why do we presume that [she] does not work? Raising a family is probably the hardest job around—and it certainly

takes more than forty hours a week. No one talks about the middle-class woman who hires household help so she can go to Vic Tanny's or play bridge and returns home in time to cook frozen dinners ... But the ADC mother is always pictured as unconcerned with her children's needs. And if she stays home to raise her children herself, she is lazy.

Insisting on mothers'—rather than experts'—rights to authority and on the inherent value of maternal care across race and class, Blankley stated, "Only a mother knows if her family will run reasonably if she is gone fifty hours a week. She should never be forced to work away from home."[64]

Both public policy experts and the American public in the second half of the twentieth century began to demonize poor mothers, especially those who did not work for wages and who accepted federal funding. Presidential candidate Richard Nixon described the United States between 1963 and 1968 as a nation "deluged by government programs for the unemployed, programs for cities, programs for the poor." In a revolting conversation picked up in released Oval Office tapes then-President Nixon said to his aides: "We're going to [place] more of those little Negro bastards on the welfare rolls at $2400 a family ... Work, work, throw 'em off the rolls."[65] Later twentieth-century Americans kept alive the earlier ideals of time efficiency and goodness and clock watching and temporal discipline as a marker of assimilated immigrants. In 1975 journalist Susan Sheehan wrote a profile of "A Welfare Mother" published in The New Yorker, in which she critiqued a New York-dwelling Puerto Rican mother of nine children fathered by a number of different men. Unabashedly portraying her as a Welfare Queen, Sheehan depicts Carmen Santana as unproductive, undisciplined with time, and extravagant: "She is at ease with time, which is to say that she pays as little attention to it as possible ... it would never occur to her to turn the time to her advantage by reading or sewing." In this influential article that she turned into a book, Sheehan portrays the welfare mother (and immigrant) as financially naïve, childlike, entitled, casual about committing welfare fraud, and undeserving of federal assistance.[66] Ronald Reagan, president from 1980 to 1988, only reinforced these antimaternalist ideas and policies. He regularly associated poor women with fraud and supported a national data bank to tease out welfare cheats. The Welfare Queen was the ultimate out-of-control woman and—as Solinger points out—"a grasping female, one taking more than her share"—which we have seen in stereotypes of the Irish American Catholic mother, along with other offensive antimaternalist depictions. White, middle-class Americans in the 1970s also lumped the Welfare Queen in with sexual liberation and "women libbers," another threatening group.[67] President Bill Clinton's 1996 welfare reform law further punished mothers by increasing poverty, lowering income for single mothers, and leaving states free to eliminate welfare entirely.[68]

Rickie Solinger has superbly explored the question of why Americans believed in the Welfare Queen in the 1970s, concluding that it was a way to explain the "welfare mess" and welfare's role in "national problems, local chaos, and personal grievances."[69] She also points to racism and white anxieties about the successes and continuing threats of the civil rights movement, which in the 1950s included the Montgomery Bus boycott following Rosa Parks' refusal to give up her seat to a white man on a Montgomery, Alabama, bus three months after Emmett Till's murder, and the "Little Rock Nine's" integration of Central High School in Little Rock, Arkansas.[70] The civil rights movement in the 1960s' United States chalked up landmark activism and victories, including the Southern freedom riders and their anti-segregation protests; the 1963 March on Washington and Martin Luther King Jr.'s "I Have a Dream" speech; the Civil Rights Act of 1964, the Voting Rights Act of 1965, and the Fair Housing Act of 1968; along with the tragic assassinations of Malcolm X and Martin Luther King, Jr.[71]

Like racism and the anti-civil rights movement backlash, antimaternalism fed into the depiction of the Welfare Queen: these were, after all, mothers—including African American and other mothers of color—claiming their right to be mothers, their right to public assistance, and their rights as citizens. As sociologist Susan Hertz stated in her study of Minneapolis welfare rights activists of this era, organizers increasingly used the term "citizens" or "first-class citizens" as a way to emphasize that "welfare mothers should be regarded as people entitled to the full privileges and enfranchisements of their nation." Hertz also noted that members of welfare rights groups were anxious to be recognized as mothers, women dedicated to the "full-time bearing and raising of children," children who were their own.[72] This desire echoes the earlier ideas of maternalists who believed that raising children was a unique and critically important contribution that mothers as citizens made to the nation.

Although earlier generations of Americans recognized and honored the very real physical risks that women assumed when they became pregnant and gave birth, despite an alarming rise in maternal and infant mortality, this health hazard that women and mothers shoulder is often overlooked. After a plummeting rate of infant mortality in the years between 1915 and the 1990s, today the United States ranks 32nd out of the 35 wealthiest nations in its infant mortality rate, driven largely by the deaths of black babies, who are more than twice as likely to die as white infants. The United States is one of only 13 countries where the rate of maternal mortality is worse than it was a quarter-century ago. Black women are three to four times more likely to die from pregnancy or childbirth-related causes than are white women. Racial bias in the medical system combined with the daily stress of racism take a serious toll on the health of African American women. According to *The New York Times*, reporting on several ground breaking studies: "For black women in America, an inescapable atmosphere of societal and systemic racism can create a kind of toxic physiological stress, resulting in conditions—including hypertension and pre-eclampsia—that lead directly to higher rates of infant and maternal death."[73] Even for white women, the journey to becoming a mother can be much harder than anticipated. One mother in her mid-thirties told me that she has a number of white friends who have lost babies—including at 22 weeks and at 32 weeks. "Being able to be a mother was not guaranteed," she reflected.[74]

Some of the anxieties that fueled antimaternalism in the 1920–1960 period are still with us, including concerns about feminism, a perception of men's loss of status and masculinity, racial tensions, and fears about immigration. The Trump administration's separation of parents (most of them mothers) and children at the United States–Mexico border between 2017 and 2020 under his "zero tolerance" policy is a contemporary manifestation of antimaternalism directed at immigrants. Beginning in El Paso, Texas, in 2017, the Justice Department detained and criminally charged all adults who crossed the border without permission. When parents arrived with young children, the children were taken from them, and parents were unable to track or reunite with their children because the government failed to create a system to facilitate reunification. Between April 19 and May 31 of 2018, the Trump administration separated nearly 2,000 children from their parents or legal guardians, with no plan for reuniting families. Although after public uproar President Trump rescinded the family separation policy later in 2018, the removed children experienced filthy living conditions, health crises, abandonment, and trauma. The official government count of children separated from their parents or guardians under the Trump administration's family separation policy was 4,368.[75] The American Civil Liberties Union identified more than 5,500 families who had been separated under President Trump. Since President Joe Biden assumed office in January 2021, a task force of federal agencies has been working to identify and reunite children who are still separated from their parents. As of this writing, 1,700 families have still to be reunited.[76] How could any mother not be gut wrenched to witness these painful separations of mothers from their children?

Julie Stephens has considered "Mother Hate" and its current manifestations in a type of nationalist politics associated with the alt-right. Circulated in social media, the mainstream press, and conservative political rhetoric, this contemporary expression of antimaternalism draws its fuel from a familiar narrative about threatened masculinity and nationhood.

> The masculinity-in-crisis narrative ... is not new. It seems to resurface in periods of war or economic crisis where there is income insecurity, labour-market instability and a cultural fear of symbols of the "foreign," variously located in immigration, race or gender. ... The masculinity-in-crisis narrative runs that feminism and women in power (playing the women card or the gender card) have undermined and enfeebled men, corrupted traditional ideals of maleness, and marginalised and feminised men.

Some of these contemporary, online discourses blame mothers for making sons too sensitive, fragile, pliant, and mother-focused: "In the alt-Right imaginary," Stephens writes, "mothers are endowed, on the one hand, with super-powers—domineering and damaging due to their over-investment in their children—and denigrated as weak, unreliable, narcissistic and neglectful on the other." Stephens points to the group A Voice for Men, who portray mothers as smothering and mother love as pathological, as one expression of alt-right mother hate. One virtual image from A Voice For Men displays an angry mother about to slap her very young son across the face, with the caption: "Men are raised to hate women, you say? I wonder who the hell is raising all these filthy misogynists?"[77]

At the same time some contemporary voices have twisted the term maternalism—defined by historians as "women's capacity to mother ... care, nurturance and morality"— into an insulting depiction of controlling and manipulative behavior.[78] *Urban Dictionary*, a crowd sourced online dictionary for slang words and phrases, defines maternalism as

> A type of toxic behavior most commonly exhibited by middle aged women which seeks to control or discredit a person through a sustained campaign of infantilisation [*sic*], gaslighting and intense focus on the target's perceived flaws or disabilities. Through this the perpetrator sets themselves up as a protective mother figure of an otherwise capable adult to whom they are usually not related.[79]

It is true that *Urban Dictionary* has been criticized for hosting and failing to remove offensive submissions, including ones containing racist and sexist content. The creator, Aaron Peckham, states that the site's audience skews toward 15- to 24-year-old males.[80] Yet, what this *Urban Dictionary* definition suggests is that while the alt-right are disseminating ideas that mothers/women in power are feminizing and undermining men, some in the progressive community are doing the same, associating maternalism with combative female right-wingers and controlling middle-aged women. Once again, we see the powerful threat that mothers/maternity/maternalism can represent for men.

On the policy and legislative front, the rejection of President Joe Biden's efforts to overhaul the nation's family policy has been resounding. His original Build Back Better Agenda (through the proposed American Families Plan) intended to invest in subsidies to increase the availability of childcare and make it more affordable; fund free universal pre-school for all three- and four year-olds; and extend the Democrats' child tax expansion that was included in the COVID-19 relief law. The plan received no support from Republicans, despite the fact that they have long positioned themselves as the party of family values. "The last time we had any sort of a comprehensive childcare system was World War II," Julie Kashen, director of women's economic justice at The Century Foundation, an independent progressive think tank, stated. She suggested that the new legislation would have made concrete America's value for families and the work of raising children: "We say we value families, we say we value children, but this will actually demonstrate that we as a country do."[81] An Ashville, North Carolina parent concurred, writing in a local newspaper editorial:

> President Biden is showing an unprecedented level of trust for parents. He knows that we know best how to take care of our kids when given the resources to do it. There's no better way to do this than invest in families to jump start economic mobility and ensure a better future for our children. President Biden is valuing parents at the level we deserve.[82]

The needs of parents and children are very real. The United States is one of six countries in the world without a national guarantee of paid parental leave. We spend just 0.2 percent of our gross domestic product on childcare for our youngest children, compared with 0.7 percent among other member nations of the Organization for Economic Co-operation and Development. We have a far higher child poverty rate than most other wealthy nations.[83] Currently, 57 percent of families with children under the age of six have no viable choices for childcare where they live. Public pre-school programs serve only 44 percent of four-year-olds. Nearly four in five private sector workers have no access to paid family leave. In its original version and $3.5 trillion budget, President Biden's plan would have guaranteed that no middle-class family would pay more than seven percent of their income for high-quality childcare up to age five, and that working families most in need would have free childcare. In addition, the Build Back Better Agenda would have instituted 12 weeks of paid family and medical leave, to help improve the health of new mothers and reduce wage loss.[84] The American Families Plan would have extended key tax cuts in the American Rescue Plan that would have benefited lower- and middle-income workers and families, including the Child Tax Credit, the Earned Income Tax Credit, and the Child and Dependent Care Tax Credit.

Instead, in August 2022, the U.S. Congress passed the Inflation Reduction Act of 2022, which expands Medicare benefits, lowers health care costs, and addresses global warming—all good things.[85] However, all of the benefits that would have supported families, mothers, and children were stripped from the bill, at the very same time that Republicans and conservatives have been rolling back abortion rights state by state, and professing their support for the unborn, mothers, and families. Republicans and conservatives were united in opposition to the family supportive legislation: every Democrat in the U.S. Congress voted for the American Rescue Plan, and every Congressional Republican voted against it. Thus, we have just passed a historic crossroads where President Biden and most Congressional

Democrats tried to implement desperately needed family supportive policies for the long term, yet Republican politicians pushed back, the same politicians who consider themselves pro-family and pro-life.

Why can't the United States enact family supportive policies? Some economists argue that racial fragmentation is the answer, along with an American attitude to the poor that views them as lazy "others" rather than as underprivileged members of their own group. The Welfare Queen trope has obvious resonance here, as does anti-feminist thought that echoes President Richard Nixon's 1971 veto of a bipartisan universal childcare bill as "communal approaches to child rearing over against the family-centered approach."[86] The failure to pass family supportive policies and the overturning of women's right to abortion are, I would argue, both clear manifestations of antimaternalism.

Not surprisingly, one of the contentious debates over the proposed legislation was whether eligibility for the Child Tax Credit should include a work requirement. Right-wing policy makers took to the internet, airwaves, and newspapers to oppose the Child Tax Credit's lack of a work requirement, some arguing for this reason that working-class families oppose it: "they want to feel that their benefits were earned," writes Patrick T. Brown, a family policy fellow at the conservative Ethics and Public Policy Center, which is committed to "defending the family in theory, in policy, and in practice."[87] This argument ignores the fact that caregiving *is* work, work that makes essential contributions to families and societies, and that most people are working hard every day to provide for their children.[88] Here we have white, powerful men making decisions that affect women's lives: women's right to reproductive choices, when women should return to work in a pandemic, or whether mothers should be in the labor force or at home with their children. Expert management of mothers' schedules and lives is playing out here, once again.

When I observe my two daughters, born in the 1980s, with their sons, born in 2017, 2018, 2020, and 2021, I reflect upon my own experiences as a young mother and what has changed in those 30-some years, what has become easier and what has become more difficult. White, well educated, and professional they are, as I was, privileged mothers. They are married to men who are supportive, plan and cook the meals, and share with them much of the heavy lifting that the early years of parenting requires. Like I did, they negotiate daily childcare responsibilities with their husbands. They have homes and adequate financial resources, involved grandparents on both sides, and work that is interesting and rewarding. I struggled more finding my professional way, piecing it together as I earned my Ph.D. and followed my husband to his jobs. Like me, my daughters have relied on a combination of day care centers and babysitters/nannies, and unlike me, they have experienced the stress of working from home with young children during the pandemic. Still in their reproductive years, they have lost the constitutional right to abortion that my generation possessed for a half century. Although I hoped they would not experience the childcare guilt I did, as young mothers they do, and especially feel guilty when they see mothers who are home with their children. They are time pressed, face high work demands, and like I did, often feel pulled in multiple directions. "Even when you're with your children," my older daughter told me, "You are being pulled the other way. Feeling like you can't be fully present and enjoy that time, there is someone else [at work] who needs you." Mothering has changed their lives dramatically: "The idea that the child would fit into our lives, that concept really doesn't work," my younger daughter told me. "They are fully in charge."

What I know as an older mother and a grandmother is that children grow up and create homes and families of their own, and that time opens up again, but sometimes it is not enough time. I could use ten more years in my career, but I don't have them. The idea of the doubled temporality of motherhood—in which time feels both timeless and fleeting, in which children grow away and independent from the mother who stays behind at home—resonates for me.[89] It was one of my motivations for writing this book. My daughters are doing a much better job than I did of staying on their professional paths, but as they recognize, that comes with its own costs, in stress and overload. As a grandmother both observing their loving care of their sons and trying to lend a helping hand, I remember viscerally the physical labor, sleep deprivation, and anxious need to keep these small beings safe that I experienced as a young mother. On the policy side, little has changed in the past 30-some years to make the lives of mothers easier. My daughters have access to more work-sponsored parental leaves than I did, but our country still lacks a national paid family and medical leave program along with universal pre-schools for all three- and four-year-olds. We have made progress since the 1980s, but not as much as some of us hoped, and there have been losses. There is still much work to do.

The Radical Idea of Mothering

Some contemporary maternal theorists suggest that mothers can reclaim their power and help Americans reconsider the values and time utilization that structure our lives. Karen Davies traced the ways that the unemployed Swedish women she interviewed in the 1980s challenged what they considered masculine constructs of linear time. They did this by rejecting wage labor as the overriding structure; prioritizing time over money; valuing time with their children; and finding arrangements—like part-time work or self-employment—that allowed more balance in their lives.[90] Like the early to mid-twentieth-century mothers who ignored the experts' admonitions about time regulation, these late-twentieth century mothers followed their own values to find ways to spend more time with their children.

In their 2016 anthology *Revolutionary Mothering*, editors Alexis Pauline Gumbs, China Martens, and Mai'a Williams assert that the *idea* of motherhood is radical in its insistence on the interdependence of humanity, and on our need to survive. The editors believe the book presents the radical concept of "mothering—creating, nurturing, affirming, and supporting life." They use the term "radical mothering" and describe mothering as a liberating practice and a queer thing: "mothering could be the queerest thing that humans do," Gumbs contends. The editors define queer as "that which fundamentally transforms our state of being and the possibilities for life." Gumbs writes: "Black mothering is already a queer thing ... Because we were never meant to survive." Paraphrasing feminist writer Audre Lorde she states, "We were never meant to survive, and if mothers are part of why we are here (and they are), then they are the queerest of us all."[91] This vision of what mothering is and could be is tied to the radical women of color tradition. It is also secured to an analysis that is anti-colonial, anti-racist, anti-patriarchal, and anti-capitalist. Radical mothering strives for a world, or many worlds "where we might exist and thrive as each other's beloved." It does not limit mothering to women. In some ways it hearkens back to ideas of maternalism, which held that because of being mothers and caregivers, women were more effective as voters, policy makers, administrators, and workers. It is true that since 1960 and certainly after the millennium, attitudes and policies in the United States have been slowly evolving—men are more involved in child care, same sex couples are raising children more equitably, reproductive technology is making parenthood available to more people, transgender mothers are giving birth, paid family leave is becoming more common. How the pandemic will influence this forward movement is, at the time of this writing, still unclear. But if nothing else, the COVID-19 pandemic should have driven home to us the radical idea of the interdependence of humanity, an idea core to the concept of care and mothering, and to ideas about time and its finiteness.

Abigail Palko contends that, like race and gender, the institution of motherhood is also a social construction: "Maternal ideology ... imposed oppressive notions of proper womanhood and acceptable maternal behaviors." She envisions a "third space" in which women can safely and successfully mother, one in which women's reproductive decisions are respected, women claim their voices as mothers, and mothers and children have access to the healthy, beneficial environments in which they will thrive. She maintains that in their collective fictional works, Irish women writers of the 1990s created a "maternal imaginary" which represents "authentic mothering," as opposed to Rich's "institutional mothering." Authentic mothering is, in Palko's estimation, a woman mothering according to *her* understanding of the situation's demands. The state can help women access authentic mothering: authentic mothers "became mothers to the potential nation, the nation that would recognize the full citizenship of women, which would in turn support authentic mothering."[92]

Some feminist theorists argue the need for a mother-centered feminism. Julie Stephens suggests a renewed maternal feminism based on an ethic of care rather than a goal of empowerment. Maternalizing feminism does not need to stigmatize non-mothers or undermine the other rights and needs of women. Instead, it could broaden the focus to include care for children, the elderly, refugees, the marginalized, and exploited, along with the health of the planet. This could help move us, Stephens believes, from dominant, privatized versions of mothering, to a more collective vision.[93] Andrea O'Reilly has coined the term "matricentric feminism" to denote a mother-centered feminism that considers the category of mother as distinct from the category of woman. She contends that the challenges mothers face—many of which I have described in this book—speak to women's roles and identities as mothers. A mother-centered feminism would recognize that, would promote the specific needs of mothers.[94]

Molly Ladd-Taylor has advocated for a new political discourse calling for mothers' human rights. She notes that in 1995, when Hillary Rodham Clinton memorably declared in Beijing that women's rights are human rights at the Fourth World Conference on Women, she had a great deal to say about mothers. "We are the primary caretakers for most of the world's children and elderly," Clinton stated. "Yet much of the work we do is not valued—not by economists, not by historians, not by popular culture, not by government leaders." Over two decades later, Ladd-Taylor argued, "the circumstances of large numbers of mothers in the United States are so dire that we cannot afford not to talk about mothers' human rights." For evidence she points to the shockingly high maternal mortality rate in the United States, which as noted is increasing and puts African Americans at four times the risk of dying from childbirth-related causes as whites. Unwanted interventions and efforts to protect the fetus/unborn deny pregnant women's "liberty and security of person."[95] Caregiving labor continues to be unrecognized, unremunerated, and excluded from the GDP. Mothers face a wage penalty that ensures they earn less than men and childless women. All of these, Ladd-Taylor asserts, are human rights violations.

For the past eight years at Rutgers University, I have taught a course on the history of motherhood in the United States. I always end the class with a collaborative brainstorming creation of "a Motherhood Manifesto," stimulated by the question: "What do women need to mother?" My 2020 students came up with the following list: in their words, mothers need to be able to survive (in reference to marginalized mothers, whose societal structures are formed against their very survival). Mothers need safety on all fronts—environmental, legal, emotional, and/or access to safe spaces. Mothers need access to contraception, to birthing information and their options for giving birth. Mothers need bodily integrity and autonomy in the eyes of the law.

They need choice; women need the choice whether or not to mother. They need community; single and poor mothers need recognition that they too are deserving of motherhood. We must all combat the idea of the "unfit," "bad" mother. In Rich's *Of Woman Born*, she explains that mothers cannot love unconditionally, and thus, they can feel and express negative emotions just like anyone else. Mothers need understanding. They need both informal support systems (through their communities) and formal support, such as federal funding for childcare, and paid maternity leave. Federal recognition of mothers must encompass every variation of mothering which includes, but is not limited to, immigrant mothers, transnational mothers, lesbian mothers, transgender mothers/parents so they are not overlooked as they often are in conversations about motherhood. Finally, mothers need access to time, both for work, themselves, and their child(ren). These are the voices of the future, which seems to me a fitting note on which to end this book.

Notes

1 Julia Grant, *Raising Baby by the Book: The Education of American Mothers* (New Haven, CT, and London: Yale University Press, 1998), 12.
2 Rebecca Jo Plant, *Mom: The Transformation of Motherhood in Modern America* (Chicago, IL: The University of Chicago Press, 2010), 13. Grant also concludes that most women applied expert prescriptions selectively: see Grant, *Raising Baby by the Book*, 138.
3 Mrs. W.I., Michigan, April 15, 1924 to the U.S. Children's Bureau, reprinted in Molly Ladd-Taylor, ed., *Raising a Baby the Government Way: Mothers' Letters to the Children's Bureau, 1915–1932* (New Brunswick, NJ, and London: Rutgers University Press, 1986), 166–167.
4 Plant, *Mom*, 2. Ladd-Taylor identified these as the four fundamental principles of maternalism. Molly Ladd-Taylor, "Mothers' Rights are Human Rights: Reflections on Activism and History," *Journal of the Motherhood Initiative for Research and Community Involvement*, Vol. 5, No. 1 (Spring 2014): 21–34. See 25.
5 Molly Ladd-Taylor and Lauri Umansky, eds., *'Bad" Mothers: The Politics of Blame in Twentieth-Century America* (New York: New York University Press, 1998).
6 Jodi Vandenberg-Daves, *Modern Motherhood: An American History* (New Brunswick, NJ, and London: Rutgers University Press, 2014), 150.
7 Vandenberg-Daves, *Modern Motherhood*, 3.
8 Vandenberg-Daves, *Modern Motherhood*, 169.
9 Joan Tronto, "Time's Place," *Feminist Theory*, Vol. 4, No. 2 (August 2003): 119–138; Rita Felski, "Telling Time in Feminist Theory," *Tulsa Studies in Women's Literature*, Vol. 21, No. 1 (Spring 2002): 21–28.
10 Felski, "Telling Time in Feminist Theory," 23; See also Tronto, "Time's Place," 121.
11 Tronto, "Time's Place," 125.
12 Tronto, "Time's Place," 127.
13 Jessica D. Johnson Carew, "Mothers of the Movement: Black Motherhood and the Political Power of Grief in the 2016 Presidential Election," in Jennifer Schenk Sacco, ed., *Women of the 2016 Election: Voices, Views, and Values* (Lanham, MD: Lexington Books, 2019), 139–156.

14 Tronto, "Time's Place," 133.
15 Dana Luciano, *Arranging Grief: Sacred Time and the Body in Nineteenth-Century America* (New York and London: New York University Press, 2007), 172–174.
16 See Tronto, "Time's Place," 131–132 on remembrance. She cites Hannah Arendt as a feminist who suggested that remembrance is another possible action feminists could take, in contrast to forgiveness or reparation.
17 See Mary K. Trigg, *Feminism as Life's Work: Four Modern American Women through Two World Wars* (New Brunswick, NJ, and London: Rutgers University Press, 2014), 182; 48–49: Mary Ritter Beard, *Woman as Force in History: A Study in Traditions and Realities* (New York: The Macmillan Co., 1946).
18 Much has been written about the "mommy wars." For one example see Leslie Morgan Steiner, ed., *Mommy Wars: Stay-at-Home and Career Moms Face Off on Their Choices, Their Lives, Their Families* (New York: Random House, 2006). With two-thirds of American families now reliant on the mother's income, this debate may have shifted to ideological battles over parenting strategies, as the intense debate over Amy Chau's *The Battle Hymn of the Tiger Mother*, suggests. See Ladd-Taylor, "Mothers' Rights are Human Rights," 23; Heather Boushey, "The New Breadwinners," *Shriver Report*, September 10, 2009; Amy Chau, *The Battle Hymn of the Tiger Mother* (New York: Penguin Press, 2011).
19 Tatjana Takseva, "One is not Born but Rather Becomes a Mother: Claiming the Maternal in Women and Gender Studies," *Journal of the Motherhood Initiative*, Vol. 10, Nos. 1 & 2 (May 2019): 27–44; Andrea O'Reilly, *Matricentric Feminism: Theory, Activism, and Practice* (Ontario, Canada: Demeter Press, 2016). Although there is ample scholarship on the politics of motherhood in the United States, much of it focuses on early twentieth-century maternalism and the white, middle-class mothers who promoted it. Ladd-Taylor, "Mothers' Rights are Human Rights," 24.
20 Samira Kawash, "New Directions in Motherhood Studies," *Signs*, Vol. 36, No. 4 (Summer 2011): 969–1003. See 997.
21 Takseva, "One is not Born," 29, 32.
22 Elizabeth Freeman, "Time Binds; or, Erotohistoriography," *Social Text*, Vol. 23, Nos. 3–4 (2005): 57–68. See 62.
23 Fanny Soderback, "Revolutionary Time: Revolt as Temporal Return," *Signs*, Vol. 37, No. 2 (Winter 2012): 301–324. See 303.
24 De Beauvoir, *The Second Sex*, [1949], 1997, 616. Quoted in Soderback, "Revolutionary Time," 301.
25 Quoted in Robert Kuttner, "Review of the Overworked American, Juliet Schor," *The New York Times*, February 2, 1992. See Juliet B. Schor, *The Overworked American: The Unexpected Decline of Leisure* (New York: Basic Books, 1992). On contemporary overwork among Americans pre-COVID-19 see Derek Thompson, "Why Americans are Always Running Out of Time," *The Atlantic*, December 23, 2019; Derek Thompson, "The Religion of Workism is Making Americans Miserable," *The Atlantic*, February 24, 2019.
26 Lyn Craig, *Contemporary Motherhood: The Impact of Children on Adult Time* (London and New York: Routledge, 2016).
27 See Arlie Russell Hochschild, *Time Bind: When Work Becomes Home and Home Becomes Work* (New York: Holt, 1997, 2001) and *The Second Shift: Working Families and the Revolution at Home* (New York: Penguin, 1989, 2003, 2012); Joan Williams, *Unbending Gender: Why Family and Work Conflict and What to Do about It* (New York: Oxford University Press, 2000) and *Re-shaping the Work-Family Debate: Why Men and Class Matter* (Cambridge, MA, and London: Harvard University Press, 2010); Faye J. Crosby, Irene Hanson Frieze, Joan C. Williams, and Monica Biernat, eds.,

The Maternal Wall: Research and Policy Perspectives on Discrimination against Mothers (New York: Wiley, 2004); and Ann Crittenden, *The Price of Motherhood: Why the Most Important Job in the World Is Still the Least Valued* (Picador, 2010).

28 Andrea O'Reilly, "Certainly not an Equal-Opportunity Pandemic: COVID-19 and Its Impact on Mothers' Carework, Health, and Employment," in Andrea O'Reilly and Fiona Joy Green, eds., *Mothers, Mothering, and COVID-19* (Ontario, Canada: Demeter Press, 2021), 41–52.
29 See Ann Crittendon, *The Price of Motherhood*.
30 Patricia Cohen, "Recession's Toll on Women Points to a Lasting Setback," *The New York Times*, November 18, 2020.
31 Jessica Grose, "Mothers Are the 'Shock Absorbers' of Our Society," *The New York Times*, October 14, 2020.
32 Cohen, "Recession's Toll on Women Points to a Lasting Setback."
33 Claire Cain Miller, "When Schools Closed, Families Turned to the Usual Backup Plan: Mothers," *The New York Times*, November 18, 2020.
34 E-mail in my possession, received July 21, 2021.
35 UN Women, "COVID-19 and its Economic Toll on Women: The Story Behind the Numbers," September 16, 2020, https://www.unwomen.org/en/news/stories/2020/9/feature-covid-19-economic-impacts-on-women.
36 Courtney Connley, "In 1 Year, Women Globally Lost $800 Billion in Income Due to COVID-19, New Report Finds," *CNBC*, https://www.cnbc.com/2021/04/30/women-globally-lost-800-billion-dollars-in-income-due-to-covid-19.html.
37 Connley, "In 1 Year."
38 Claire Cain Miller, "How Same-Sex Couples Divide Chores, and What it Reveals about Modern Parenting," *The New York Times*, May 16, 2018.
39 Isabel Sawhill and Morgan Welch, "In Georgia, Family or Culture War?" *The New York Times*, November 30, 2020.
40 Kristen Hicks-Roof, "The Continuous Clock: A Working Academic Mother during COVID-19," *Journal of the Motherhood Initiative*, Vol. 11, No.2/Vol. 12, No. 1 (Fall 2020/Spring 2021): 265–276.
41 Mona Harrington, "Mothers, Politics, and Public Policy," *WSQ: Women's Studies Quarterly*, Vol. 37, Nos. 3 & 4 (Fall/Winter 2009): 329–333. See 332. See also Jennifer L. Borda, "Workplace and Social Justice: A New Feminist Movement for Labour and Love," in O'Reilly and Green, eds., *Mothers, Mothering, and COVID-19*, 83–99.
42 Sabrina Tavernise, Claire Cain Miller, Quoctrung Bai, and Robert Geberoff, "Why American Women Everywhere Are Delaying Motherhood," *The New York Times*, June 16, 2021.
43 In this chapter I have woven through quotations from a conversation I facilitated on May 31, 2021, with a group of white women in their thirties and forties.
44 Claire Cain Miller, "The Costs of Motherhood Are Rising, and Catching Women Off Guard," *The New York Times*, August 17, 2018.
45 Damien Cave, Emma Bubola, and Choe Sang-Hun, "Long Slide Looms for World Population, with Sweeping Ramifications," *The New York Times*, May 22, 2021.
46 From conversation conducted May 31, 2021.
47 Margaret Renkl, "The Mother's Day Trap," *The New York Times*, May 7, 2018.
48 Julie Stephens, "Mother Hate: The Anti-Maternal Fantasies of the Alt-Right," *Arena Magazine*, No. 160 (June/July 2019): 36–39. See 36.
49 From conversation conducted May 31, 2021.
50 Jessica Hische Twitter feed, May 12, 2021. This feed had 107 retweets, 69 quote tweets, and 1,326 likes on May 12, 2021. All other quotes from conversation conducted May 31, 2021.

51 Julia Kristeva and Arthur Goldhammer, "Stabat Mater," *Poetics Today*, Vol. 6, Nos. 1–2 (1985): 133–152. See 133–134.
52 Kristeva and Goldhammer, "Stabat Mater," 142.
53 Anne LaMott, *Operating Instructions: A Journal of My Son's First Year* (New York: Ballantine Books, 1993), 215.
54 Interview with SR, June 2018.
55 Jorie Graham, "Lapse," Graham, in *Place: New Poems*. New York: HarperCollins, 2012, 71–74. See 72.
56 Rachel Zucker, *Mothers* (Denver, CO: Counterpath, 2014), 102.
57 Patti Smith, *M Train* (New York: Penguin Books, 2015), 208–209.
58 Rickie Solinger, *Beggars and Choosers: How the Politics of Choice Shapes Adoption, Abortion, and Welfare in the United States* (New York: Hill and Wang, 2001), 142.
59 Solinger, *Beggars and Choosers*, 143.
60 Solinger, *Beggars and Choosers*, 144.
61 Solinger, *Beggars and Choosers*, 144; Mink, *The Wages of Motherhood*, 142.
62 Solinger, *Beggars and Choosers*, 145.
63 Solinger, *Beggars and Choosers*, 148.
64 Quoted in Solinger, *Beggars and Choosers*, 149.
65 Quoted in Solinger, *Beggars and Choosers*, 154.
66 Susan Sheehan, "A Welfare Mother," *New Yorker*, September 29, 1975, 42–99. Discussed in Solinger, *Beggars and Choosers*, 155–157.
67 Solinger, *Beggars and Choosers*, 156–170. Quote from 167.
68 Peter Edelman, "The Worst Thing Bill Clinton Has Done," *The Atlantic*, March 1997.
69 Solinger, *Beggars and Choosers*, 165.
70 "Civil Rights Movement Timeline," History.Com, https://www.history.com/topics/civil-rights-movement/civil-rights-movement-timeline, downloaded July 12, 2021. See also Bridget Gurtler, "Daisy Bates: The NAACP," in Mary K. Trigg and Alison R. Bernstein, eds., *Junctures in Women's Leadership: Social Movements* (New Brunswick, NJ, and London: Rutgers University Press, 2016), 23–38.
71 "Civil Rights Movement Timeline."
72 Quoted in Solinger, *Beggars and Choosers*, 166.
73 Linda Villarosa, "Why America's Black Mothers and Babies are in a Life-or-Death Crisis," *The New York Times*, April 11, 2018.
74 Conversation conducted May 31, 2021.
75 Southern Poverty Law Center, "Family Separation: A Timeline," updated March 23, 2022, https://www.splcenter.org/news/2022/03/23/family-separation-timeline, downloaded April 1, 2022.
76 Southern Poverty Law Center, "Family Separation: A Timeline." See also Jonathan Blitzer, "A Mother, Separated from Her Children at the Border, Comes Home," *The New Yorker*, May 5, 2021.
77 Stephens, "Mother Hate," 36, 37, 38.
78 Seth Koven and Sonya Michel, eds., *Mothers of a New World: Maternalist Politics and the Origins of the Welfare State* (New York and London: Routledge, 1993), 4, 6.
79 Urban Dictionary, https://www.urbandictionary.com/define.php?term=maternalism, accessed September 10, 2021.
80 Clio Change, "Why Urban Dictionary is Horrifically Racist," *The Nation*, July 5, 2017.
81 Quoted in Keya Vakil, "The Pandemic 'Blew the House of Cards All the Way Down for Mothers. Can Joe Biden Build it Back Better?" *The Keystone*, August 27, 2021. Updated August 30, 2021. Accessed September 14, 2021.
82 "As Third Child Tax Credits Hit Bank Accounts, Republican Senate Candidates' Opposition is Even More Toxic," NCDP, September 15, 2021.

83 Bryce Covert, "There's a Reason We Can't Have Nice Things," *The New York Times*, July 21, 2022.
84 Fact Sheet, The White House, "The American Families Plan," April 28, 2021, https://www.whitehouse.gov/briefing-room/statements-releases/2021/04/28/fact-sheet-the-american-families-plan/.
85 "Summary: The Inflation Reduction Act of 2022," https://www.democrats.senate.gov/imo/media/doc/inflation_reduction_act_one_page_summary.pdf, downloaded August 19, 2022.
86 Covert, "There's a Reason We Can't Have Nice Things."
87 Patrick T. Brown, "Some Parents Say No to a Bigger Child Credit," *The New York Times*, September 16, 2021; "EPPC Welcomes Patrick Brown as Fellow in Family Policy," June 1, 2021, https://eppc.org/news/eppc-welcomes-patrick-t-brown-as-fellow-in-family-policy/.
88 "Democrats Pour Cold Water on Joe Manchin's Suggested Work Requirement."
89 Luciano, *Arranging Grief*, 122.
90 Karen Davies, *Women, Time and the Weaving of the Strands of Everyday Life* (Aldershot, Hampshire: Gower Publishing Co., 1990), 239.
91 Alexis Pauline Gumbs, China Martens, and Mai'a Williams, eds., *Revolutionary Mothering: Love on the Front Lines* (Oakland, CA: PM Press, 2016), xv, 115, 119–120. See Audre Lorde, "A Litany for Survival," The Poetry Foundation, https://www.poetryfoundation.org/poems/147275/a-litany-for-survival; and Audre Lorde, "Man Child: A Black Lesbian Feminist's Response," from Audre Lorde, *Sister Outsider: Essays by Audre Lorde* (Berkeley, CA: The Crossing Press, 1984), 72–80.
92 Abigail L. Palko, *Imagining Motherhood in Contemporary Irish and Caribbean Literature* (New York: Palgrave Macmillan, 2016), 219, 225–226, 3, 32–41.
93 Stephens, "Mother Hate," 38–39.
94 O'Reilly, *Matricentric Feminism*.
95 Ladd-Taylor, "Mothers' Rights are Human Rights," 21, 22, 27, 28.

Reference List

Beard, Mary Ritter. *Woman as Force in History: A Study in Traditions and Realities*. New York: The Macmillan Co., 1946.

Borda, Jennifer L. "Workplace and Social Justice: A New Feminist Movement for Labour and Love." In Andrea O'Reilly and Fiona Joy Green, eds., *Mothers, Mothering, and COVID-19*. Ontario, Canada: Demeter Press, 2021, 83–99.

Boushey, Heather. "The New Breadwinners," Shriver Report, September 10, 2009.

Carew, Jessica D. Johnson. "Mothers of the Movement: Black Motherhood and the Political Power of Grief in the 2016 Presidential Election." In Jennifer Schenk Sacco, ed., *Women of the 2016 Election: Voices, Views, and Values*. Lanham, MD: Lexington Books, 2019, 139–156.

Cave, Damien, Emma Bubola, and Choe Sang-Hun. "Long Slide Looms for World Population, with Sweeping Ramifications." *The New York Times*, May 22, 2021.

Chau, Amy. *The Battle Hymn of the Tiger Mother*. New York: Penguin Press, 2011.

Cohen, Patricia. "Recession's Toll on Women Points to a Lasting Setback." *The New York Times*, November 18, 2020.

Connley, Courtney. "In 1 Year, Women Globally Lost $800 Billion in Income Due to COVID-19, New Report Finds." *CNBC*. https://www.cnbc.com/2021/04/30/women-globally-lost-800-billion-dollars-in-income-due-to-covid-19.html.

Craig, Lyn. *Contemporary Motherhood: The Impact of Children on Adult Time*. London and New York: Routledge, 2016.

Davies, Karen. *Women, Time and the Weaving of the Strands of Everyday Life*. Aldershot, Hampshire: Gower Publishing Co., 1990.
de Beauvoir, Simone. *The Second Sex*. New York: Knopf, 1952.
Edelman, Peter. "The Worst Thing Bill Clinton Has Done." *The Atlantic*, March 1997.
Felski, Rita. "Telling Time in Feminist Theory." *Tulsa Studies in Women's Literature*, Vol. 21, No. 1 (Spring 2002): 21–28.
Freeman, Elizabeth. "Time Binds; or, Erotohistoriography." *Social Text (3–4)*, Vol. 84–85 (2005) 3: 57–68.
Graham, Jorie Graham. "Lapse." In *Place: New Poems*. New York: HarperCollins, 2012, 71–74.
Grant, Julia. *Raising Baby by the Book: the Education of American Mothers*. New Haven, CT and London: Yale University Press, 1998.
Grose, Jessica. "Mothers Are the 'Shock Absorbers' of Our Society." *The New York Times*, October 14, 2020.
Gumbs, Alexis Pauline, China Martens, and Mai'a Williams, eds. *Revolutionary Mothering: Love on the Front Lines*. Oakland, CA: PM Press, 2016.
Harrington, Mona. "Mothers, Politics, and Public Policy." *WSQ: Women's Studies Quarterly*, Vol. 37, Nos. 3&4 (Fall/Winter 2009): 329–333.
Hicks-Roof, Kristen. "The Continuous Clock: A Working Academic Mother during COVID-19." *Journal of the Motherhood Initiative*, Vol. 11, No.2/Vol. 12, No. 1 (Fall 2020/Spring 2021): 265–276.
Kawash, Samira. "New Directions in Motherhood Studies." *Signs*, Vol. 36, No. 4 (Summer 2011): 969–1003.
Koven, Seth and Sonya Michel, eds. *Mothers of a New World: Maternalist Politics and the Origins of the Welfare State*. New York and London: Routledge, 1993.
Kristeva, Julia and Arthur Goldhammer. "Stabat Mater." *Poetics Today*, Vol. 6, Nos. 1–2 (1985): 133–152.
Kuttner, Robert. "Review of the Overworked American, Juliet Schor." *The New York Times*, February 2, 1992.
Ladd-Taylor, Molly, ed. *Raising a Baby the Government Way: Mothers' Letters to the Children's Bureau, 1915–1932*. New Brunswick, NJ and London: Rutgers University Press, 1986.
Ladd-Taylor, Molly and Lauri Umansky, eds. *'Bad" Mothers: The Politics of Blame in Twentieth-Century America*. New York: New York University Press, 1998.
Ladd-Taylor, Molly. "Mothers' Rights are Human Rights: Reflections on Activism and History." *Journal of the Motherhood Initiative for Research & Community Involvement*, Vol. 5, No. 1 (Spring 2014): 21–34.
LaMott, Anne. *Operating Instructions: A Journal of My Son's First Year*. New York: Ballantine Books, 1993.
Luciano, Dana. *Arranging Grief: Sacred Time and the Body in Nineteenth-Century America*. New York: New York University Press, 2007.
Miller, Claire Cain. "How Same-Sex Couples Divide Chores, and What it Reveals about Modern Parenting." *The New York Times*, May 16, 2018.
Miller, Claire Cain. "The Costs of Motherhood are Rising, and Catching Women Off Guard." *The New York Times*, August 17, 2018.
Miller, Claire Cain. "When Schools Closed, Families Turned to the Usual Backup Plan: Mothers." *The New York Times*, November 18, 2020.

O'Reilly, Andrea. *Matricentic Feminism: Theory, Activism, and Practice*. Ontario, Canada: Demeter Press, 2016.
O'Reilly, Andrea. "Certainly not an Equal-Opportunity Pandemic: COVID-19 and Its Impact on Mothers' Carework, Health, and Employment." In Andrea O'Reilly and Fiona Joy Green, eds., *Mothers, Mothering, and COVID-19*. Ontario, Canada: Demeter Press, 2021, 41–52.
Palko, Abigail L. *Imagining Motherhood in Contemporary Irish and Caribbean Literature*. New York: Palgrave Macmillan, 2016.
Plant, Rebecca Jo. *Mom: The Transformation of Motherhood in Modern America*. Chicago, IL: The University of Chicago Press, 2010.
Renkl, Margaret. "The Mother's Day Trap." *The New York Times*, May 7, 2018.
Sawhill, Isabel and Morgan Welch. "In Georgia, Family or Culture War?" *The New York Times*, November 30, 2020.
Smith, Patti. *M Train*. New York: Penguin Books, 2015.
Soderback, Fanny. "Revolutionary Time: Revolt as Temporal Return." *Signs*, Vol. 37, No. 2 (Winter 2012): 301–324.
Solinger, Rickie. *Beggars and Choosers: How the Politics of Choice Shapes Adoption, Abortion, and Welfare in the United States*. New York: Hill and Wang, 2001.
Steiner, Leslie Morgan, ed., *Mommy Wars: Stay-at-Home and Career Moms Face Off on Their Choices, Their Lives, Their Families*. New York: Random House, 2006.
Stephens, Julie. "Mother Hate: The Anti-Maternal Fantasies of the Alt-Right." *Arena Magazine*, No. 160 (June/July 2019): 36–39.
Takseva, Tatjana. "One is not Born but Rather Becomes a Mother: Claiming the Maternal in Women and Gender Studies." *Journal of the Motherhood Initiative*, Vol. 10, Nos. 1 & 2 (May 2019): 27–44.
Tavernise, Sabrina, Claire Cain Miller, Quoctrung Bai, and Robert Geberoff. "Why American Women Everywhere Are Delaying Motherhood." *The New York Times*, June 16, 2021.
Trigg, Mary K. *Feminism as Life's Work: Four Modern American Women through Two World Wars*. New Brunswick, NJ and London: Rutgers University Press, 2014.
Tronto, Joan. "Time's Place." *Feminist Theory*, Vol. 4, No. 2 (August 2003): 119–138.
UN Women. "COVID-19 and its Economic Toll on Women: The Story Behind the Numbers." September 16, 2020. https://www.unwomen.org/en/news/stories/2020/9/feature-covid-19-economic-impacts-on-women.
Vakil, Kaya. "The Pandemic 'Blew the House of Cards All the Way Down' for Mothers. Can Joe Biden Build it Back Better?" *The Keystone*, August 27, 2021.
Vandenberg-Daves, Jodi. *Modern Motherhood: An American History*. New Brunswick, NJ and London: Rutgers University Press, 2014.
Villarosa, Linda. "Why America's Black Mothers and Babies are in a Life-or-Death Crisis." *The New York Times*, April 11, 2018.
Zucker, Rachel. *Mothers*. Denver, CO: Counterpath, 2014.

Index

access to free time 7
acculturation 171
adolescence 38, 161
African American: authors 110; culture 2, 104; Gold Star Mothers 11, 126, 136; lynching plays 128; motherhood 116, 120; women activists 111
African slavery 154
Aid to Dependent Children 203
alcoholism 169, 175, 179, 192
alienation 122
alternative: approaches to pregnancy 45; birth movement 43; childbirth movement 48; mothering 43
American: battle fatigue 1; black family 31; Civil Liberties Union 206; cultural identity 194; culture 9, 27, 58, 80, 151, 181, 191; Depression 61; endurance 58; literature 61, 174; motherhood 10, 86, 105; racism 109; Rescue Plan 208; Revolution 126, 165
American Exodus: A Record of Human Erosion in the Thirties (Lange & Taylor) 79–80
American Frugal Housewife (Child) 17
American Woman's Home (Beecher sisters) 159
amnesia 122
anamnesis 122, 195
Anglo Saxon: culture 153; Protestants 11
anti-:black state violence 108; Catholic 152–156, 165; consumerist 67; domestic 112; feminist 16; feminist thought 209; immigration legislation 165; lynching movement 108; lynching plays 122
antimaternalism 4, 16, 48, 105, 135, 151, 191–200; definition of 1; and policy 202–208

antimaternalist ideas 37, 193–194, 204; message 28, 104
antimaternalists 38
antimaternal narratives 56
assimilation 32, 152–153, 158, 171, 173, 180

babyhood 29, 202
Beard, M. 36, 194
bearing and rearing of children 1
bed sharing 38
Beecher, Catharine 17–18, 25
behaviorism 41
Beloved (Morrison) 104, 115
Biblical ideas 18
birth control 73–74, 105, 203
Black Bourgeoisie (Frazier) 174
Black cultural nationalist 138
Black Lives Matter 2, 143n72
black Mammy 109–110
Blessed Virgin Mary 174
Blue Blood (play by Johnson) 113
Boston's Immigrants 1790–1880: A Study in Acculturation (Handlin) 169
Bradley, M. T. 11, 107, 120, 127–137, 193
breastfeeding 10, 27, 39, 43, 45–47
breast milk 45
Bringing Up Babies: A Family Doctor's Practical Approach to Child Care (Walter) 42
British colonialism 176
broken citizens 5
Brooklyn's Jack Frost Sugar Company 168
Brown University 24
Brown v. Board of Education of Topeka case 127
Build Back Better Agenda 207–208
business sphere 18

capitalism 17, 37, 56, 138
caregiver(s) 20, 22, 179, 211
caregiving 8, 20, 36, 67, 70, 191, 209; obligations 198
Caste and Class in a Southern Town (Dollard) 30
Catholic Church 11, 162–164
Catholicism 11, 152, 162–164, 175
Century Foundation 207
Cheaper By The Dozen (Frank Jr. and Ernestine) 25
Cherokee 58
Chicago Defender 109, 133
child bearing 16, 198, 202–203
childbirth 42–45, 68, 74–75, 151, 205–206
childcare 7, 34, 169, 196–197; centers 68, 197; free 208–210; manual 27; responsibilities 198, 209; solitary 68; system 207; universal 209
child guidance 27
Child Labor Amendment of 1924 74
child rearing 6, 16–17, 20, 158, 191, 198, 209
childrearing 6, 76
child-rearing 16, 21, 40, 42–43, 158, 162; methods 16
Children's Bureau 28, 35, 73–75, 192
"Child's Daily Time Cards" 28
Christian mother 18
chrononormativity 47
civil rights: leaders 38; legislation 128; movement 103, 127–128, 130, 202, 205
clockdriven approach 43
clock time 18, 20, 32, 48, 158
clockwork rationality 56
Closing Door (Grimke) 115
code-switching 23
Cold War 40, 42, 47
colonialism 161, 179, 194
colonization 62, 152, 154, 164; of the mother 62
Common Sense Book of Baby and Child Car (Spock) 40–41
communism 68, 92, 192
consumer culture 34
consumerism of the 1920s and 1950s 5
Contemporary Motherhood: The Impact of Children on Adult Time (Craig) 196
cotton strike 77
COVID-19: (pandemic) 8, 11, 194, 196–197, 211; relief law 207

critiques of motherhood 4
crucifixion 116
cultural: critics 3, 17, 112, 154; shift 192
culturally marginalized 181, 191

de Beauvoir Simone 5, 8, 21, 36, 39, 191, 194–195
dehumanization 56, 135, 137
Department of Agriculture 65
Depression (the Great) 30, 56
depression years 3, 10
Derricotte, T. 44, 48
Discipline and Punish (Foucalt) 19
discrimination 2, 124, 128; class 103
"disordered" families 30–32, 170
domestic: labor(s) 21, 24, 36, 67, 81, 181, 193, 198; service 158–160, 163, 170, 172; sphere 18; *see also* business sphere; virtues 81; vision 19
domesticity 1, 21, 56, 68–70, 76, 80, 93, 121; Gilbert on domesticity 25; symbols of 67; virtues of 3; women's 26
"Don'ts for Doting Mothers" 38
"double shift" 7

ecofeminism 43
economic: crisis 35, 57, 87, 206; discourse 18; exploitation 171; justice 30
emigration 153, 157, 160, 179
emotional immediacy 57
eroticism 6
erotogenic zone 6
Ethics and Public Policy Center 209
ethnic oppression 176
Eurocentric: models of motherhood 116; notions of motherhood 11
European fascism 5
evangelicals 60
experiences of motherhood 23, 56, 87
Extreme Domesticity (Fraiman) 80

familial role 4
family separation policy (of Trummp Administration) 206
famine 153, 194
Farm Security Administration 10, 60, 68–69, 77, 92
Farm Security Administration Photographic Project 60
Farrell, J. T. 173–175
fascism 40

feeding schedule 31, 46
female: lactation 45; self-determination 157
Feminine Mystique (Friedan) 38–39
feminism 193–195; and mothers 2, 193–195
feminist movement 4, 39, 43
feminists 7, 22, 26, 193
feminist writers: de Beauvoir, S. 5; Friedan B. 5
fertility 40, 62, 75, 196, 199
field photographer 57
First Lady of Engineering (Gilbreth) 25
First World women 167
fixed temporality 139
foster care 90, 92
foster families 87, 91
Foucault, Michael 19
Foucaultian time discipline 46
Franklin D. Roosevelt's New Deal legislation 29
Freeman, Elizabeth 19, 47, 195
Freud, S. 6, 86, 179
Friedan, Betty 36, 39–40, 191, 193–194
FSA Photographic Project 72, 82, 92
FSA project 60

gaslighting 207
gender: discrimination 181; inequality 3; roles 3, 168; -segregated work force 3
Generation of Vipers (Wylie) 36, 173
genocide 105, 154, 193
geographic mobility 41
Gilbreth, L. 24–27
Godey's Ladies Book (Schultz) 160
Grapes of Wrath (Steinbeck) 62
Great: depression 10, 57, 60, 82, 103; famine 162; *see also* Great, Hunger; hunger 176; migration 33, 103
Greeley, A. 177–179
grief 110, 118–120, 123–126, 134–139
grievability 136–137

Hagood, M. J. 66–67, 71, 75
Handbook of Public Assistance 203
helicopter mums 1
heterosexual couples 198
hippy culture 42
Hitler 36, 40, 42, 47
Holocaust 193
Home-Maker and Her Job (Gilbreth) 25, 26
homemaking 26, 198

Homo faber 21
homosexuality 192
household labor 25
housework 7, 21, 25–26, 29, 32, 67, 172
How the Irish Became White (Ignatiev) 154
hyperrationalism 42

ideal mothering 3, 112
Ignatiev Noel 154, 172
"I Have a Dream" speech 205
Immigrant Life in New York City (Ernst) 169
immigration 5, 153, 156–157, 161–162, 206
industrial capitalism 47, 76
infantilisation 207
Inflation Reduction Act of 2022 208
instinct (maternal) 4, 17, 20, 41, 45, 59, 107
institutional support 1
intermarriage 166
Irish: Catholicism 2, 178; Catholic women 155, 171; emigration 157–158, 160, 162, 166; families 169–171; history 164–165; immigration 154; mothers 152; penitential guilt 163; Republican Army 164; Republican Brotherhood 164; women's emigration 158
Irish American: antimaternalism 174; Catholic men 152; Catholic women 152, 168; culture 152; women 9, 158, 160, 166–167, 170, 176, 180

Johnson, G. D. 113–115
Johnson-Reed Act 165
juvenile delinquency 106

Killing the Black Body (Roberts) 105
Kristeva, J. 103, 116–117, 201
Ku Klux Klan 165

labor: discrimination 167; force participation 38, 196; market 3, 196; protections 159
Ladies' Home Journal 37
La Leche League 39–40, 46
Lange's: biography 56–58; experiences of motherhood 86–93; field notes 66; gender politics 62; images 56, 62–63, 67–68, 71–72, 81, 86, 93; marriage 170–171, 196–198; photographs

Index

10, 56, 61, 67–68, 77, 80, 82, 91–93, 122
lesbian and gay couples 198
Letters to Mothers (Sigourney) 6
Let Us Now Praise Famous Men (Agee and Evans) 3, 85
Levy, David 37–38
literal translation 28
Look magazine 36, 83
love substitute 38
lynching 108–111, 120, 128–129, 133; drama(s) 113; plays 9, 11, 112–113, 116, 122, 137; victim 109, 118
lynch mobs 108, 137

Madonnas of the Fields 72
male: sexual dysfunction 1; unemployment 4
'male-kind of time' 8
Mama's Baby Papa's Maybe (Spiller) 103
Mammy monument 109
Man with Two Mothers (film) 178
marital dissolution 167
market capitalism 18
Mary Jemison Study Club for Mothers 27
Mary's sorrow 116–118, 137, 163, 164
masculinity 29–30, 37, 40, 42, 61, 162, 168, 175, 179–180, 206
maternal: care 8, 19, 22–23, 58, 68, 70, 72, 108, 134, 204; control 1; effect 192; grief 10–11, 107–108, 116–117, 119, 126, 135, 137–138, 163; ideal 2–4, 105, 111, 126; identity 23; influence 5, 17, 37; love 58, 64, 92, 107, 111, 122, 136; mortality 42; pain 103; power 48, 62, 106, 115, 132, 137, 181; pride 64; regeneration 117; rejection 107; status 5; suffering 119; tasks 20
Maternal and Child Health Association in Springfield 39
maternal-child relationship 192
maternalism 26; definition of 207; ideas of 3
maternalist: ideas 3; narratives 3; thinking 3
Maternal Overprotection (Levy) 36
maternity 21
"matriarchs" 106, 170, 174, 176–180
May Day demonstrations (of 1933) 57
medical leave program 210
memorial photographs 120–122

menopause 45
men's mental health 4
menstruation 45
mental weaning 5, 71
Mexican Mother in California (Lange) iv, 64
midwifery 44
Migrant Mother (Lange's photo) iv, 58, 59, 61, 70, 73, 82, 85, 86, 93
miscarriage 75, 111
misogynist interpretations 5
mixed marriages 173
modernization 27, 192
momism 5, 6, 36, 173
moral: development 4; motherhood 4, 36, 111
morality 3, 120, 157, 207
Mormons 60
Morning (Graham) 115
mother(s): African American 10, 31, 64, 103–105, 112–113, 124, 139, 152, 158, 191–193, 203; Agrarian 73; black 2, 30–31, 104–106, 112–114, 118–119, 124, 135, 137–138, 203; black single 38, 138; blaming 4; -blaming 107, 179–180, 203–204; -centered feminism 212; -child bond 56; discretion 28; emotions 73; feminist 1; Gold Star 107, 122–127, 134–136, 194; identity 23; immigrant 2, 6, 32, 33, 43; -infant bonding 68; -infant relationship 6; Irish American Catholic 2, 9, 11, 152, 162–163, 166, 173, 179–181, 204; itinerant 2, 10, 56, 75, 81, 103; itinerant rural 75, 85, 91, 166, 203; Japanese-American 64; Jewish-American 33; love 10, 17, 36, 107, 111, 136, 192, 207; marginalized 1, 2, 212; middle-class 9, 27, 36, 41, 43; migrant 2, 6, 31–33, 43, 62, 67, 75, 87, 151, 166–167; migratory 2, 10, 58, 65, 67, 72, 91, 137; multiracial 72; non-wage-earning 32; over-attentive 5; poor 2; professional educated 1; refrigerator 107; rural 2, 10, 33, 73–76, 92–93; rural migratory 56; self-sacrificing 35–37; single 6, 7; teenage 1; time 73; working-class 12, 191
Mother and Two Children on the Road (Lange) 78
motherhood: construction of 3; critics of 5; devaluation of 1; ideal 11, 47, 88, 93, 152, 162; meanings of 2;

narrative of 27; patriotic 37; scientific 1; tenets of 17
mothering 27, 41, 201; authentic 211, 212; institutional 211; perfect 199; responsibilities 104
"mother-love" 27
"mothers' boy" 38
mothers' obligations 23
Mothers of the South (Hagood) 3, 66, 71, 75
Mothers of the South: Portraiture of the White Tenant Farm Woman (Hagood) 66
Mothers Who Must Earn (Anthony) 171
mourning and melancholia 153, 179
"*Moynihan Report*" 31
multicultural motherhood 64

Nation (McClean) 90, 104
national: consciousness 61; identity 3, 180
National Association for the Advancement of Colored People 107
National Association of Colored Women 110
native-born Americans 151, 165, 171
natural: childbirth 10, 43–44; motherhood' 43; schedule 41
Nazis 1, 40
Nazism 5
Negro Family in the United States (Frazier) 30
Negro Family: The Case for National Action (1965 report) 30
Negro Family: The Case for National Action (Moynihan) 169
Negro-Mother's Cradle-Song (Young) 124
Newsweek 130
New Yorker 120, 204
New York National Federation of Business and Professional Women's Clubs 25
New York Post 132
New York's Museum of Modern Art 90
New York Times 197, 199, 205
Nursery and Child's Hospital 152
nurturance 3, 20, 62, 72, 106–107, 112, 120, 134, 137, 180, 207

Oedipus complex 6
Of Woman Born (Rich) 6, 12, 62, 213
Of Woman Born: Motherhood as Experience and Institution (Rich) 6

Olsen, T. 34–35
oppression 1, 20, 65, 119, 130, 171, 177, 191, 193
orchestrated schedules 56
Organization for Economic Co-operation and Development 208
Our American Babies: The Art of Baby Care (Whipple) 41
Overworked American (Schor) 195
Oxfam International 197

paid parental leave 208, 210
parent: education 5, 31, 35; education movement 35
Parents (magazine) 77
patriarchal control of motherhood 62
patriarchal structure 7
patriotic motherhood 38
patriotism 125, 165
Pedagogies of Crossing (Alexander) 139
personal care 23
personality disorders 106
Philadelphia Press 110
photography history 81–83
physical suffering 4, 113
pneumonia 121
political: activism 137; participation 126; subjectivity 126, 138
post:-Famine 160; -Freudian 17, 175;-industrial society 5
pregnancy and childbirth 42, 45, 74
preschool education 27
President Franklin D. Roosevelt 60
President Joe Biden 206–207
President Trump 206
Price of Motherhood: Why the Most Important Job in the World is Still the Least Valued (Crittenden) 196
primary object of love 6
Principles of Scientific Management (Taylor) 24
private sphere 18, 22, 56
Problems in Administration of Public Welfare Programs 203
productivity 10–11, 19–20, 24–25, 47, 79, 156, 191, 201
progressive ideas 5
promaternal narrative 56, 72
pronatalist ideology 40
Protestant: American culture 174; culture 2; theology 18
Psychological Care of Infant and Child (Watson) 16

226 Index

psychological development 6
psychoneuroses 1
"psychoneurotics" 37

racial: bias 205; caste system 109, 114; inequality 31, 65; injustice 65; justice 125, 127, 134–135; norms 65; power relations 65; stereotypes 107; tensions 206; violence 107, 111–112, 127, 130
racialization: of Irish 152–155, 158–159, 172
racism 104–205; portrayal of 65
racist: society 116; violence 115, 118, 120, 137
Radical mothering 211
rebellion 116, 137, 164
redemptive value 104
relationship with time 196
remembrance and memory 108, 120–127, 193–194
reparation movements 193
reproduction 8, 12, 158
reproductive: choices 209; freedom 105–106; justice 105; technology 211; years 210
Republican Motherhood 126
resurrection 117
reverse emigration 167
Revolutionary Mothering (Gumbs) 137–138, 211
Rich, A. 6, 12, 43, 62, 73, 89, 151, 181, 192–193, 211, 213
Rights of Infants (Ribble) 107
Roberts, R. S. 121–122
rural: American families 56; economy 74; poverty 56–57, 79, 171

Safe (play by Johnson) 113–116
same sex couples 211
scientific motherhood 4, 16, 20, 29, 40, 56; definiton of 10; proponents of 8, 10, 45, 47, 68, 112, 191; redefinition of 42; tenets of 33
scientific mothering 48
Second Sex (de Beauvoir) 8, 21, 194–195
second shift 26
selflessness 192, 200
self-sacrifice 4, 17, 103, 111, 113, 122, 163, 181, 191–192
sentimentality 4
sexual: desire 17; division of labor 8; repression 4

Silences (Olsen) 89
Sinn Fein 164
slave auctions 104
slavery 103–104, 106, 109, 115, 126, 138–139, 152, 159, 193, 203
slave trade 119
slave-trading 139
social: acceptance 164; control 19, 191; discipline 20; exclusion 152; injustice 118, 126; movements 36, 42, 193; power 19; reformers 3; roles 3, 92; welfare 5; work 27, 57
Souls of Black Folk (Du Bois) 109
Spock, B. 40–42
("Stabat) Mater Dolorosa" 116–118, 137
sterilization 105, 138
Strecker, E. 37
Stryker, R. 60–61
Studs Lonigan (Farrell) 173–175
suburbanization 40
suicide 111

tax cuts 208
Taylorism 24–25
temporal: control 46; modernization 19; regulation 10, 16, 20, 23, 46–48, 201
temporalities of care 20, 22–23, 62
temporality 7, 20, 22–23, 191, 210
temporality of violent racial practices 139
"tender mother" 6
That Most Distressful Nation: The Taming of the American Irish (Greeley) 177
Their Mothers' Sons: The Psychiatrist Examines an American Problem (Strecker) 37
This Is Her First Lynching (March painting) 120
time: access to 7–8, 87, 89, 90; binds 47; card 28; discipline 16–20, 27, 29–30, 32–33, 40–41, 43, 46, 56, 62, 80, 191; efficiency 4, 12, 16, 19, 24, 29, 47, 191–192, 199, 204; immigrants and 156, 158; management 4, 16–18, 25, 199; mothers 195–202; poverty 3, 8, 9; and race 105
toilet training 41
tuberculosis 121, 171
Tulare County Mother and Child (Lange) 71
Tulsa Race Massacre (of 1921) 108

U.S.: Children's Bureau 28, 29, 67, 73–75, 192; civil rights movement 120; Library of Congress 59
Uncle Tom's Cabin (Stowe) 115
United States Department of Labor 28
"universal motherhood" 17
unpaid household labor 7
Urban Dictionary (online dictionary) 207
urban modernity 107

Van Der Zee, J. 120–122
Victorian construction of motherhood 4
Virginia's Arlington National Cemetery 122
Virgin Mary 116–118, 163–164, 174, 178, 180
visual construction of motherhood 56
voluntary childlessness 8
voting rights 5, 128

wage: -earning wives 29; -earning women 7, 30
wage loss 208
"Wages for Housework" campaign 7
Washington D.C 109, 113
WASP culture 156–159, 172, 179, 181
Watson John 16, 34, 110, 191
welfare: cheats 204; mess 205; moms 1; reform 204; rights 203, 205; state 3, 29

well-baby clinics 67
Western: capitalists 19; culture 151; intellectual traditions 62
While the Mothers are Working in the Fields (Lange) 69
White Angel Breadline (Lange) 88
White Anglo-Saxon Protestant (WASP) culture 151
white culture 106, 191
whiteness 154–155, 171–173
White Protestant Americans 152, 155
white supremacy 120, 138, 165
Woman As Force in History (Beard) 36
womanhood 163, 199, 203, 211
woman suffrage 156
women's: fertility 105; gender studies 194–195, 212–213; paid labor 3, 197–199; responsibilities 3; subordination 21; traditional labors 1
Women's Committee of the Council of National Defense 123
working-class families 56, 209
World War I 107–108, 110, 122, 124, 127, 153, 164–165, 174, 194
World War II 10, 17, 36, 38, 40, 42, 60, 79, 92, 137, 164, 166, 168, 173, 207
Wylie, P. 35–37, 173, 191

Xenophobes 153
xenophobia 166

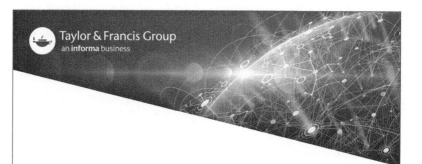

Taylor & Francis eBooks

www.taylorfrancis.com

A single destination for eBooks from Taylor & Francis with increased functionality and an improved user experience to meet the needs of our customers.

90,000+ eBooks of award-winning academic content in Humanities, Social Science, Science, Technology, Engineering, and Medical written by a global network of editors and authors.

TAYLOR & FRANCIS EBOOKS OFFERS:

A streamlined experience for our library customers

A single point of discovery for all of our eBook content

Improved search and discovery of content at both book and chapter level

REQUEST A FREE TRIAL
support@taylorfrancis.com